CHILD SAFETY ON THE INTERNET

by
The Staff
of *Classroom Connect*

with Vince Distefano

Gregory Giagnocavo, Editorial Director
Dorissa Bolinski, Editor

CLASSROOM CONNECT

Internet made easy in the classroom™

Lancaster, Pennsylvania
Email: connect@classroom.net
URL: http://www.classroom.net

From the
publishers of

Internet made easy in the Classroom™   and

Prentice Hall PTR
Prentice-Hall, Inc.
A Simon & Schuster Company
Upper Saddle River, New Jersey 07458

Design and layout: John Svatek
Contributing Writers: Tim McLain
            and Chris Mautner
Indexer: Kim Conlin
CD-ROM Production: Nathanael Waite
            and Jay Walters
Project Manager: Les Miller

Production supervision: Mary Sudul
Cover design: Talar Agasyan
Cover design director: Jerry Votta
Manufacturing manager: Alexis R. Heydt
Acquisitions editor: Mary Franz
Editorial Assistant: Noreen Regina
Copy editor: Laurie Benda

ISBN 0-13-569568-X

Prentice-Hall International (UK) Limited, *London*
Prentice-Hall of Australia Pty. Limited, *Sydney*
Prentice-Hall Canada Inc., *Toronto*
Prentice-Hall Hispanoamericana, S.A., *Mexico*
Prentice-Hall of India Private Limited, *New Delhi*
Prentice-Hall of Japan, Inc., *Tokyo*
Simon & Schuster Asia Pte. Ltd., *Singapore*
Editora Prentice-Hall do Brasil, Ltda., *Rio de Janeiro*

**The CD-ROM to accompany this item
is available from the issue counter**

Classroom Connect - Prentice Hall

Educator's Internet Companion

Child Safety on the Internet

Family Internet Companion

Internet Homework Helper

CONTENTS

10 POLICE THE NET   209

A ACCEPTABLE USE POLICIES   227

SAFE SURFING
ON THE INTERNET

Foreword

I'm really glad you're reading this book.

The subject of "safety" on the Internet has been a popular one for quite some time. Some people feel that the Internet has no place in schools or even homes due to "online danger." Nothing terrible will physically happen to a child while he or she is online, but perhaps you've seen articles or heard reports that describe some of the indecent material and unsavory aspects of the online world. Well, it's true—there is quite a bit of inappropriate material and inappropriate behavior online. But denying access to the Internet and missing out on such a great information, communication, and learning resource is not the answer. Understanding and dealing with negative issues is a better way to protect your children.

Since the Internet is really the sum of all its parts—the millions of people all over the world who use the Internet—it should come as no surprise that each of us will find material online that we won't like. As in real life, there are some down-right undesirable things "out there" on the Internet. But again, as in real life, those things are in the minority and are far outweighed by the excitement, information, human inter-action, and learning value that the Internet offers.

But fear of the Internet still exists. Each year, I speak all across North America to thousands of parents, teachers, and students on the great value of the Internet. I feel fortunate to share some time and excitement with these folks wherever I go. Yet, I still meet people who don't want children to have access to the Internet. Since I am so convinced of the Internet's great value and benefit to educating children, such conversations disturb me a great deal. I have a sincere concern for the children who are kept away from the greatest techno-logical tool since the birth of the personal computer. I hope this book will help provide a way to deal with the legitimate concerns about the Internet so all children can have access in a safe environment.

. . . .

About this book

Please don't fear the Internet. Don't be scared that you or your children will be harmed by going online—anymore than you fear going to the mall or taking a bus ride. But do the sensible thing—prepare yourself and your children to handle problem situations, should they arise. This book helps you to get prepared—and to prepare children—to benefit from the Internet without fearing its unsavory side. And quite frankly, staying safe is usually a matter of common sense.

We'll show you how to keep children from accessing unde-sirable information using specially designed filtering software, how to talk to them about the "bad stuff" that is online, and learn what to do if they accidentally stumble across inappropri-ate material. There's a section dealing with the proper and safe way to participate in chat rooms and online meetings. We've even developed a set of online safety rules and a written agree-ment you may want to adopt for children using the Internet. I think you'll find them extremely helpful.

Child Safety on the Internet will give you the confidence to feel that you and your children can stay safe as you "surf" the Net. So, don't miss out. Come on in—the water's fine!

Gregory Giagnocavo
Director, Classroom Connect
Email: jgg@classroom.net

P.S. Thanks for your Interest in our book. If you'd like to share your online experiences related to safety issues and chil-dren using the Internet, please send me an email. I get hundreds of messages a week, but I promise I'll do my best to respond to each and every message.

Preface

Larry Magid, Syndicated Columnist, *Los Angeles Times*

I recently took my family to New York, where we caught a Broadway play, visited museums, and walked around town. Inevitably, we passed some adult theaters and bookstores and other places that were not appropriate for kids to enter. My kids know that such places are off-limits, likewise they know to beware of high-crime areas in a city like New York. In addition, they know the safe way to behave around strangers and in public: It's all part of being "street smart."

The Internet can be compared to a big city that contains many fun and educational areas for children, as well as places you'd want them to avoid. Children who surf the Net must be "Net smart"—they have to know how to behave around strangers and to stay away from potentially dangerous areas.

Before stressing the dangers of the Internet, I want to emphasize that the vast majority of Internet and commercial on-line service sites are safe. Many are downright wholesome. Like a virtual city, the Internet houses museums; universities; libraries; shops; and even churches, mosques, and synagogues.

In actuality, it is extremely rare for a child to get into physical danger in cyberspace. The bad news is that there are a lot of places online that are inappropriate for children, and it's sometimes difficult for parents to know how to keep their kids from wandering into this territory. Areas of concern are located on the World Wide Web, in newsgroups, and in online "chat" areas. A chat area is like a party line in which several people converse in real time by typing and reading comments that are instantly transmitted to all who are tuned in. Chat sessions are particularly troublesome because they are live and there is no way to screen material before it is posted.

Most commercial online service forums or bulletin boards are appropriate for family viewing. Offensive material is usually removed by the staff. But this is not necessarily true with chat sessions, and it's definitely not true on the Internet, which is not maintained by a single company or organization. Some sexually explicit private bulletin boards also exist, but in most cases, they attempt to keep children out.

The issue of protecting children online is different from that of online distribution of child pornography, where adults use online services to distribute images of children engaged in sexual activities. Regardless of whether this type of material is made available to children or adults, it is illegal to produce, distribute, or possess it online or in any other form.

Basically, there are three potential online dangers to children. They might access something inappropriate, a pedophile might try to lure them into contact, or they may be harassed.

First, it is possible for children to access sexually explicit or violent material. Anyone who knows where to look can find newsgroups and World Wide Web sites that feature sexually explicit descriptions or images. Some, like *Playboy* and *Penthouse* sites are fairly mild by today's standards. Others contain obscenities that would be offensive to most adults and potentially disturbing to children.

Second, however slight, there exists the danger that a child might do something that could create a risk of physical molestation. There are actually a few cases in which pedophiles have used bulletin boards and chat sessions to lure a child into face-to-face encounters. A recent FBI sting operation caught several people allegedly using America Online to arrange such meetings.

Children must be told to never give their full name, address, phone number, or any other identifying information to anyone they "meet" via the Internet—even if they believe that they're in touch with another child. A person who claims to be a 14-year-old girl could really be a 40-year-old man.

Children should never arrange a face-to-face meeting with someone they meet online without parental approval. If the parents agree to such a meeting, it should occur in a public place with a parent present.

Third, harassment and emotional abuse is also an issue. Although most people online are polite, there are a few who use abusive language or are otherwise belligerent and hostile. I've witnessed some cases in which children have been verbally insulted for asking innocent questions on a computer-related bulletin board.

There are basically two ways to protect your children online—parental involvement and parental control of the technology. As a parent, you should be involved in your childrens' Internet use and establish usage rules. Don't use the PC as an electronic babysitter. You don't need to stand over your kids' shoulders at all times, but if you're concerned about what your kids are doing online, keep the machine in a communal room rather than in the child's bedroom. Children are less likely to do something they know is wrong if other family members are walking into and out of the room.

Technological child-safety solutions on commercial online services include parental control, or "blocking," features that allow parents to keep children out of certain areas. For example, chat sessions can be blocked, or you can restrict your child from entering certain bulletin boards. Currently, the Internet doesn't have such controls, but there are many software packages designed to provide some of these functions.

SurfWatch Software, for example, has a Macintosh and Windows program that blocks Internet newsgroups, Web sites, file libraries, and chat areas that are known to contain sexually explicit material. The program knows over 1,600 such sites and is also able to block other areas, based on certain combinations of words that are generally associated with X-rated sites. The program's site-blocking list is automatically updated while you're online. (**Note: SurfWatch is included free with the CD-ROM at the back of this book.**)

Likewise, CyberPatrol offers similar features. With this program, adults can customize restrictions to reflect school, community, and personal standards. Any Internet World Wide Web, gopher, ftp, Usenet news, and Internet Relay Chat (IRC) site and resource can be filtered. In response to the child safety issue, commercial online services are also integrating similar software and developing technology to allow parents to prevent children from accessing certain areas of the Internet.

A coalition of organizations, computer companies, Internet providers, and online services have developed the Platform for Internet Content Selection (PICS). It is a "viewpoint-neutral technology platform that will empower organizations and individuals to categorize and selectively access information according to their own needs," states a coalition spokesperson. The idea is to provide a labeling system that makes it possible for parents to automatically block certain types of sites.

The National Center for Missing and Exploited Children will provide information to anyone interested in learning more about how adults can protect children in cyberspace. For a free copy of my booklet "Child Safety on the Information Highway," you can contact them at 800-843-5678 (an excerpt is included in Chaper 3 of this book). The full text of that booklet, as well as links to organizations and companies working on this issue, is also available from my World Wide Web home page at http://www.larrysworld.com.

. . . .

Online Rules for Kids

- ◌ Do not give personal information such as your address, telephone number, parents' work addresses or phone numbers or the name and location of your school without your parents' permission.
- ◌ Tell your parents right away if you access any information that makes you feel uncomfortable.
- ◌ Never agree to get together with someone you "meet" online without first checking with your parents. If they agree to the meeting, be sure that it occurs in a public place, and bring your mom or dad along.
- ◌ Never send a person a picture or anything else without first checking with your parents.
- ◌ Do not respond to any messages that are mean or in any way make you feel uncomfortable. It's not your fault if you get a message like that. If you do, tell your parents right away so they can contact the online service.
- ◌ Talk with your parents and set up rules for going online. Decide upon the time of day, the length of time and appropriate areas to visit.

In general, the amount of positive and beneficial material available to children and adults on the Internet far outweighs the bad. But make sure your children understand and agree to abide by these rules before they venture onto the Internet. Remember, a little planning and foresight can help you avoid an unpleasant situation. By taking charge of the Internet, you and your children can best enjoy this great and growing repository of information.

Larry Magid
Syndicated Columnist, *Los Angeles Times*
magid@latimes.com
URL: http://www.larrysworld.com

CHILD SAFETY ON THE INTERNET

MAKING THE NET SAFE

As we approach the millennium, the importance of the Internet as a global communication tool and source of information becomes ever more apparent. Today's youngsters will need to become well-versed in this medium to achieve their full potential as they climb the educational ladder and enter the working world. While the media has exaggerated some of the Net's dangers, there *is* a "dark side" to the Internet that you will want your children to avoid.

This book gives you the necessary tools to prevent your children and students from gaining access to harmful online information or being the victim of an ill-minded adult Internet user. When you finish this book, you should realize that the Internet is not something to fear; rather, it's an educational tool that can help your children learn and teach them responsibility.

THE INCREDIBLE GROWTH AND POPULARITY OF THE INTERNET

Think back a few years to 1993 or 1994. Do you remember hearing the word "Internet"? How often did "the Net" come up in conversations at work, school, or church? How many newspaper or magazine articles about the World Wide Web did you read? How many friends or relatives kept in touch with email? Did you know anything about modems, Internet Service Providers, hyperlinks, and search engines? If you are like most of us, you probably had no idea that these terms existed, let alone understood them.

What do you know about the Internet *today?* Chances are, you know quite a bit more than you did just a year ago, even if you are not a "power user" who checks for new email messages every hour. You cannot escape it. The Internet has hit prime time, and now it seems that everyone has an email address or home page on the Web. Evidence of the Net's pervasiveness is everywhere. Schools, businesses, nonprofit organizations, and government agencies are all leaping into cyberspace. And the young programmers and Internet entrepreneurs who help them get there become millionaires overnight.

Major magazines and newspapers such as the *New York Times, USA Today,* and *Business Week* and cable networks such as CNN run daily features about cyberspace. In fact, now you can read articles from the *Times* about cyberspace while you are *in* cyberspace! That speaks volumes. It seems like everybody everywhere is getting "wired"—signing on with an Internet Service Provider and surfing the Net. A brave new world truly has arrived, and it is time to begin making sense of it.

Even if you have not spent a whole lot of time online, you probably know that:

- The Internet brings millions of people around the world together via computers, modems, and telephone lines. This global network is the sum of all those millions of people who use its resources.
- Millions of pages of information, graphics, and even multimedia sound and video programs await your exploring eyes on the World Wide Web.

- Electronic mail, known as email, combines the best properties of the phone, fax machine, and postal letter and can help you become more efficient at work and school—for very little cost.
- You do not have to be a "computer geek" to get online and start to reap the benefits. In fact, most newer computers come equipped with modems and free "all-in-one" software kits that make it easy to connect to the Net. Internet pioneers never would have guessed it could be this simple.
- Finding resources is getting easier despite the Internet's tremendous growth, thanks to powerful search engines, topical indexes, directories, and information "agents" that can help you find the information you need.

THE POWER OF THE INTERNET FOR FAMILIES AND SCHOOLS

So, the Net is everywhere. But what does it offer to children, families, and schools? And is it worth any possible risks to children? If you are a parent or educator who has spent some time surfing the Net or reading about the online world, you already know the answer to these questions. Here are some of them.

- Thousands of educational resources exist on the Internet, including government data, historical documents, classic novels, scientific experiments, images from space, newspapers and magazines, and much more. Many of these great resources were put online by parents, teachers, and students *especially* for enhancing education and empowering people to become lifelong learners. And most of it is still free.

More people go online every day. According to a study released by the Emerging Technologies Research Group in January 1996:

INFO BYTE

- 9.5 million Americans use the Internet.
- 8.4 million of those users are adults.
- At least one million are children.
- More people use the Internet at home than at work.
- About half of all users got online in 1995.

Schools are getting online too—and fast! According to the U.S. Department of Education:

- About 50 percent of all public schools in the United States have at least some Internet access.
- Last year, about 35 percent did.

⚬ The Net can put you in touch with experts from all walks of life—professional peers, computer specialists, public officials, scientists, writers, researchers, and business people.

⚬ Endless opportunities exist for young minds to collaborate, share ideas and visions, and compare cultures and customs. Quite simply, the Internet's flexibility and immediacy is creating powerful new ways of communicating with each other.

⚬ Knowing how to use the Internet will be extremely valuable for today's young people, who will be tomorrow's "knowledge workers" and technical pioneers. They will almost certainly be expected to know how to telecommunicate and to gather digital information.

⚬ Families can explore the Internet from their own home and extend their learning opportunities well beyond the school walls and calendar.

Given all this, why would any parent or school decide *against* Internet access? Because sometimes things happen or appear online that just are not appropriate for children. Perhaps you have heard disturbing reports in the media about the Internet's "red light" districts, online pedophiles, or credit card scams. You may have read a newspaper article or seen a news broadcast that makes you think the Internet is mainly a place to trade pornography, find recipes for making bombs, or download illegal software. Perhaps you believe that there are just too many risks and that your child can survive just fine without the Internet. "Better safe than sorry," you may say.

THE NET'S DARK SIDE REFLECTS THE REAL WORLD

Yes, the Internet does pose some problems when it comes to allowing children to go online—mainly because the network does not exist in a vacuum, but in the same "real world" we

Figure 1
The Internet is home to hundreds of electronic magazines, but some are inappropriate for youngsters.

inhabit, warts and all. Just because it exists "on computers" does not protect the Internet from all of the social problems we encounter every day. Sure, computers comprise the Internet, but there are *people* sitting at those keyboards. The activities and behavior of those people mirror the "real world." The Net is an open, diverse culture, with no rules forcing those who put materials online to adhere to certain standards.

What types of material might parents and teachers find objectionable? Internet sites that contain nudity, pornography, and violent or degrading images are tops on most people's list. Some of these materials are illegal, while others are similar to photos in *Cosmopolitan* or *Sport Illustrated's* swimsuit issue. (See Figure 1.)

Hundreds of adult stores selling everything from condoms to lingerie have set up shop on the Net. Adult nightclubs and 900 numbers advertise their services via newsgroup postings and Web

The World Wide Web has become a showcase for the talents of teachers and students around the globe. According to the Web66 International Schools Registry:

- The number of school districts with sites on the World Wide Web increased from about 50 to more than 400 in 1995.
- Nearly 3,000 individual secondary and primary schools have sites on the Web.

INFO BYTE

Figure 2
You wouldn't want your child hanging out at this "mall."

home pages. Many offer graphical catalogs or free sample pictures that any visitor may view, while others require users to establish credit card accounts ahead of time or use an online payment system. (See Figure 2.)

Materials that are not necessarily pornographic or illegal but that may conflict with your family's values or your personal sensibilities also dot the Internet landscape. Just like the real world, the virtual world contains all kinds of propaganda, hate literature, and even some inflammatory art and photography. (See Figure 3.)

It is easy to spot the inappropriateness of porn or hate literature. But plenty of online material is not offensive; rather it is inappropriate when accessed in a school setting, such as sports, movies, and music sites. The last thing parents and teachers want is for youngsters to use their Internet time to hang around Melrose Place chat rooms or the Zima Web site.

Even at "safe" sites with no nudity, violence, or other inappropriate material, parents and teachers must grapple with certain "information knowledge" issues. No gatekeeper decides what information is suitable for the Net and what is not. Anyone may post anything. Sarcastic parodies of Web sites such as the White House site have evolved, creating the possibility of confusing a child who may believe this is the "real" White House Web site. Is the child able to judge whether the information is reliable? What are the original author's intentions? In our hurry

CHILD SAFETY ON THE INTERNET

6

to embrace this technology, are students relying too much on online resources and not using materials that may be more accurate, in-depth, reliable, appropriate, and easier to obtain?

The interactive components of the Internet pose similar problems. The powerful, global, one-to-one or many-to-one communications features of email, newsgroups, and online chat carry a price. Although there are only a few reported cases in which adults have abused the immediacy and anonymity of email by preying on unsuspecting or trusting youth, not everyone in a chat room is a friend.

Thanks to the Net's interactivity, young people can get advice on sensitive, personal issues such as health, sex, or careers from strangers. But free advice is not always good advice.

Children's first steps into the Net's interactive world most often involve email. It is simple, easy to control, text-based: What could happen? But do you know how your students or children are using email? Are they following online rules and common-sense guidelines? Or could they be giving away too much personal information about themselves to someone they do not really know? Could they be using email for careless and harmful activities that incite trouble in the online world, trouble that could hurt people? (See Figure 4.)

Children often use the Internet to forge friendships with other young people, near or far. But as many child psychologists will tell you, even these seemingly innocuous online "keypal" relationships should be supervised by adults. Why? Because as with real-world companions, parents should know a little bit about their children's "virtual" friends. But this isn't easy; you

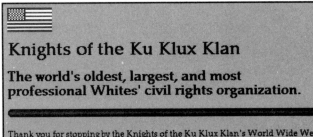

Figure 3
Not every site that could be inappropriate for children on the Internet is pornographic. Some contain hate literature or inflammatory art and photography.

```
alt.support.breastfeeding
alt.support.cancer
alt.support.cancer.prostate
alt.support.cant.urinate.in-public
alt.support.cerebral-palsy
alt.support.crohns-colitis
alt.support.depression
alt.support.depression.manic
alt.support.depression.seasonal
alt.support.diabetes.kids
alt.support.diet
alt.support.dissociation
alt.support.divorce
alt.support.dwarfism
```

cannot meet them or their parents, or learn more about them from your son's or daughter's teachers.

When friendships sour in real life, you can step in and offer some adult wisdom and insight to preserve friendships, or maybe even break off negative relationships. What about your child's online relationships? Do you know who their new Internet friends are and what they discuss? Are the relationships healthy? Is your child being used by an older online "friend"?

IF ONLY IT WERE HARDER TO FIND THE BAD STUFF . . .

Some experienced Internet users often inaccurately assert that to find bad stuff on the Internet you have to go looking for it. (More on that in Chapter 1.) If that is so, then students using World Wide Web search engines to find information for papers, book reports, and school projects should be able to avoid inappropriate materials by entering keywords related *only* to the subject at hand, right? Wrong.

Even targeted keyword searches can yield links to inappropriate sites. Look closely at the results of the Web search in the screen capture in Figure 5. We searched for feminism resources, using only *feminism* as the keyword, via WebCrawler (http://webcrawler.com) and got plenty of links that *looked* useful, including hyperlinks to book reviews, the National Organization for Women home page, and resources from the *New York Times.* Fine. But we also got a link to the "Hardcore Porno Page."

Even if an adult is present or if special blocking software is in place to prevent a youngster from actually *following* this link, those words alone can cause concern, distress, or panic in a youngster. And unscrupulous Net users know how to present their information so search engines find and return what amounts to very bold advertising copy. Some search engines display the first 100 words of sites, so the people putting pornography online write a sexually suggestive description of the site that gets right to the point. Those 100 words can be quite objectionable under any circumstance—yet another case of getting the bad with the good.

There is more at stake than protecting children from the seedier side of the online community. Teachers and school administrators are often more concerned about Internet safety than any other group, and rightly so. They must protect *themselves,* their parental or professional standing, and the school district. One negative online

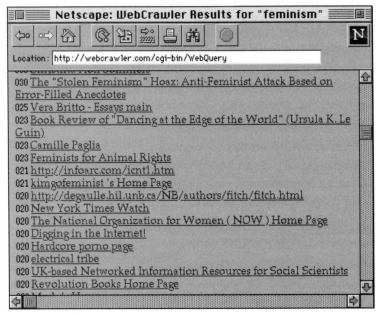

Figure 5
An Internet search on the seemingly innocuous topic, *feminism,* returned these results, including a disturbing link to something called the "Hardcore Porno Page."

INFO BYTE

Adults are not the only ones who abuse the Net. *The Washington Post* reported that a college student sent email messages to child welfare and psychology groups on the Internet accusing a fellow student's mother (he never met the student or mother) of abuse. He urged people to call the mother "and tell her you are disgusted and you demand that she stops." Family and school officials are outraged and a lawsuit may ensue.

The student's defense? "You should be able to write what you want on the Internet, whether it's true or not. . . ."

incident, even if precautions have been taken, could create problems for a school trying to integrate the Net into the curriculum.

The same things that make the Internet a great place to explore and learn also present risks for children and for the adults responsible for their well-being. Giving kids access to the Internet is not like handing them a book, magazine, or the latest educational CD-ROM. You cannot possibly screen all of the Internet ahead of time or guess what your kids might do online. Although television programs and movies contain plenty of violence and sex, you can restrict access to the TV or VCR without worrying too much about denying your children access to the benefits of educational programming. Quite simply, the Internet is a very, very powerful entity that puts the world at your fingertips. It demands absolute responsibility and accountability of its users—young and old.

The Internet is a powerful source of global information, most of it educational and all of it just a mouse click away. Denying our children some familiarity with it borders on irresponsibility. But the Net cannot replace quality teaching, constructive social interaction, or family support and encouragement.

**From
*Child Safety
on the
Information
Highway***

Traditionally, online services have been oriented towards adults, but that's changing. An increasing number of schools are going online, and, in many homes, children are logging on to commercial services, private bulletin boards, and the Internet. . . . Millions of people communicate through electronic mail (email) with family and friends around the world, and others use the public message boards to make new friends who share common interests. Most people who use online services have mainly positive experiences. But, . . . there are some risks. The online world, like the rest of society, is made up of a wide array of people. Most are decent and respectful, but some may be rude, obnoxious, insulting, or even mean and exploitative.

Children and teenagers get a lot of benefit from being online, but they can also be targets of crime and exploitation in this as in any other environment. Trusting, curious, and anxious to explore this new world and the relationships it brings, children and teenagers need parental supervision and common sense advice. . . .

"Although there have been some highly publicized cases of abuse involving computers, reported cases are relatively infrequent. Of course, like most crimes against children, many cases go unreported, especially if the child is engaged in an activity that he or she does not want to discuss with a parent. The fact that crimes are being committed online, however, is not a reason to avoid using these services. To tell children to stop using these services would be like telling them to forgo attending college because students are sometimes victimized on campus. A better strategy would be for children to learn how to be "street smart" in order to better safeguard themselves in any potentially dangerous situation."

—The Center for Missing and Exploited Children

USE THIS BOOK TO MAKE THE NET SAFE FOR CHILDREN

This book will help you separate fact from fiction. You will be able to get past all the hype, the inaccuracy, and the sensationalism surrounding the dark side of the Internet and understand the real issues. You will be able to find strategies for making sure your children are safe, teaching them to protect themselves, and handling incidents if they occur.

This book does not purport to tell you how to raise your children or what you should teach your students. Nor is our objective to promote censorship, suggest what is wrong or right, or promote any type of moral agenda.

Our simple goal is to paint a complete picture of the Internet world. How you bring young people into this world is entirely up to you.

WHAT YOU WILL FIND IN EACH CHAPTER

Chapter 1 acquaints you with some of the risks and dangers of the most common inappropriate materials on the Net—pornography—and where they are most likely be found. You will also learn about the "cyberporn" controversy and the new telecommunications law and how it might, or might not, apply to the Internet.

Chapter 2 tells you about some other dangers on the Net—pedophiles, distributors of hate literature, scam artists, and more.

Chapter 3 provides practical, hands-on, real-world steps you can take to ensure that your young ones stay safe online. It includes an overview of new software tools, for example CyberPatrol, that allow parents and teachers to control access to material on the Internet.

Chapter 4 brings you up to speed on the basics of online Netiquette, a set of informal rules for behaving and interacting with others on the Internet. Learn them yourself and then teach them to your children.

Chapter 5 educates you about the one policy that most schools use to set the rules for Internet use—acceptable-use policies. Learn how to design one fitting your school's needs or how to create rules for home use of the Net.

Chapter 6 covers the safety and security measures commercial online services such as America Online offer for parents and teachers.

Chapter 7 tells you why teaching your children to become information literate is a vital survival and safety skill, especially on the Internet.

Chapter 8 describes numerous kid-safe movements and organizations which seek to make the Net a better place for kids to explore.

Chapter 9 provides valuable "Net detective" tips and advice for parents and teachers who want to keep tabs on their computers and their kids.

Chapter 10 focuses on a topic rarely mentioned in Internet safety discussions—what to do when, despite your best efforts, something bad *does* happen to a youngster on the Net. How do you deal with the aftermath?

A list of Internet sites related to the subjects addressed in the chapter, as well as any other useful information, is located at the end of each chapter.

At the end of this book, you will also find a handy glossary of terms, a useful index, and several appendices that contain more detailed documents and information. Best of all, you will find a comprehensive directory of safe Internet sites for children. Be sure to read through Appendix D, "Using SurfWatch," if you plan on installing and using the SurfWatch software included with this book.

INFO BYTE

Schools are facing a great liability at the present time—they can be sued for almost anything a child might see on the Internet if the parent feels it is indecent . . . that's a very scary thought to me.

—*Donna Fernandez, Dallas Independent School District, from the World Wide Web in Education mailing list*

The fact that crimes are being committed online. . . is not a reason to avoid using these (online) services. To tell children to stop using these services would be like telling them to forgo attending college because students are sometimes victimized on campus.

—from *Child Safety on the Information Highway*

DON'T PULL THE PLUG ON THE NET!

This book does not aim to push any sort of agenda except one—we want to persuade you *not* to pull the plug on Internet access for young people. Despite its negatives, the Net is just too valuable as a learning tool to warrant the severance of access.

If you want to read further, The National Center for Missing and Exploited Children publishes a free brochure by Larry Magid, called *Child Safety on the Information Highway* (a short portion of which is excerpted on page 11). It explains why legitimate concerns about Internet safety should not keep adults and children from taking advantage of the Net's opportunities. A copy may be found on the Internet at the address below.

REFERENCES

Magid, Larry. "Child Safety on the Information Highway." [Online] Available http://www.larry'sworld.com.

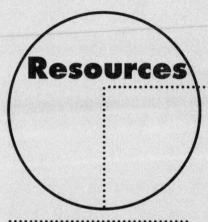

Resources LEARN MORE ABOUT IT!

INTERNET BASICS

Don't fret if you are not using the Internet yet! Not *everybody* is online and we were all beginners once. Consult the following resources to learn what the Internet is and how to use it.

Books

▣ **Zen and the Art of the Internet**
Brendan Kehoe
Prentice Hall
ISBN: 0–13–452914–6
URL: http://www.prenhall.com/~ray/list/internet.html

▣ **The Internet Unleashed 1996**
SAMS Development Group
Macmillan Publishing USA
ISBN: 1–57521–041-X

▣ **Internet For Parents**
Karen Strudwick, John Spilker, and Jay Arney
Resolution Business Press
ISBN 0–945264–17–8
URL: http://www.halcyon.com/ResPress/parents.htm

Internet Sites

▣ **Internet Basics**
URL: http://www.sen.ca.gov/www/leginfo/docs/orient/
help1_intro.html

□ **EFF's (Extended) Guide to the Internet: A Round-Trip through Global Networks, Life in Cyberspace, and Everything. . .**
http://www.nova.edu/Inter-Links/bigdummy/bdg_toc.html

□ **The Unofficial Internet Book List: The Most Extensive Bibliography of Books about the Internet**
URL: http://www.northcoast.com/savetz/blist.html

□ **Starting Points for Internet Beginners**
URL: http://www.acad.bg/beginner/beginner.html

□ **Internet Basics by Roy Tennet**
URL: http://unixg.ubc.ca:7001/00/i-guides/i-basics.txt

EDUCATION ON THE NET

Try out some of the following resources if you're a little further along on the Internet learning curve and you want to use the Net to help your children or students enhance their education.

Books

□ **Educator's Internet Companion**
Staff of Classroom Connect
Wentworth Worldwide Media, Inc.
ISBN: 0–932577–10–5

□ **Educator's World Wide Web Tourguide**
Staff of Classroom Connect
Wentworth Worldwide Media, Inc.
ISBN: 0–932577–16–4
URL: http://www.classroom.net

□ **Internet for Teachers**
Douglas R. Steen, Mark R. Roddy, PhD, et al.
Resolution Business Press
ISBN: 0–945264–19–4
URL: http://www.halcyon.com/ResPress/teacher.htm

▣ **Education on the Internet: A Hands-On Book of Ideas, Resources, Projects, and Advice**
Jill H. Ellsworth
Macmillan Publishing USA
ISBN: 0–672–30595-X

....

Internet Sites

▣ **Classroom Connect on the 'Net**
URL: http://www.classroom.net

▣ **Web66: A K–12 World Wide Web Project**
URL: http://www.web66.coled.umn.edu/

▣ **24 Hours in Cyberspace**
URL: http://www.cyber24.com

▣ **International Registry of K–12 Schools on the Web**
URL: http://www.web66.coled.umn.edu/schools.html

▣ **EdWeb Home Page**
URL: http://www.edweb.cnidr.org:90/

▣ **ERIC—Educational Resources Information Center**
URL: http://www.ericir.syr.edu

▣ **OER—Online Educational Resources**
URL: http://www.quest.arc.nasa.gov/OER/

▣ **Get Connected to Learning Using the Internet**
URL: http://www.ericir.syr.edu/ICONN/ihome.html

....

Videos/Kits

▣ **The Internet Revealed**
Classroom Connect
A four-video series
800-638–1639

▣ **The Educators' Essential Internet Training System**
Classroom Connect
A training kit with trainer's manual, slide presentation, workbooks, videos, CyberPatrol software, and Internet access
800-638–1639

Chapter

1

THE INTERNET'S DARK SIDE

Although the Internet offers a
wealth of great educational and
entertainment material for children
and adults alike, it is also home to
some unsavory and possibly
threatening material. A knowledge
of these dangers and knowing
where they may reside can help
parents and teachers protect their
youngsters while still allowing them
to explore the numerous "good"
resources the Net has to offer.

WHAT ARE THE DANGERS OF THE NET?

Just as you can find "good" and "bad" people in your neighborhood, shopping malls, and even schools, you can find good and bad things on the Internet. It would be great if we could let children freely explore and learn online without worry, but the reality is that the Net offers some material that is unsuitable for children.

But what exactly are these online dangers and why do you need to know anything about them, other than the fact that they exist? Well, just remember the old saying: "Keep your friends close, but your enemies closer." Knowing what kind of inappropriate materials are on the Net and where they are likely to reside will help you keep your children away from them.

After reading this chapter, you will be able to:

Q» Get a firsthand, accurate view of the "darker" side of the Internet.
Q» Discuss with your children specific areas, services, or sites that are off-limits.
Q» Alert fellow Net-connected parents or teachers to sites and activities that should be avoided.
Q» Speak knowledgeably about Internet safety, filtering, and censorship with parents, educators, school boards, activists, lawmakers, and others.

IS THE NET AS DANGEROUS AS PEOPLE THINK?

The Internet is often not what people expect when they first log on. Some believe it to be worse than it actually is; while others do not understand all the fuss about it. People simply have not had a chance to catch up with this new communications medium. At first, they know only what they read or hear from others. Many base their perceptions on experiences with commercial online services, such as America Online, which is not the Internet, though it does offer limited access to it. For others, flurries of Internet articles, exposés, and reports in the media—many inaccurate or sensationalized—leave them understandably confused as to what's really going on in cyberspace.

THE INTERNET'S BACK ALLEYS

While this book will alert you to the objectionable materials online, where they're found, and how they're retrieved, it will not get *too* specific. This book is not a primer for finding and downloading such materials, so we will not provide the addresses of the objectionable sites we reference.

This book also will not cover bulletin board services (BBSs), many of which contain explicit adult content. BBSs are different from the Internet in that most of them are local, for-pay services. Establishing a connection to your Internet Service Provider will not enable you to log in directly to a BBS. Rather, you must be a paying member of the BBS before you can connect to and use the service. We focus on the inappropriate materials typically found on the Internet because the Net is more easily accessible to children.

In regards to commercial online services such as America Online or Prodigy, we will discuss the pitfalls of online chat rooms and email. Commercial services generally pose fewer immediate dangers for children because much of the content in services is controlled. However, they all offer access to Internet newsgroups, Web sites, and email, so many of the same Internet hazards also apply when you use commercial online services to get on the Net.

After reading the following sections, it may seem as if objectionable materials are pervasive and unavoidable. They're not! The Net offers hundreds of thousands of valuable, educational materials—resources you just cannot find anywhere else, which is why so many schools are getting

INFO BYTE

I was not very aware of what the Internet was before I got online. I thought it would pretty much be like the online services, such as Prodigy, Compuserve, etc. I thought the language and content would be 'moderated' or something. . . boy, what a shock to get a dose of reality! I really don't allow my children ([ages] 15, 11, 7) any unsupervised time on the Net.

—Carolyn Huesman, Churubusco, Indiana

I suppose I had the preconceived ideas of the "super-highway" that most adults had—smut, pornography, a fun thing to play with, and not really an educational tool . . . once I found out that the Internet had a lot of good educational content, I did allow [my children] to access the Net with my guidance. In fact, if you find pornographic material, you have to be looking for it specifically. I have been on the Internet for a little more than a year and I have not even come close to porno-graphic material!

—Anna & Gerry, Merrimack, New Hampshire

online. Many people actually *do* spend months or years surfing the Net without getting into unwanted situations. And, as you will learn in later chapters, you can take steps to steer children away from the kinds of online content we cover next.

PORNOGRAPHY FINDS A HOME ON THE NET

Of all the online dangers—except perhaps pedophiles—pornography gets the most attention. Issues surrounding pornography—morality, First Amendment rights, women's rights, and psychological effects—usually incite heated debate. The debate becomes even more intense, though, when the issue is *online* porn—porn that can be easily downloaded every day directly into thousands of homes, with few restrictions or barriers.

Most online pornography is found either on the graphically intensive World Wide Web or in Usenet newsgroups, where you can post images as well as text. Some ftp (file transfer protocol) and gopher sites contain pornographic or other objectionable images, but they do not seem to be nearly as popular or problematic as the Web or Usenet.

WHY BAD STUFF IS GETTING EASIER TO FIND

Many Internet users still believe that the risks of accidentally stumbling across pornographic materials online are few and that those who do encounter such materials probably set out to find them in the first place.

It used to be true that you really had to search for pornography online—there were only a few Usenet newsgroups devoted to exchanging graphics and even fewer Web sites. You had to know how to decode messages—graphics were temporarily converted to text format, so you needed to patch together long strings of nonsensical text and apply a converter to form a viewable picture. A few programs were available for actually *viewing* the pictures but they were not always easy to find or use.

Not many Web-site owners or hosts were brazen enough to post pornographic images and almost no commercial enterprises

---

INFO BYTE

This list of content categories blocked by a service called Specs For Kids offers an at-a-glance overview of the online materials considered inappropriate for kids. Each category includes a brief definition of the range of materials, from the minor to the extreme.

Sex	From sexual connotations to human intercourse
Nudity	American beach to gratuitous full nudity
Violence	Hitting (no blood) to gratuitous torture or death
Profanity	Common use of what is considered sacred
Hatred	Group degradation
Obscenity	Vulgar slang
Mature Themes	Suicide, drugs, tattooing and explosives, etc.
Text & Literature	Lengthy literature with mature adult themes
Gambling	Stories about gambling to actual betting
Games	Fantasy—competitive and adventure
Advertising	Commercial and credit card solicitation
Religion	Informational and opposing to recruiting
Politics	Informational and opposing to recruiting
Cartoon Violence	Violence with blood to gratuitous torture
Alt. Lifestyles	Informational, promotions to recruiting

> In all of my countless hours of surfing the Internet, I
> have yet to see my first dirty picture. I guess that's
> because I haven't been looking for any. When I go
> looking on the Net, I invariably find what I'm looking
> for. I'm sure that filthy-minded people . . . can find
> smut, if that's what they're looking for.
> —*Post to k12.teacher chat newsgroup*

used the Web to sell pornographic images, magazines, or videos.
Locating, converting, and viewing images was a long, arduous
process that usually discouraged most people from continuing
their efforts. Besides, when 2400 or 9600 baud modems were
the norm, who had time to download graphics? Even a small
graphic could take half an hour. Few children had access to an
Internet account, but even if they did, it was improbable that
they could carry on such activity for hours without being discovered by a parent or teacher.

Things have changed, though. Now it is much easier to find
and download pornography. As our keyword search back in the
Introduction demonstrated, you can even find it without looking.

What has changed to make online smut more easily available? At the most basic level, it is the law of supply and
demand. The Internet simply makes getting porn more conve-
nient for those who previously had to go to a store and pay for
magazines or videos. Never mind that minors may not be dis-
suaded by things like ID checks or the cover price of newsstand
pornography. Adults are demanding it, so the supply has risen
to meet that demand.

On the more technical side, modem speeds of 28.8 baud,
which enable people to upload and download graphics quickly,
are becoming the norm. Soon, ISDN or cable Internet lines
will become more affordable and widespread—pumping digital
information into households and schools faster than anyone
could have imagined. We can guess at some other factors that
lead to more computer porn: cheap color scanners, inexpensive
computers and mass storage devices, an increase of adult
CD-ROM products that provide endless fodder for porn
traders, and new Web technology that makes it easy to set up

powerful commercial servers or connect Web sites directly to adult bulletin board systems.

· ·

THE EXCHANGE OF PORN ON NEWSGROUPS

We now present a little background on Usenet newsgroups before discussing their dangers. There are about 13,000 active Usenet newsgroups or worldwide "discussion" groups. These Internet bulletin boards (not to be confused with bulletin board systems or BBSs) are places where people of similar interests can post "articles" for other visitors to read.

The "news" or traffic in these groups comes from a dizzying array of sources, including many networks that technically are not even part of the Internet. But they all have at least one thing in common: They all had to go through an "official" procedure to become widely distributed, accepted groups on the Internet. Proposed groups must go through a long voting procedure. The Usenet community discusses the proposed groups and votes whether to accept them.

Groups in these nine categories are not really regulated by any kind of central authority. They are self-policed, with a system of checks and balances that help control organization and content. Some are even moderated, which means volunteers regularly check all posts before being distributed. Messages that are inappropriate or off-topic are not posted. Moderators

---

Newsgroups fall into roughly nine main content categories:

INFO BYTE

alt.	alternatives to mainstream groups
comp.	computer professionals and hobbyists
k12.	groups for educators and students
sci.	science applications and research
news.	pertaining to the Usenet network itself
misc.	miscellaneous themes not easily classified under the other categories
soc.	socializing and discussing social issues
rec.	arts, crafts, hobbies, sports, and other recreation
talk.	groups with lots of debate on politics, religion, etc.

INFO BYTE

To read about the latest proposed groups, learn more about Usenet voting and membership, or check on the status of groups considered for inclusion, visit the following newsgroups.

news.announce.newsgroups
news.groups.questions
news.groups.reviews

make rules or guidelines available to all participants and firmly but fairly enforce them.

Another newsgroup hierarchy has emerged, however, and has grown considerably over the past few years—the alt or alternative newsgroup category. Generally, these groups are *not* moderated. In fact, anybody can create and run one and any host can decide to carry or not carry a particular alt group. The alt groups are, by and large, the ones you should watch out for!

Pornographic images are exchanged through roughly 50 major, active newsgroups—and most are within this alt hierarchy. These groups, though few compared with the entire Usenet hierarchy of 13,000, generate a lot of Internet traffic, receiving hundreds or thousands of new posts each day. Besides the alt.binaries.pictures groups, there are others in which graphics are posted and traded, including a range of newsgroups starting with alt.sex. Most of them are easily identifiable by their names. (See Figure 1.1.)

Almost all of the images within these groups come from print sources. In fact, people in these groups are probably responsible for more copyright violations than almost anyone else on the Internet! Participants use image scanners to convert photos from glossy magazines into digital GIF or JPEG graphical formats, then upload them through their news servers for the whole world to share. Graphic files are also frequently copied from adult CD-ROMs, bulletin board services, and Web sites and then posted.

Some ISPs or Usenet-news providers refuse to carry the most offensive of these explicit newsgroups, while others keep the channels wide open. If you're ever unsure as to what groups your ISP offers, call for more information on their policies or scan through the full group list yourself to see the content. Many service providers at least attempt to control the sheer amount of images trading in these groups by restricting posts to a certain file size, such as 20K, but breaking one large graphic file into smaller pieces (or saving images at lower resolution) gets around these minor annoyances.

It's pretty easy to spot a graphical file in a newsgroup and determine its content without downloading and viewing it. First, they usually have quite obvious file names, such as sexy.gif or hot.jpg. Files split into segments are labeled like this, one per line: sexy.gif ($\frac{1}{3}$), sexy.gif ($\frac{2}{3}$), and so forth. And as you have just seen, most are also followed by a .gif or .jpg extension, indicating that they are graphic file formats. Many contain special Usenet "shorthand" to help describe the photo—such as

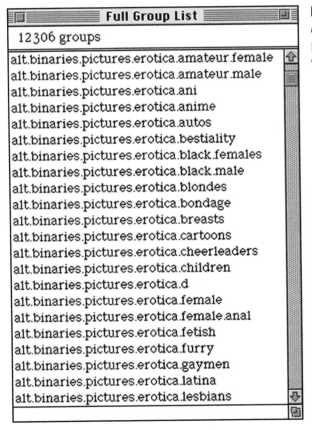

Figure 1.1
Most Usenet groups containing pornographic text and images are easily identified by their names.

M/M/F. Almost all have short descriptions included as the subject line of an image post or as a separate text message.

A range of programs now make it easy to enter these newsgroups, download files, and encode and decode them into viewable pictures. Powerful newsreader programs such as News-Watcher or NewsXPress automatically put together segmented files. Then, with a decoder program such as uuUndo, you need only drag the encoded file over an icon to instantly decode it. Double-click to launch a graphics viewer program, and you have your picture. Some of these viewers even offer slide-show features, so you can browse through a whole directory or folder full of images.

Most computer-savvy kids would have no trouble figuring out how to do this. But if they could not, there are plenty of people within these newsgroups who freely offer technical assistance. In some newsgroups, individuals "lurk" or hang out with the express purpose of offering help to those having trouble downloading, decoding, and viewing images. One wonders about their intentions.

To some, this process is still too difficult, but the constant evolution of Internet software is making it easier to obtain newsgroup images. Newer Web browsers such as Netscape 2.0 offer built-in newsreaders that let you access newsgroups right from the browser window. Graphics are automatically downloaded, decoded, and displayed in the newsgroup window.

If young people cannot find graphics just by surfing around, then they can use a Web search engine called DejaNews, which allows them to scan Usenet posts in much the same way as searching for Web sites.

Finally, it is worth noting that, unlike the Web, Usenet porn purveyors do not need any special connections, equipment, or even a hosting service to "publish" pornography on the Internet. There are fewer checks along the way to prevent objectionable materials from being distributed. Although building a Web page is easier than it used to be, not everyone can put up a Web page yet. And even if they could, the owners or "landlords" of those Web servers often watch for content that puts them at risk. Anybody with newsreading software and a Net connection, however, can publish anything that can be converted to digital information whenever they want. People with lots of experience and creativity can even post anonymously, making it impossible for investigators to trace them.

CASE STUDY: COMPUSERVE'S NEWSGROUP WOES

Despite America Online's overwhelming use by families, it is often the first name that comes to mind when you think of online porn on major commercial services. But CompuServe has also had its share of headaches. In 1995, pressured by the German government, CompuServe shut down its access to over 200 newsgroups. Among the blocked groups were the usual alt.binary offenders, but other, more tenable groups were also banned, including alt.politics.sex, alt.recovery.addiction.sexual, alt.religion.sexuality, alt.sex.historical, clari.news.crime.sex, and clari.news.gays.

German officials insisted that these newsgroups clearly broke many of the nation's laws. As expected, "cyber rights activists" around the world immediately criticized CompuServe for abandoning too easily the Net's principles of free information exchange.

PORN BUSINESS ON THE WEB

The Web seems a natural choice for those purveying indecent materials over the Internet. Since it is literally a point-and-click environment, you can be instantly transported to a whole new online realm with one (possibly accidental) touch of a mouse. Graphics display easily—you do not need extra viewer software or decoders. You can easily bookmark sites so that you can return anytime or you can set up your own page with collections of lusty links.

How many Web sites contain pornographic materials? This is anyone's guess. It is much more difficult to keep up with the daily addition of new Web sites than growth in other areas of the Net. Every day it seems as if yet another Net-head establishes his very own "Babe of the Week" page.

Smutty content on the Web ranges from swimsuit model photos and lingerie ads, to online versions of *Hustler*, *Penthouse*, and *Playboy*, all the way to hardcore magazines.

Figure 1.2
Most adult-oriented Web sites open with a warning explaining that the content within is not meant for minors. Others do not, but often such notices just entice people to enter the site.

Most of these sites are located in the .com, or commercial, domain. (See Figure 1.2.)

Realize that any graphic on any Netscape screen can be instantly saved to disk (or its location copied for future reference) by clicking and holding down your mouse pointer on the graphic. If you do want to search for pornography or any other objectionable materials, you have many more powerful tools at your disposal. Enter a long string of keywords (try *naked, nude, explicit, adult, xxx, porn, hot, babes*) into the WebCrawler search engine **(http://webcrawler.com)** and see what you find. You'll get links to thousands of sites—many standing directories of links to other sites offering sexual content. Some even provide critiques, ratings, or listings of the "best sex sites on the Net"— those with free graphics usually get the highest marks.

Even worse, online smut is fast becoming a big business, as hundreds of sites establish for-pay services every month. To subscribe to one of these Web services, users must call ahead with credit card information or set up special online payment accounts. They get passwords so they can freely access and download all images. Even though you have to be a paying member to get to most of the "good" adult files or areas, almost all of these services have a separate "Guest" area where nonsubscribers can preview the types of materials they'll receive if they send payment right away. Offering "visitor" areas is usually a thinly disguised way of luring even more people to a site.

CHILD PORNOGRAPHY THRIVES

Child pornography is the least common but most dangerous of the offensive materials online. It cannot be produced without actual physical abuse or molestation. Recent police raids of child porn rings, however, provide evidence that it may be even more rampant than previously thought. The Internet's global nature complicates law-enforcement efforts, since it connects users to parts of the world where child porn is either legal or decriminalized.

Because of the zero-tolerance environment for child pornography, most child porn activity on the Internet is underground. Graphics are privately exchanged within small circles of collectors, as opposed to being placed in widely accessible areas on the Web or in newsgroups. Be warned, though, that there are several renegade Usenet newsgroups that may house child pornography. With just a little nudging from the local community to make them aware of such activity, many Internet Service Providers or Usenet newsfeeds will usually remove these groups from their newsfeeds or delete then posts.

INFO BYTE

In the United States and Canada it is illegal to produce, distribute, or own pornography involving minors under any circumstance or in any form. In recent years, offenders have been caught and prosecuted more frequently. Those found guilty face up to 10 years in prison and a $10,000 fine. Child pornographers have no claim to free speech protection under the First Amendment.

If you encounter child pornography in any form, be sure to notify your Internet Service Provider or the organization hosting the offending materials. Contact the National Center for Missing and Exploited Children by calling 800-843-5678.

CASE STUDY: CHILD PORN ON AMERICA ONLINE

One of the biggest online child porn cases in recent years did not involve the Internet, but the commercial service America Online. According to an Associated Press article in *USA Today*, the FBI raided 120 homes across the United States and arrested dozens of people after a two-year investigation of child pornography activities in AOL.

The FBI issued a statement asserting that "the utilization of online services or bulletin board systems is rapidly becoming one of the most prevalent techniques for individuals to share pornographic pictures of minors, as well as to identify and recruit children into sexually illicit relationships." America Online reportedly cooperated with authorities in uncovering illegal activity, which occurs mainly through email correspondence between users, most often initiated in one of the live chat rooms.

Despite such highly publicized busts, however, concerns still abound about child pornography on America Online. Critics of AOL, the largest of the "Big Three" commercial services, state that anyone can create a private "chat room" on the service and trade images without much fear of reprisal. AOL specifically prohibits child porn and similar activities in its Terms of Service (TOS) agreement, which each member must sign. But if no one complains or AOL is unaware of such activities, the criminal activity could continue unchecked.

Besides, thousands of people logon to AOL with temporary trial accounts—those diskettes that offer 10–15 free hours and seem to be everywhere. They can also access the service with copies of AOL "hacker" programs that let them log on without real accounts, so the TOS agreement becomes meaningless.

Children's rights and safety activist and writer Barry Crimmins spent considerable time researching the degree to which child porn was prevalent and available on the service. During his many hours logged on to the service, Crimmins claims to have encountered numerous chat rooms "obviously created by, and for, pedophiles," including rooms where child porn was openly exchanged and rooms with titles such as "DadsNDaughtrs."

He reported that he was even sent materials without asking for them. Crimmins claims he frequently notified AOL of the child porn activity, even forwarding the images to company representatives as proof, but AOL said it was unable to do anything about most of the activity since it occurred via private email.

In its defense, AOL replied that only a small percentage of its members are involved in illegal activities, that its TOS specifically prohibits such activities, and that violators are turned over to the authorities when they are discovered. Further, the company stated that employees constantly scan the service for such chat rooms, but by the time one chat room can be shut down, several new ones are created. The complete text of Crimmins' testimony, including responses from staff at America Online, can be found on the Web.

We experienced such activities firsthand within America Online chat rooms. While we were in a Macintosh computing chat room, a participant emailed every person in the room a compressed folder containing several explicit, full-color images, including a grotesque murder scene and explicit sex photos. The folder containing the graphics was sent by AOL email, and there was no initial indication of its contents. There was no member profile available for the sender, and email sent to him or her returned with an error.

America Online reports that it is working on improving its technology, procedures, and staff training in order to help reduce or eliminate these kinds of activities. Until then, even if only a fraction of what Crimmins reports is true, parents and educators need to be especially wary of the America Online chat rooms. See the section in Chapter 3 on how to control or completely deny access to these chat areas.

Working both under my own name and undercover (often with a profile that clearly stated I was 12 years old), I have been sent over a thousand pornographic photographs of children via AOL. I have seen every possible type of sexual degradation of children, from toddlers to teens.

—Barry Crimmins
excerpt from Senate testimony on cyberporn

INFO BYTE

THE ARRIVAL OF PORNOGRAPHIC MOVIES

In addition to graphical images, a growing portion of pornography providers are moving toward putting video clips online. Video is becoming more common for many of the same reasons image files are common now—faster connections and better viewers, as well as cheaper yet faster computers that enable users to run full motion, color video on their PCs with good results. Also, with inexpensive audio and video hardware and software kits available for any kind of computer, it is easier than ever to hook up a VCR, cable connection, or even satellite feed to a PC and record digital movies.

Like GIF or JPEG files, pornographic movies are most often encountered on Web sites or in certain Usenet newsgroups. Movie files usually have suffixes such as .mpg, .mov, .avi, or .dl, which indicate the video format in which they are saved. You need special movie players to watch them, though some newer programs can convert a wide variety of movie formats. New browsers such as Netscape will soon eliminate the need for any external viewers—which at least slow down the process. Right now, with a freely available plug-in, Netscape 2.0 can play QuickTime movies without viewers "inline," which means it will appear right on the browser screen. Other movie formats will soon follow.

Even though they are highly compressed, video clips still take up a lot of space. Downloading a single 30-second clip via a 14.4 modem might take half an hour and 1.5 megabytes of hard drive space. They also require lots of RAM to play properly without crashing the computer. Youngsters will not likely go undetected when downloading, storing, and playing these movie files.

THE POWER OF PORNOGRAPHIC TEXT

A picture can speak a thousand words, but a thousand words of explicit, hardcore, pornographic text can be pretty powerful stuff, too. There are plenty of places online where wild fictional stories, hands-on sex guides or manuals, and candid personal accounts can be found and downloaded. Most of this material is comparable to the text in magazines such as *Penthouse Forum,* where "sex-savvy" individuals swap stories of their adventures and brag of their prowess. Of course, more extreme examples can be found, too, including rape fantasies, anal sex instructions, or violent, perverted fiction.

Some "adult" text is found right where you would expect it—in the alt newsgroups or on the Web. But many other areas of the Net can house such materials. Since they are such a good medium for storing and serving text documents, some of the "private" ftp and gopher sites contain large collections of pornographic documents, many of which are archived from Usenet discussions.

Much pornographic text on the Internet, however, is not really stored anywhere—it is created on-the-fly via IRC (Internet Relay Chat) or similar online chat sessions or is contained within private email correspondence. IRC is a method for communicating in "real time" with other users, similar to chat rooms in Prodigy or AOL. Messages you type on your computer appear on the screens of all the other users in the same "virtual room" or channel.

Fortunately, it is easier to avoid receiving explicit text via email or IRC than it is to avoid it on the Web or Usenet. If someone insists on sending your child offensive email, you can at least demand that he or she stop, call the authorities, notify the individual's service provider, or—all else failing—simply change your email address. In chat rooms, you can set controls to ignore messages from certain individuals, leave the particular room and set up your own private, invitation-only chat area, or simply forgo IRC completely, since it is among the least useful of online educational tools. (We will discuss these topics in more detail later in this book.)

Before we take a look at some of the places you will want your young ones to avoid, read this brief overview of media events surrounding objectionable materials online. We will begin by taking a quick look at the "cyberporn" controversy, which brought concerns about objectionable material to the forefront. Then we will briefly explain the Telecommunications Reform Act, which has serious implications for every person using the Internet.

TIME MAGAZINE AND THE CYBERPORN CONTROVERSY

Now that you have a clear picture of the nature of pornography on the Net, we will discuss the controversy over cyberporn and its effects. *Time* magazine's now infamous "cyberporn" issue brought Internet pornography to the forefront. (See Figure 1.3.) In the cover story, titled "On a Screen Near You: Cyberporn," *Time* reporter Philip Elmer DeWitt drew upon research conducted by a team at Carnegie Mellon University. This research team, led by undergraduate Marty Rimm, published a study called "Marketing Pornography on the Information Superhighway: A Survey of 917,410 Images, Descriptions, Short Stories, and Animations Downloaded 8.5 Million Times by Consumers in Over 2000 Cities in Forty Countries, Provinces and Territories."

The study painted a bleak picture of the Internet landscape. The Rimm report stated that 83.5 percent of all the images within Internet newsgroups were pornographic. DeWitt wrote that trading explicit graphics was "one of the largest (if not the largest) recreational applications of users of computer networks." The article also relayed the study's assertion that much of the online pornography went well beyond merely depicting naked men and women engaged in sexual acts. In fact, one could find pedophilia, bondage, sado-masochism, defecation, and bestiality images in numerous Usenet newsgroups, without trying too hard. It came to the following conclusion:

> The appearance of material like this on a public network accessible to men, women and children around the world raises issues too important to ignore—or to oversimplify. Parents have legitimate concerns about what their kids are being exposed to and, conversely, what those children might miss if their access to the Internet were cut off. Lawmakers must balance public safety with their obligation to preserve essential civil liberties.

The study's findings were soon adopted by various conservative special interest groups and politicians as powerful proof that the Internet and commercial online services must be closely regulated and policed by the government. Critics of the *Time* article and the Rimm study, however, began debunking Rimm's study within days in efforts to discredit the *Time* article. Among the critics were Donna L. Hoffman and Thomas P. Novak, researchers and marketing experts who specialize in Internet communications. They examined Rimm's report and found it to be misleading on many counts.

For one thing, asserted Novak and Hoffman, the study counted graphics on adult BBSs (bulletin board systems), which are generally *not* freely accessible to Internet users, along with Usenet pornographic images. To gain access to an adult-oriented BBS, you must subscribe with a credit card. The critics maintained that in actuality less than 1 percent of all files posted to Usenet newsgroups are pornographic—quite a difference compared to the study's assertion that more than 80 percent of Usenet images are pornographic.

Other researchers investigated Rimm's background. They soon discovered a 1990 letter from Rimm to the Atlantic City Casino Commission claiming that he had hacked a casino's computer system and found potentially damaging information about the activities of certain government officials. They also

Figure 1.3
This *Time* magazine cover story ignited the controversy surrounding pornography on the Internet. Although the statistics cited in the article were frightening, many researchers immediately set out to debunk what they believed were misleading, inflammatory claims.

INFO BYTE

Rimm study critics Hoffman and Novak explain their interest in the cyberporn debate on their Web site.

"Our objective is to provide a forum for a constructive, honest, and open critique process. We do not debate the existence of pornography in 'cyberspace,' though we do dispute the findings presented in the Rimm study and the Time article concerning its extent and consumption on the Internet. . . . The critically important national debate over First Amendment rights and restrictions on the Internet and other emerging media requires facts and informed opinion, not hysteria.

"Both the Rimm study and the Time cover story contain serious conceptual, logical, and methodological flaws and errors. These flaws and errors are sufficiently severe that neither the Rimm study nor the Time cover story should be taken seriously by policy makers considering issues involving the Internet and the so-called 'Information Superhighway.'"

—Donna L. Hoffman and Thomas P. Novak
Internet researchers and marketing experts

learned about a book that Rimm had published called *The Pornographer's Handbook: How to Exploit Women, Dupe Men, and Make Lots of Money.* Rimm claimed the book was meant only as satire, but critics claim it undermines his objectivity as a researcher on the subject.

Rimm published a counter-critique in which he addressed many of the questions, claims, and assertions made by Hoffman and Novak in their evaluation of his study and the *Time* article. The counter-critique provides some good arguments in defense of the study.

In the end, however, it is not important which study is accurate or which percentage is correct or how much pornography *really* is online. If only a dozen pornographic images existed on the Internet, you still would not want children to download them. Even though the article and the research it was based on created controversy—warranted or not—some good *did* result from it. The article was among the first in a major print publication to cover key issues and make pertinent statements about the environment of the online world. It captured the attention of people who had not really thought at all about online pornography or dangers to children.

ABOUT THE NEW TELECOMMUNICATIONS LAW

Most of the Telecommunications Reform Act of 1996, a bill signed into law February 8, 1996, by President Clinton, focuses on deregulating advanced telecommunications and information technologies to open U.S. markets to more competition.

Of interest to those concerned about cyberporn is Section 501, "Communications Decency Act of 1996." This section amends federal legislation so that obscenity laws can now include computer communications and the Internet. It makes it a federal crime to expose minors to "indecent, filthy or patently offensive" material. Violators could face up to two years in prison and a $250,000 fine.

In June 1996, a unanimous vote of 3–0 by the United States Court of Appeals ruled that the Communications Decency Act is unconstitutional. According to Judge Sloviter, "the CDA is patently a government-imposed content-based restriction on speech, and the speech at issue, whether denominated 'indecent' or 'patently offensive,' is entitled to constitutional protection." The issue will most likely be finally settled by the Supreme Court.

Despite its unsure status, the law still highlights several key issues in the Internet porn debate. The specific language of the bill covers the following types of communications via computer networks:

> The transmission of any comment, request, suggestion, proposal, image, or other communication which is obscene, lewd, lascivious, filthy, or indecent, with intent to annoy, abuse, threaten, or harass another person.

Internauts around the world protested the Communications Decency Act by changing the background colors on thousands of Web sites to black to symbolize mourning. Some also proudly displayed "Free Speech Online" blue ribbons.

The bill also covers these types of communication:

> Any comment, request, suggestion, proposal, image, or other communication that, in context, depicts or describes, in terms patently offensive as measured by contemporary community standards, sexual or excretory activities or organs, regardless of whether the user of such service placed the call or initiated the communication.

What counts as obscene or indecent? The bill refers to the Obscene Publications Act of 1959 and 1964 for definition. In short, an article is deemed obscene if:

> The effect of any one of its items is, if taken as a whole, such as to tend to deprave and corrupt persons who are likely, having regard to all relevant circumstances, to read, see or hear the matter contained or embodied in it. The language of the Obscene Publications Act has been interpreted so that an *article* can include computer diskettes, CD-ROMs, video tapes, and audio cassettes.

WEAKNESSES OF THE TELECOMMUNICATIONS LAW

One major problem with the law is that it was constructed using pieces of other, older legislation, including the 1934 Communications Act, which was designed to regulate broadcast radio and TV. The Internet is not quite a broadcast medium, nor is it a print medium.

Questions remain as to how the test of community standards can be applied over a freely accessible, *global* network of computers. Obscene content can be downloaded from computers in other communities or countries where community standards may be much different. Besides, how will the law affect people who use the Internet within the privacy of their own homes? Materials that have been protected by the Constitution and established as legal through precedent can suddenly become *illegal* when available in digital format.

The other, more important problem is the bill's vagueness. Its broad language was immediately challenged by senators such as Patrick Leahy of Vermont, dozens of groups such as the American Civil Liberties Union, major communications companies, even the Speaker of the House, Newt Gingrich. According to the bill's provisions, *any* activity or material containing language about sexual activities that could potentially be witnessed by a minor online—including email, online chat, and Web pages—could be illegal. Critics point out that adults risk prosecution even if minors willfully seek out objectionable materials by posing as adults. See Figure 1.4 for how many Net users reacted the law.

The feared result is that the law would lead to a worldwide "chilling effect." Until now, the Net has provided a wonderful way to share ideas and thoughts with others—one of the main reasons for its dramatic growth. The online world is already a large, active forum for people with all sorts of interests, including religion, health, and politics. However, publishers, content providers, online experts, and everyday citizens will feel inhibited when it comes to open discussion and debate on important issues. The opportunity for bringing people of different cultures and beliefs together—of getting citizens actively involved in politics and government—could be lost as people begin to fear the repercussions of speaking out and voicing opinions.

Figure 1.4
People concerned about free speech on the Internet protested the Telecommunications Reform Act of 1996 by placing blue ribbons on their Web sites.

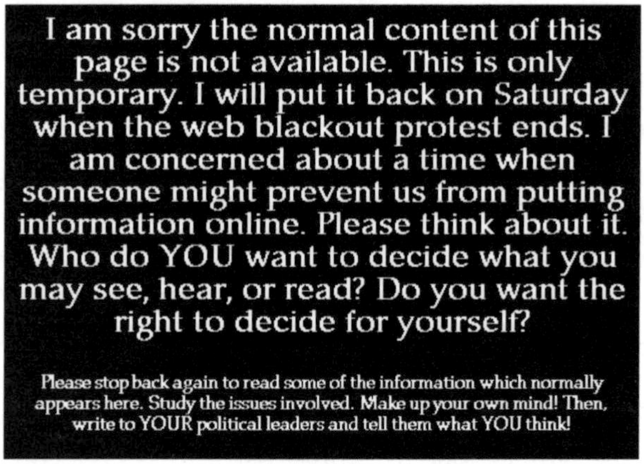

Figure 1.5
A black background on a
Web site signifies protest of
the Telecommunications
Reform Act of 1996.

I am sorry the normal content of this page is not available. This is only temporary. I will put it back on Saturday when the web blackout protest ends. I am concerned about a time when someone might prevent us from putting information online. Please think about it. Who do YOU want to decide what you may see, hear, or read? Do you want the right to decide for yourself?

Please stop back again to read some of the information which normally appears here. Study the issues involved. Make up your own mind! Then, write to YOUR political leaders and tell them what YOU think!

Control could also come from other corners. Powerful interests or individuals may abuse or manipulate online communications laws to silence opposition and promote their own views, or to extend those laws into the realms of print and broadcast media. Will Big Brother watch our every online move? Will we receive email from government officials stating that we are to immediately remove our pages from the World Wide Web? Where will the lines be drawn? (See Figure 1.5.)

WHAT THE LAW MAY MEAN TO YOU

Technically, the new law may make it illegal to provide objectionable material over computer networks. But it is doubtful that it will really offer you much protection or peace of mind when it comes to children finding inappropriate material.

First, in the practical sense, the law won't help you protect your child if he or she does access something harmful. Once explicit graphics have been downloaded and viewed, once a makeshift bomb has exploded in someone's face, once a recipe for LSD has been tested, the damage has already been done. The law will not replace adult interest, concern, and vigilance concerning children's online activities.

Second, the Internet is a truly difficult beat for *any* cop. Many legal analysts predict that the law would be loosely enforced because of the sheer number of cases that could erupt and the difficulty of prosecuting them. With millions of users from different countries and states—each with different sets of laws, community standards, and definitions of obscenity—many new layers of government and law enforcement will have to be established.

In a society already teeming with crowded prisons, overwhelmed courtrooms, swollen bureaucracies, and general distrust of lawmakers and politicians, the law may be a bit overambitious.

Finally, the law is being challenged by lawmakers, judges, millions of citizens, and dozens of large corporations with deep pockets. Even educators responsible for keeping students away from inappropriate materials are speaking out against it. General feelings in the K–12 online community are that most attempts to regulate the Internet are overly broad and may actually decrease the effectiveness of the law—if any.

For now, we'll have to wait until the issue is finally settled by the Supreme Court.

....

REFERENCES

Crimmins, Barry. "Testimony from July 24, 1995 Senate Judiciary Committee Hearing on Cyberporn." [Online]. Available http://www.cdt.org/policy/freespeech/crimins72495.html, February 3, 1996.

DeWitt, Philip Elmer. "On A Screen Near You: Cyberporn." *Time*. 3 July 1995: pp. 38–43.

Hoffman, Diane L. and Thomas P. Novak. "The Cyberporn Debate." [Online] Available http://www2000.ogsm.vanderbilt.edu/cyber-porn.debate.cgi#danger, March 1, 1996.

Hoffman, Diane L. and Thomas P. Novak. "A Detailed Critique of the TIME Article: 'On a Screen Near You: Cyberporn' (DeWitt, 7/3/95), Version 1.01" [Online] Available http://www2000.ogsm.vanderbilt.edu/dewitt.cgi, July 1995.

Jespen, Dee. "Testimony from July 24, 1995 Senate Judiciary Committee Hearing on Cyberporn." [Online] Available http://www.cdt.org/policy/freespeech/724list.html, February 3, 1996.

NewView, Inc. "Comprehensive Ratings Categories." [Online] Available http://www.newview.com/demo/dscntg.html, February 2, 1996.

United States Senate, House-Senate Conference Committee on Telecommunications Reform. *Telecommunications Reform Act of 1996*, 104th Congress, 2nd sess. §652. Washington: GPO, 1996.

Resources LEARN MORE ABOUT IT!

Related Internet Sites

☐ **U.S. Telecommunications Reform Act of 1996 (S. 652)**
URL: http://thomas.loc.gov/cgi-bin/query/z?c104:s.652.enr:

☐ **Challenge to the Communications Decency Act of 1996 in *United States District Court Eastern District of Pennsylvania ACLU, et.al. v. Janet Reno***
URL: http://www.aclu.org/court/cdacom.html

☐ **National Public Radio Stories on the Telecom Bill and Exon Amendment**
URL: http://www.well.com/user/srhodes/telecom.html

☐ **Center for Democracy and Technology**
URL: http://www.cdt.org/

☐ **The Internet Censorship page at EPIC (Electronic Privacy Information Center)**
URL: http://epic.org/free_speech/censorship/

☐ ***Time*'s "Cyberporn" Cover Story**
URL: http://pathfinder.com/@qGCGnxFxyAMAQG60/time/magazine/domestic/1995/950703/950703.cover.html

☐ **The Cyberporn Debate—Hoffman and Novak's Critique**
Includes links to dozens of online resources that critique or evaluate the Rimm study and provide additional information.
URL: http://www2000.ogsm.vanderbilt.edu/cyberporn.debate.cgi

☐ **Marty Rimm's Critique of the Hoffman/Novak Critique**
URL: http://TRFN.pgh.pa.us/guest/mrcrit.html

◻ **The Rimm Study**
"Marketing Pornography on the Information Superhighway:
A Survey of 917,410 Images, Description, Short Stories and
Animations Downloaded 8.5 Million Times by Consumers in
Over 2000 Cities in Forty Countries, Provinces and
Territories"
URL: http://TRFN.pgh.pa.us/guest/mrstudy.html

◻ **Yahoo Index of Cyberporn Debate Links**
URL: http://www.yahoo.com/News/Journalism/Censorship/
The_Cyberporn_Debate/

Chapter 2

DANGEROUS MINDS

When considering inappropriate material for children on the Internet, most people immediately think of pornography.

In truth, smut is not the only thing you'll want your children to avoid. Antisocial attitudes and behavior, as well as grotesque or violent images, can be even more damaging to a young mind.

PORNOGRAPHY IS NOT THE ONLY DANGER . . .

Although it gets a lot of attention, pornography is not the only thing to worry about when it comes to children and the Internet. It is, however, the most common form of "adult" entertainment on the Net and seems to be the type of online material many adults are most concerned about keeping away from children. Certainly the media pays a lot of attention to it.

But ideas can be as dangerous as images. So can people with antisocial tendencies who want to lure others into their circle. In this chapter we will discuss those "other" online materials from which you will want to protect your children.

THE APPEAL OF THE GRUESOME

Many of us have felt a strange curiosity about gruesome scenes or events. How many of us have tried to sneak a peek as we slowly pass an auto accident on the highway? For some reason, looking upon these things satisfies a morbid curiosity, perhaps because it gives us a closer look at death without actually placing our own lives in danger. But seeing photos or depictions of death, dismemberment, or violent degradation can be incredibly damaging to young people, especially when no adult is present to help them make sense of what they see.

Despite this, numerous Web sites cater to those looking to satisfy this curiosity by offering gruesome, explicit close-up shots

Figure 2.1
Sites with grotesque or bizarre material can be disturbing to very young children.

of suicides, murders, autopsies, hangings or lynchings, car accidents, and any other bloody, gory scene. (See Figure 2.1.)

Some people seem to put these images online with the sole purpose of shocking, horrifying, or outraging other Internet users. The content of one particular newsgroup typically includes pictures of corpses or mutated animals.

Other objectionable materials online include books on how to torture or trap animals or people, execution techniques, biographies that glorify brutal serial killers, and images or text from exploitation movies and books. (See Figure 2.2.) Many of the same things we talked about concerning pornography—locations, graphic file formats, viewers, saving images, and so forth—apply here as well.

THE TACTICS OF ONLINE PEDOPHILES

Pedophiles are individuals who are attracted to and seek out children for sexual encounters. Parents and teachers have always been wary of the dangers of child molesters hanging out on street corners or near playgrounds. Children are taught from a very young age not to accept car rides or gifts from strangers.

Figure 2.2
Some sites glorify deviant behavior and criminals. This can be confusing to a child who may question what is truly "right and wrong" behavior.

Now, those who would abuse or molest children have another way to contact them—through online correspondence. As is so often the case, several heavily reported incidents of adults luring children into face-to-face meetings via email or online chat have brought to national attention this danger and the increased need for caution.

We now realize that children who would normally be very cautious of "stranger dangers" on the street can quickly forget that there may be dangerous people on the other end of the modem, too. It is all too easy for an adult to pose as a child, establish a friendship, and pry personal information, such as phone numbers or street addresses, from trusting children or even adults. We usually do not have the benefit of observing an online "friend's" nonverbal communication, knowing them instead only by what they *choose* to tell us.

In some situations, online predators may not even need to pose as children—they can easily trick youngsters who are simply naive or overly trusting of strangers. Consider this testimony from Dee Jespen, speaking at the July 24, 1995, Senate Judiciary Committee Hearing on Cyberporn. Jespen is president of Enough is Enough!, a nonprofit women's organization opposing child pornography and illegal obscenity.

> A friend . . . tells how her husband intercepted a suspicious [email] letter from a distant state addressed to their 16-year-old daughter. The letter proved to be from an adult man to whom the young girl had given her real name and address over her computer. This electronic predator began his letter by asking the girl to describe her fantasies, and then described his. He went into graphic, vulgar sexual detail. At first the teenager laughed about it, but quickly realized that it was no laughing matter, for her obscene "pen pal" could show up on her doorstep one day to fulfill his fantasy. She made the dangerous mistake of giving out her real name and address to an unknown person through her home computer.

Adult perpetrators may also take advantage of children for reasons besides sexual encounters. They may try to get information from children to help them case your home for burglaries or to sell you something. The potential hazards are limited only by the imaginations of criminals and swindlers.

It is easy to understand how online predators might scare families right off the Internet. Take heart, though—the actual frequency of adults attempting to or actually harassing, molesting, or prying information from children is very low, especially when compared with the enormous amount of user traffic on the Net. The dangers to children in our own towns and neighborhoods are still much greater than those of the online world. Besides, if all the caring, friendly, well-mannered Internauts out there abandon the online world because of a few bad apples, the bad apples will have won.

HATE LITERATURE AND PROPAGANDA

The Internet community prides itself on being one in which ideas are openly discussed and debated. One of its main claims to fame is as a place where people of all walks of life are welcome, and (to quote a famous Net saying) "nobody knows you're a dog." All sorts of people with different views, personalities, and backgrounds frequent the Internet—people who would otherwise go largely unnoticed or have no soapbox or pulpit *without* the Net. (See Figure 2.3, for example.)

Unfortunately for families trying to encourage principles of decency and kindness as well as open-mindedness, this atmosphere includes individuals who promote hate, racism, and other

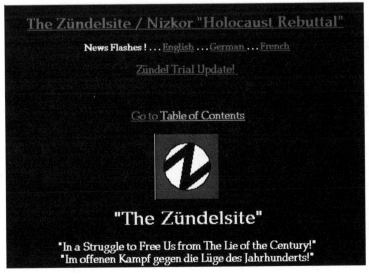

Figure 2.3
The Net is a global forum in which people from all walks of life can exchange ideas and philosophies. Unfortunately, it can also act as a posting board for people who want to spread dangerous propaganda.

Figure 2.4
Some militant and extremist
organizations actually recruit
members via the Internet.

The CNG is an cell-based White Nationalist organization.
It's battleground is the Internet. The CNG develops
propaganda, distributes propaganda, and recruits for
real-world organizations.

CNG Material

* The CNG Manifesto
* CNG Information
* CNG Divisions
* CNG Propaganda
* The Homosexual Threat
* The Original CNG Guide
* Suggestions for USENET Strategy

dangerous antisocial views. For example, numerous Web sites
host propaganda claiming that there was no Holocaust, that
homosexuals should be removed from society, and that whites
are superior to all races. See Figure 2.4.

Newsgroups are especially favored among many bigoted,
extremist individuals, offering them a way to be heard where
there may not be any other "acceptable" or even legal way.
Often, certain Usenet newsgroups become overwhelmed with
racial "flame wars"—somebody will post a discriminatory message with the intent to incite an online race riot. Insults, racist
statements, and hateful messages are thoughtlessly flung back
and forth until a moderator steps in or people tire of it.

EXPOSURE TO DISSIMILAR VIEWS

On the less drastic side, there are thousands and thousands of
people whom you or your children may encounter online who
hold political, religious, or social ideas and beliefs that directly
conflict with your own. You can find them in newsgroups, chat
rooms, or Web pages. Some may even try to send you email
explaining their opinions. (See Figures 2.5 and 2.6.)

In fact, exposure to people of varied backgrounds usually
turns out to be a positive educational experience, especially as
children become older and more independent. It can be positive if parents are present to help children understand some of
the strange or different people or things they encounter.

Trouble arises when youngsters are repeatedly exposed to such information behind their parents' backs. Young children are quite impressionable. It is all too easy for them to find and read propaganda for one cause or another, accept casual or thoughtless comments at face value, become amenable to "values" that conflict with their family's, or develop distorted, one-sided views of the world.

Figure 2.5
Children freely surfing the Net may access information that conflicts with your family's religious or political views. By supervising your child's Internet activity, you can be prepared to answer any questions he or she may have when they find something controversial.

Figure 2.6
Political views of every type are presented on the Internet.

"DANGEROUS" INFORMATION FOR YOUNG MINDS

The "battle cry" of the Net has traditionally been "Information wants to be free," but some kinds of information stored online can be physically dangerous in the hands of naive or curious youngsters. The more-obvious examples include recipes for making bombs or drugs, instructions for performing self-abortions, or inaccurate information about sex or reproduction. Some of these materials are strictly tongue-in-cheek, but others are meant as reference guides. (See Figure 2.7.)

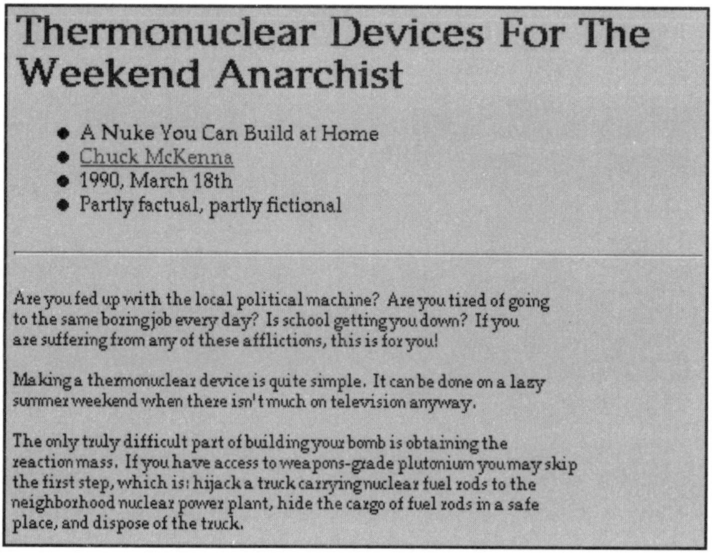

Figure 2.7
Yes, a few Internet sites explain how to make bombs and other destructive devices. But these types of plans have always been available in print form in libraries and government archives.

> # Thermonuclear Devices For The Weekend Anarchist
>
> * A Nuke You Can Build at Home
> * Chuck McKenna
> * 1990, March 18th
> * Partly factual, partly fictional
>
> ---
>
> Are you fed up with the local political machine? Are you tired of going to the same boring job every day? Is school getting you down? If you are suffering from any of these afflictions, this is for you!
>
> Making a thermonuclear device is quite simple. It can be done on a lazy summer weekend when there isn't much on television anyway.
>
> The only truly difficult part of building your bomb is obtaining the reaction mass. If you have access to weapons-grade plutonium you may skip the first step, which is: hijack a truck carrying nuclear fuel rods to the neighborhood nuclear power plant, hide the cargo of fuel rods in a safe place, and dispose of the truck.

CASE STUDY: BOMB MAKERS

Two cases have popped up already in which youths used bomb-making information downloaded from the Internet with disastrous results. According to the January 13, 1996, *Australia Newswire*, a teenager gained accessed to an Internet newsgroup from school to learn how to make the bomb which "exploded into his chest at his backyard birthday party."

The *New York Times* reported another case involving three 13-year-old boys from Syracuse, New York. Reportedly, the boys were charged with "plotting to set off a homemade bomb in their junior high school after getting plans for the device on the Internet." They were caught with fertilizer, diesel fuel, and other bomb-making materials, police reported.

An ironic note about these kinds of incidents is that plans, recipes, or books on making bombs, explosions, traps, poisons, and other weapons of warfare are quite often widely available in print form in libraries or government archives. As with pornography, most "dangerous" literature begins and continues life on paper until someone decides to digitize it, giving it new life on the Net.

Other materials many parents will find objectionable include Web sites or newsgroups advocating, displaying, or providing information on alternative lifestyles and sexual behavior, depression or suicide, drug use, anarchy or antisocial behavior, or anything else that might conflict with their personal values or culture. (See Figures 2.8 and 2.9.) Some parents may not take issue with the information per se, but would rather have the opportunity to talk to their teenagers first.

SCAM OPERATORS, FRAUD, AND HACKERS

Many "enterprising" Internet users—probably the same folks who run 1-900 sex lines or real estate or insurance fraud scams in the "real world"—have discovered that the Internet can also be a great tool for making a quick buck.

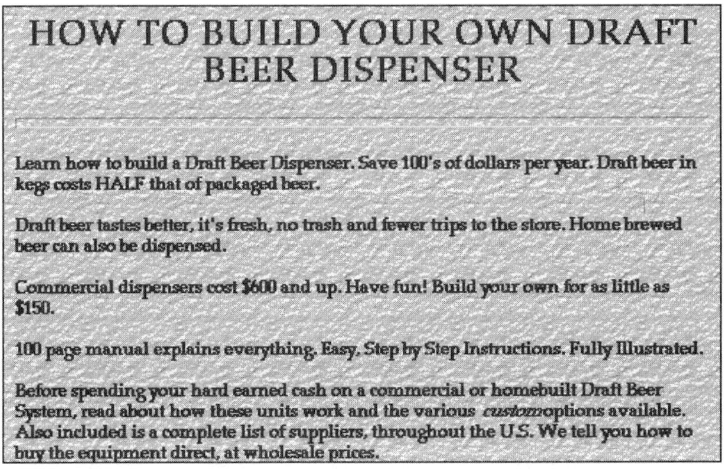

HOW TO BUILD YOUR OWN DRAFT BEER DISPENSER

Learn how to build a Draft Beer Dispenser. Save 100's of dollars per year. Draft beer in kegs costs HALF that of packaged beer.

Draft beer tastes better, it's fresh, no trash and fewer trips to the store. Home brewed beer can also be dispensed.

Commercial dispensers cost $600 and up. Have fun! Build your own for as little as $150.

100 page manual explains everything. Easy, Step by Step Instructions. Fully Illustrated.

Before spending your hard earned cash on a commercial or homebuilt Draft Beer System, read about how these units work and the various *custom* options available. Also included is a complete list of suppliers, throughout the U.S. We tell you how to buy the equipment direct, at wholesale prices.

Figure 2.8
In addition to containing information about making explosive devices, some Web sites explain how to make beer, wine, alcohol and even illegal drugs.

Figure 2.9
Most teenagers face tough decisions regarding drug and alcohol use, and try to do the right thing. Understandably, parents may be concerned about Web sites that advocate alcohol and recreational drugs.

Welcome to HIGH TIMES
Finally! Somewhere you can relax, light a phattie, and enjoy the atmosphere
LET US BEGIN THE JOURNEY...

NEWSFLASH

The Net's anonymity, massive audience, and widespread reach make it tempting for many people to run all sorts of online moneymaking schemes. (See Figure 2.10.) The most common of these is the "pyramid" system, where a small handful of people collaborate to make tons of money from unsuspecting victims who think they too are part of the plan. (See Figure 2.11.) Incredulous claims, including "Earn one million in one year!" or "Receive $1,000 a day for doing NOTHING!" are common.

Also be wary of any offers for cheap cable access, free long distance, discounted cellular phone or credit card accounts, unbelievable real estate deals, and clubs that require large membership fees.

On a less-ambitious scale, some individuals simply hang out in commercial online services using hacker software and then "phish" for accounts, posing as service guides in an attempt to get unsuspecting users to reveal their passwords or account information.

If your children spend any amount of time online, they should be told that most things that sound too good to be true probably are. A good rule of thumb is for the whole family to refrain from engaging in *any* online business activity, especially with people or companies you have never seen or heard of. Few people actually get rich from online business endeavors, and almost none of them do so in any of the above-mentioned ways.

PIRATED SOFTWARE OR "WAREZ"

Another dubious online activity to be avoided is "warez" trading.
Warez is online slang for illegally copied and distributed programs—software piracy, in other words. Software piracy is a
serious crime, costing the industry millions of dollars per year in
lost revenue and increasing the cost of software for honest users
who pay for their programs.

Gigabytes upon gigabytes of illegal programs traverse the
Net every month, from programs such as WordPerfect and
Quicken, to games like Myst, to entire operating systems such as
Windows '95. Most of the time, though, you will not easily stumble across pirated software and suddenly find it on your hard
drive. Internet users must seek out and download illegal software, which can be a very time-consuming task even with fast
connections.

-		Rob Tremper	EXPAND YOUR EARNING POTENTIAL
-		United Biogenics	Attract Women Biochemically! (secret is ...
▷	3	Rob Tremper	RISK FREE$$$ *UNLIMITED* MONTHLY I...
-		an536409@anon.p...	Excellent SAP R3 professionals available ...
▷	2	Access Denied	_ Earn $500 or More, Paid 6 days a Wee...
-		Major News	[[[[[[[[[[[[[[[Great News]]]]]]]]]]]]]]]
▷	2	Richard Soos	Electronic Money Tree March 1996
-		justme@aloha.net	"Dear Internet Surfers...........THIS IS WHE...
-		Steve Speaks	>>>>> LIFE PLUS <<<<<
▷	3	Rob Tremper	--------EASIEST M O N E Y AROUND-------
-		Anton Sajovetz	Gourmet Foods - Southern Style
-		Kyle	Make $1000's weekly processing mail. Fr...
▷	2	Ken Chadwick	VISA CARDS & BANK ACCOUNTS GUARA...
-		John Schwartz	EMPLOYMENT HELP
▷	4	Daniel Nolan	Time to Live!
-		Rob Tremper	--D O N O T R E A D T H I S--
-		Roger Karlsson	>>>> UNLOCK THE SECRETS OF A WEALTH ...
-		Wolff	Re: GREAT OPPORTUNITY! GET IN ON IT!
-		gate	! Actually get paid $4,000 per month!
-		Mike Garner	/\/\/\ It Can't Get Any Easier Than This...

Figure 2.10
The Internet attracts
many entrepreneurs—
some offering legi-
timate services and
goods and others who
prey on peoples'
naïveté. Parents must
warn children never to
send cash or give a
credit card number to
anyone selling anything
on the Internet without
their approval.

```
                    * Work Full Or Part Time *

  * Set Your Own Income Bracket/Work For 1 Or 100's Of Companies*

            * Opportunities Available For Everyone *

         * No Selling Or Previous Experience Required*

To Receive More Information, Reply To: 104407.2560@compuserve.com
```

Figure 2.11
"Get-rich-quick"
schemes, such as this
one, proliferate among
Usenet newsgroups.

Most illegal software is secretly buried in ftp sites or bulletin board systems maintained by small circles of online friends. They don't let just anyone in—you often have to prove yourself by posting a choice program of your own. Other pirates post programs in multiple segments to Usenet newsgroups such as alt.binaries.warez.mac or alt.binaries.warez.windows, though many ISPs, fearful of liability issues, cleverly delete just one of the dozens of file segments to render the whole thing useless. Illegal software is also common on commercial online services, though most services make concerted efforts to eliminate it.

Sometimes pirated programs have been modified, so they are often buggy or virus-infected and could damage your computer. Still, many youngsters (and adults, too) are tempted when they see expensive video games such as Doom or Dark Forces free for the taking. Perhaps they think it is a victimless crime or that it is acceptable because "everybody else does it." Be sure to explain to them that people do get caught, fined, and even arrested for stealing programs. Stealing a copy of Sim City is the equivalent to stealing $40 worth of merchandise from the local convenience store.

IRC, CU-SEEME, AND OTHER "REAL-TIME" DANGERS

The last category of online dangers includes the "real-time" Internet services—Internet Relay Chat, CU-SeeMe, and real-time audio. Real-time services are excellent for communicating one-on-one with friends, peers, and online associates. With CU-SeeMe, for example, you can use the Net to visit with people from all over the world, or to network with business associates in other cities. The sound and video quality is not exactly breathtaking, but, for the cost of an Internet connection and a computer camera (about $100), you can easily get in on the cutting edge of Internet communications technology. Internet audio technology is rapidly advancing as well, with products such as NetPhone serving the same purpose as everyday phones—but without long-distance charges.

The most obvious dangers of real-time video would be adults or other children using profanity or vulgar expressions, exposing themselves, smoking or drinking, and generally carrying on in front of the camera. For now, thankfully, broadcasting video requires lots of bandwidth, so cameras have not yet made it into many households or dorm rooms.

Some entrepreneurs are prepared for that time, though, and plan to exploit this technology and the Internet to its fullest. Strip clubs and adult escort services have already devised ways to transmit live, for-pay sex services over the Internet. Since most of these services are expensive and require special software or dial-up accounts, it is unlikely many children will be exposed to it—but it is there, nonetheless.

The dangers of live audio are pretty much the same as those associated with the telephone—except you can not easily track a youngster's calling habits by checking phone bills.

Finally, IRC—fun for chatting back and forth with friends or schoolmates—can also expose kids to a whole new world of dirty language. Hundreds of people can type whatever they want back and forth, and things move pretty quickly. It is not, however, the most efficient or easy-to-use Internet tool. If you are worried about IRC but still want your child to be able to communicate online, use email instead.

Chapter 3

COMMON SENSE PROTECTION

Thus far, we have taken a long, hard look at a lot of the negative and sometimes disturbing material that children can gain access to over the Internet.

But don't be discouraged; now it's time to learn what kind of practical, hands-on actions that you can take to protect children from these dangers.

TAKING STEPS TO PROTECT CHILDREN ONLINE

So far, we have taken a hard look at some of the negative things available on the Internet—perhaps in more shocking detail than you have read anywhere else. We did not gloss over the facts or minimize the online hazards for kids—and for good reason. It is important that, as an adult responsible for the well-being of young people, you enter the online world with your eyes wide open.

Now it is time to learn what you can do to protect children from those dangers. We will offer hands-on approaches and practical advice for ensuring that the entire family can safely take advantage of the Internet's vast resources. Then we will explore some software solutions parents and educators can employ to help them in their efforts. Programs such as SurfWatch and Net Nanny make it easier to control Internet access and enable parents, teachers, and kids to spend time *learning* online instead of worrying about whether they should be online at all. Contact information for these companies is provided at the end of the chapter.

Next to learning some steps you can take right away to help keep your kids safe online, the most important thing you can learn from this chapter is that no one *single* method of achieving Internet safety will suffice. Rather, a combination of parent and teacher vigilance, direct involvement with kids' online activities, youth responsibility, community interest, and software-filtering methods all play important roles. Combine these elements with acceptable-use policies (AUPs, which we cover later in the book) and Internet youth education and the Net starts looking like a much safer place for kids.

If you have not surmised by now, creating a safer Internet depends on *everyone*—from families and schools to commercial online services to the government. Because of the far-reaching, proliferate nature of the Internet, all users and providers will have to work together. Dee Jespen talked about the need for everyone to assume responsibility for children in the new digital age as she concluded her testimony at the Senate "cyberporn" hearings. Though her speech mainly addressed online pornography, it is easy to apply her words to other online dangers.

Dee Jespens's Testimony from the Senate "Cyberporn" Hearings

In reality, we will never be able to eliminate all illegal pornography and protect all children from [it]. It is, however, imperative that we do all we can. . . in a reasoned, reasonable, yet responsible manner. . . . Some are saying that this problem is . . . parents' responsibility. Parents must become educated about the dangers. . . . Parents also need to learn more about computer technology in order to do so. But to place all the responsibility upon parents not only is unfair, it is inadequate to protect children. Parents can't be present 100% of the time to monitor their children . . . cannot monitor what happens when they are at the homes of friends, whose parents may not be as informed or vigilant. . . .

Some suggest technical screening "fixes." These are good ideas, but to say that this is the answer is again unfair and inadequate. Prior to this time, those who wanted to consume pornography had to pay for it. Are we now going to say those who do not want pornography . . . have to pay *not* to get it? Those who have in-depth computer understanding acknowledge there is no way to screen all pornographic material.

It is often asked that if much of this material is illegal (not protected speech) isn't it up to law enforcement to simply enforce the law? There should be aggressive enforcement of the pornography laws in the area of computer porn. The reality is, however, that law-enforcement resources are limited, and it is difficult to monitor and enforce this electronic outlet.

To find effective solutions to the pornography problem, it will take the combination of education, legislative action, public policy initiatives and aggressive law enforcement, as well as the exercise of corporate and individual responsibility. . . . We must all take the responsibility to protect the welfare of our nation's children. Those in the technology community should be encouraged to work diligently to find every way possible to protect children. . . . Yet we must all be committed to protecting both the free flow of material on the Information Superhighway and the children of the country.

THE KEY TO SAFETY: DIRECT SUPERVISION

Direct adult supervision is the number one way to ensure safety when using the Internet at home or school. Children are unlikely to attempt to access objectionable, noneducational materials when adults are present. And they can quickly turn to parents or teachers for guidance should they accidentally encounter pornography or other such materials.

You do not have to "stand guard," stare over a child's shoulder at the screen, and watch a child's every movement of the mouse. You should be around enough, however, so that children take your presence for granted. Besides, being with kids as they surf the Net allows parents to spend more time with their children—always a worthwhile goal.

If you are online, you will find many parents, teachers, and others who are concerned about young people and the Net. You will glean advice from the "front line"—parents whose children use or will soon be using online resources for fun and learning. This is what Timothy Linde, of New Richmond, Ohio, the father of a nine-month-old son, says about his plans to introduce his son to the Net:

> What people need most to keep in mind is that going out over the Net is the same as going outside the home. . . . Many of the same things—both favorable and unfavorable—can be found in either instance. Our son, who is only nine months, enjoys computer games. He's got a few months before he can surf the Net as well. . . . Of course, as he grows there will be a few ground rules, like not hacking into banks, no turning worm programs loose on other peoples' databases. And, of course, we will log all his activities on the Net as well.

Daniel Mahoney, of Irvine, California, trusts his son's judgment when it comes to surfing the Net—but only after much preparation. Here is what he says about young people and the Net:

> My son is only allowed to surf the Net when one of us is available to supervise. The best advice I can offer to other parents is to watch what the children are doing. There are no software packages that can guarantee that your kids won't get

into inappropriate material; there's no substitute for parental supervision. We don't have an explicit AUP; my son knows what things are likely to make me uneasy and what things I consider to be inappropriate. We have had discussions on what I will and won't allow him to access.

So far I haven't had to worry about my son going online at the houses of friends; none of his friends have computers and modems. However, I would be comfortable with him doing so, since we have talked about proper and improper uses. I have taken the time to discuss moral obligations with my son, so I am confident that he will usually be able to make appropriate decisions, even when I am not present.

If you cannot be at the computer with your children as they surf, or have not achieved a level of confidence or trust in which you would feel comfortable about them surfing alone, consider restricting access to only those times when you can be present.

INFO BYTE

Whenever I'm asked about the safety of kids on the Net, I often use this example—if you won't let your kids go to the playground all by themselves, you also shouldn't let them use the Internet all by themselves. Just because the computer's in the living room doesn't mean it's perfectly protected. . . .

The realization that the Net isn't a perfect place is often slow-coming, unfortunately. And even when it's realized, the thing that sparks that realization is usually a horrific news story. The challenge is figuring out how to make parents feel more comfortable using the Internet with their kids, and not feel intimidated by the children knowing how to use it better than Mom and Dad. Let kids impress you . . . but be there to see it.

—Brendan Kehoe, *author of* Zen and The Art of the Internet, *post to the Children Accessing Controversial Information mailing list*

BRING NET RESOURCES OFFLINE

Sometimes kids need to work on the computer, but you simply can't be there with them. One good workaround solution for these times is to bring as much as you can of the Internet's safe, educational materials to them in advance. When you *do* have time to Net surf together, download and save resources that you don't have a chance to read online. Copy documents onto your hard drive or print them out. Then your children have something with which to work and read during times when you can't directly monitor their online activity. There is usually more than enough downloadable material on any given educational site to keep them busy while you work in the backyard, make dinner, or catch up with bills and paperwork.

Parents and teachers can also take advantage of programs such as WebWhacker, which enable you to enter a Web site address and download to your computer's hard drive all the pages and links that fall under that particular address. You can "whack" single pages, groups of pages, or entire sites from the World Wide Web and then "surf" from your local desktop without an Internet connection. See Figure 3.1.

For example, you could visit the White House home page and set WebWhacker to download the whole site automatically—two, three, four, or all clicks deep, either including or excluding external links. Then kids can use any Web browser later to explore the site offline. You will know that they will not intentionally or willfully follow any inappropriate links. (You can surf a site stored on your hard drive first and then remove any objectionable pages or graphics.)

It can, however, take a long time to download an entire site. One smart strategy is to get WebWhacker started on sites while you do other things, like attend a meeting, go to a soccer game, or see a movie.

WebWhacker is available for Windows 3.x, Windows 95, and Macintosh computers and costs $49.95. More information and free demo versions are available at WebWhacker's home page:

http://www.ffg.com/whacker.html

Other parents, such as Steve Savitzky of San Jose, California, take an even more hands-on approach to pointing their children toward safe sites. Savitzky developed a custom home page for his nine-year-old daughter, Katy. He included links to all sorts of music, science, crafts, and other fun and educational sites for kids. It's called Steve Savitzky's Interesting Places For Kids. You can visit it at:

http://www.crc.ricoh.com/people/steve/kids.html

Of course, it's still possible to link to objectionable pages if your child visits your custom page with a live connection. Savitzky explains his philosophy on the site:

> Parents differ in the degree to which they try to protect their kids from various aspects of reality, including strong language, violence, beliefs and opinions contrary to their own, and so on. I am not particularly protective. . . . In general, kids are mostly inclined to be sensible. If they see something uninteresting, they'll say "Yuck!" and click the back button. In any case, they are unlikely to run into anything on the Web that's nearly as disturbing as what they can see on TV network news. Stephen C. Steel says it best: "The only long-term answer is to educate your children about pornography, hate literature, etc., so that when they come across it, they'll know how to react. The only software you can be sure they'll be running is the stuff you install between their ears."

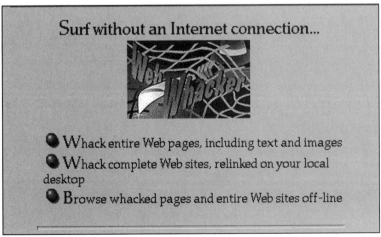

Surf without an Internet connection...

● Whack entire Web pages, including text and images
● Whack complete Web sites, relinked on your local desktop
● Browse whacked pages and entire Web sites off-line

Figure 3.1
This powerful program lets you download entire sites, including their links. This can eliminate the need for children to surf the Net blindly—all they need is right at their fingertips, on your computer's hard drive.

COMMUNICATE ABOUT COMMUNICATING ONLINE!

It is important to talk openly and honestly with children about online safety issues as you explore the Internet together. If they are old enough, get specific with them about some of the potential dangers. No matter how old they are or how much you trust them, be sure to frequently reiterate your rules against providing personal information to people on the Internet.

Child Safety on the Information Highway, a free brochure written by Larry Magid and produced by the National Center for Missing and Exploited Children, is an excellent guide, showing how parents, teachers, and any adult can get directly involved with children's online activity and talk with them about safety issues. (See Figure 3.2.) It includes specific guidelines for parents as well as youngsters. The brochure covers nearly all aspects of online child safety, so we have obtained permission to reprint it on the following pages.

The best way to assure that your children are having positive online experiences is to stay in touch with what they are doing. One way to do this is to spend time with your children while they're online. Have them show you what they do and ask them to teach you how to access the services.

While children and teenagers need a certain amount of privacy, they also need parental involvement and supervision

Figure 3.2 This helpful brochure is available free from the National Center for Missing and Exploited Children. The address is located at the end of this chapter.

Child Safety on the Information Highway

Produced by the National Center for Missing and Exploited Children and Interactive Services Association

Child Safety on the Information Highway

Whatever it's called, millions of people are now connecting their personal computers to telephone lines so that they can "go online."

Some call it cyberspace, others call it the "digital highway."

Traditionally, online services have been oriented towards adults, but that's changing. An increasing number of schools are going online and, in many homes, children are logging on to commercial services, private bulletin boards, and the Internet. As a parent you need to understand the nature of these systems.

Child Safety on the Information Highway

····································

Guidelines for Parents

By taking responsibility for your children's online computer use, parents can greatly minimize any potential risks of being online.

Make it a family rule to:

- ◐ Never give out identifying information—home address, school name, or telephone number—in a public message such as chat or bulletin boards, and be sure you're dealing with someone that both you and your child know and trust before giving it out via email.

- ◐ Think carefully before revealing any personal information such as age, marital status, or financial information. Consider using a pseudonym or "unlisting" your child's name if your service allows it.

- ◐ Get to know the services your child uses. If you don't know how to log on, get your child to show you. Find out what types of information it offers and whether there are ways for parents to block out objectionable material.

- ◐ Never allow a child to arrange a face-to-face meeting with another computer user without parental permission. If a meeting is arranged, make the first one in a public spot, and be sure to accompany your child.

- ◐ Never respond to messages or bulletin board items that are suggestive, obscene, belligerent, threatening, or make you feel uncomfortable. Encourage your children to tell you if they encounter such messages. If you or your child receives a message that is harassing, of a sexual nature, or threatening, forward a copy of the message to your service provider and ask for their assistance.

- Remember that people online may not be who they seem. Because you can't see or even hear the person, it would be easy for someone to misrepresent him- or herself. Thus, someone indicating that "she" is a "12-year-old girl" could in reality be a 40-year-old man.

- Remember that everything you read online may not be true. Any offer that's "too good to be true" probably is. Be very careful about any offers that involve your coming to a meeting or having someone visit your house.

- Set reasonable rules and guidelines for computer use by your children (see "My Rules for Online Safety," which follow, as a sample). Discuss these rules and post them near the computer as a reminder. Remember to monitor their compliance with these rules, especially when it comes to the amount of time your children spend on the computer. A child or teenager's excessive use of online services or bulletin boards, especially late at night, may be a clue that there is a potential problem. Remember that personal computers and online services should not be used as electronic babysitters.

- Be sure to make this a family activity. Consider keeping the computer in a family room rather than the child's bedroom. Get to know their "online friends" just as you get to know all of their other friends.

My Rules for Online Safety

- I will not give out personal information such as my address, telephone number, parents' work address/telephone number, or the name and location of my school without my parents' permission.

○ I will tell my parents right away if I come across any information that makes me feel uncomfortable.

○ I will never agree to get together with someone I "meet" online without first checking with my parents. If my parents agree to the meeting, I will be sure that it is in a public place and bring my mother or father along.

○ I will never send a person my picture or anything else without first checking with my parents.

○ I will not respond to any messages that are mean or in any way make me feel uncomfortable. It is not my fault if I get a message like that. If I do I will tell my parents right away so that they can contact the online service.

○ I will talk with my parents so that we can set up rules for going online. We will decide upon the time of day that I can be online, the length of time I can be online, and appropriate areas for me to visit. I will not access other areas or break these rules without their permission.

—Larry Magid

·······
Note
The full text of this brochure is available on the Web at http://www.larry'sworld.com *or in hardcopy form from either the National Center for Missing and Exploited Children or from the Interactive Services Association.*

·········
Source
Published by the National Center for Missing and Exploited Children. Reprinted with permission.

in their daily lives. The same general parenting skills that apply to the "real world" also apply online. If you have cause for concern about your children's online activities, talk to them. Also seek out the advice and counsel of other computer users in your area and become familiar with literature on these systems. Open communication with your children, utilization of such computer resources, and getting online yourself will help you obtain the full benefits of these systems and alert you to any potential problem that may occur with their use.

Talk frequently with kids about their online adventures—not from an investigative angle, but rather to find out what kinds of positive things they have discovered. Ask them questions about their Internet experiences or searches. Find out what they have (or have not) been learning. Some teachers or parents ask youngsters to keep "online learning logs" in which they write down significant new discoveries, information about keypals, or Web site addresses. Ask them to print pages from good sites they find, save pages and graphics for later viewing, or make Web-browser bookmarks for you so you can check out all the good stuff, too.

CONTROLLING ACCESS ON COMMERCIAL ONLINE SERVICES

Of course, there are dangers when children use commercial online services—just as there are when they use the Internet. Sessions on America Online, Prodigy, CompuServe, and other services should be monitored, even if simply to control the amount of time youngsters spend online with the hourly "meter running." Besides taking some of the common-sense steps we have already covered, you can employ methods of access control specific to each service.

In general, most online services have features that let parents or educators either limit or completely deny access to certain areas, such as chat rooms or bulletin boards. After reading about some of the perils of chat rooms in Chapter 1, you are probably ready to learn all you can about these features. See Chapter 6 for full details on how to use the protection tools that are available from most major commercial online services.

WORKING WITH INTERNET SERVICE PROVIDERS

Contact your local Internet Service Provider to ask about ways you or they can control children's access to objectionable materials. Some providers, concerned about protecting themselves and establishing a wide customer base of families and schools, are more than willing to work with parents, teachers, and other community members to better protect youngsters. Some may be able to offer custom newsfeeds that exclude the more offensive alt.sex groups or set up special proxy Web servers that allow access only to certain areas of the Internet.

Also, ask about your ISP's specific acceptable-use policy (AUP) or terms-of-service (TOS) agreement and how it protects their younger customers. Contact the ISP if someone poses a threat to online child safety. The offender is probably violating the terms of service of his provider, and your complaint may be enough for his ISP to take action if others have complained, too.

Finally, some service providers may even be willing to volunteer some time to speak at a parent or school gathering and help educate your community about online safety. Look for ways to get positive exposure for both your community, school, and the ISP—notify your local paper that parents in the area are working with local providers, for example. Your ISP will benefit from the publicity, and parents and children will benefit from a greater understanding of the Internet.

WHERE TO SET UP YOUR COMPUTER

The direct supervision of a child's Internet use and adult involvement are two effective methods of ensuring safe Net surfing—a third is a "smart" computer set-up. For parents and teachers who cannot observe youngsters' Internet use every second, the right computer equipment arrangement can make it easier to keep track of how young people are using computers. Here are some tips on strategic placement of computers.

- Move computers to an office or living room rather than a child's bedroom. Just as children are not typically allowed to lock doors or play with friends in private, neither should they be given adult privileges regarding computer time.

- Assume ownership of the computer. Many parents buy computers for their kids for birthdays or Christmas, which is fine, but a computer is not the same as, say, a bicycle, which will be used solely by your son or daughter. Make it clear that the computer is a *family* machine. As such, it is accessible to *all* members of the family but is ultimately controlled by you. Family computing should be democratic, but only to a point.
- In schools, arrange computers so that teachers can keep tabs on the greatest number of users at the same time and so that students can see each other's screens. This is similar to corporate "management by walking around." Traditional arrangements, such as straight rows of desks with students facing forward and a teacher at the front, probably will not be effective. Students can easily hit the "back" arrow on their browsers before you walk over and see their screens.

WATCH FOR BEHAVIORAL WARNING SIGNS

Later in this book, we will review some of the clues parents or teachers should look for to find out if youngsters are abusing their Internet access privileges, including tips for monitoring hard drive activity and finding "hidden" files. There are some other, often more telling signs that a child is breaking your rules for online activity. These signs do not necessarily have anything to do with hardware or software: look for nonverbal cues.

- Does your child become uneasy or defensive when you walk in on an Internet session?
- Do they seem overly protective of the computer or its contents, or get nervous and linger when you get on the machine?

Such changes in behavior can indicate that your son or daughter is up to something unusual. We are by no means suggesting that parents should spy on their children—just be aware of changes in attitude or behavior as they relate to computing and the Internet, just as you make an effort to notice changes in hygiene, peer relations, and self-esteem as they relate to drug use or other youth problems.

DIRECT SUPERVISION IN SCHOOLS

Since kids are directly supervised at school, monitoring their Internet use should not pose much of a problem, right? Not necessarily. The post below, from the Children Accessing Controversial Information mailing list, indicates that, when it comes to getting online at school, it is often much easier to talk about supervising children's use of the Internet than it is to actually do it.

Monitoring student Internet use in the classroom *can* be difficult, especially in overcrowded, understaffed classrooms. But it is not impossible. Try strategies such as those in the Child Safety brochure. In addition, a well-crafted AUP can help protect teachers and schools if something bad does happen.

Here is another way of looking at the issue. Schools frequently send dozens or even hundreds of students on field trips or to sporting events, let classes hold dances and other social events, and sponsor many other activities that present just as many dangers as using the Internet. Consider employing some of the same strategies for supervision as you do in those cases—seek volunteers to serve as "Internet chaperons." Work to create a similar environment in which students police themselves to protect their Internet privileges.

> Do you have one teacher by each computer, doing nothing but watching what the student is doing? That may work great if you have activities for all the other children and only one computer per class room, but seems wasteful even so. If you have a teacher supervise by looking at the screen at random intervals every five minutes or so, what is to stop the children from accessing other items when the teacher isn't looking? In other words, it seems like a false premise that a teacher can really stop a child from accessing information that isn't relevant to a particular class exercise. The costs are just too high to enforce that, if it is even possible.
>
> —John DeCarlo, McLean, Virginia, post to the Children Accessing Controversial Information mailing list

INFO BYTE

The National Council for Educational Technology (NCET), offers good advice for teachers and schools concerned about controlling Internet access to inappropriate materials in the classroom. Of special importance is making sure students and parents understand the implications of Information Technology (IT) for working life and society. Students may show less interest in using the Net as an entertainment device when they realize that time online is actually an opportunity to gain valuable knowledge and skills, to prepare to work in the Information Age, and to start networking with people who can help them succeed and attain their goals.

COMPUTER PORNOGRAPHY—WHAT CAN SCHOOLS DO?

- As appropriate, alert parents to any problems relating to computer pornography.
- Make sure that teachers can explain the arguments against pornography to pupils.
- Make sure that parents and teachers know how and where to report incidents.
- Regularly check files held on networks.
- Carefully supervise the sharing of computer disks between home and school.
- Make sure that telecommunications links are closely managed.
- Be aware that schools must be alert to the need of involving social service departments if a child's behavior at school indicates serious problems at home.
- Bear in mind that precocious or otherwise inappropriate sexual behavior may be a sign that a child is being abused.

SOFTWARE SOLUTIONS FOR CONTROLLING INTERNET ACCESS

The Internet is capitalism at its best. Thousands of parents and educators need products to help them manage Internet access at home and at school. So, entrepreneurs reasoned, if software such as Netscape enables adults to access areas like the Playboy home page, then surely it must be possible to invent software to prevent *children* from accessing those areas.

Software companies—about a half dozen of them—met that need as quickly as they could with *blocking* or *filtering* software. New products with catchy names such as Net Nanny, SurfWatch, and CyberPatrol are programs that parents and teachers can use to enter the Internet addresses of specific Internet sites they wish to block. Youngsters trying to access areas designated as blocked are quickly thwarted. And kids who wander around cyberspace will be less likely to stumble across inappropriate sites.

Teachers, parents, technology coordinators, or other adult administrators holding the passwords can still access whatever they wish, but children are effectively blocked from entering, for example, the Prostitution FAQ, Hustler's Web site, Condom Country, or even the Nintendo Home Page.

Since no parent or teacher can possibly keep up with all the inappropriate sites that spring up each week, these companies employ Net-savvy workers to constantly explore and add sites to their databases of restricted areas. Most of these products include access to these databases for no cost for the first several months, then charge subscription fees for users to stay current.

Many of these products are already in their third or fourth versions, adding excellent new filtering and administration features with each new release. Some now block *outgoing* information. For example, you can type your home phone number, address, and credit card number into the program to prevent that information from leaving your home via your Internet connection. Most of the programs also offer you the ability to control the number of hours a person spends online each day or week, enabling educators or parents to print detailed reports of who accessed what, and when.

Several programs can even regulate access to computer games and other applications stored on your computer's hard drive, such as Quicken personal finance software or gradebook programs. These programs are surprisingly "hack proof," considering the technical computer knowledge many teenagers now possess. If anyone tries to tamper with the software settings, Internet access is totally blocked, and the administrator is notified. Some of the programs even shut down the entire computer! Most are available in either single-computer or network versions, and nearly all offer steep discounts for educational organizations.

WHAT DOES PLAYBOY THINK OF ALL THIS?

How have the publishers of Internet sites containing material inappropriate for children reacted to the rush of filtering software products? Most major players such as Playboy and Hustler enthusiastically support these programs, at least in public. By giving parents the power to block objectionable sites, such publishers may believe the risk of children finding their way to their sites is removed. (See Figure 3.3.)

Of course, software filters do not protect children in quite the same way as age restrictions and local zoning laws. Parents do not have to pay for their kids *not* to be able to buy *Playboy* at the local bookstore. But they *do* have to pay to keep kids from not seeing it on the Internet.

On the other hand, numerous smaller content providers—especially those selling phone sex services or videotapes via the Net—are already trying to avoid filtering software. One such company registered the domain name www.pu55y.com, presumably as an attempt to retain a salacious site name while circumventing filtering software that would block out the real spelling of the middle portion of the domain name. Others simply intersperse text with asterisks or dashes. Fortunately, many access control programs dig deeper than the home page level to block objectionable material, so most of the time these tricks will not work. (See Figure 3.4.)

Figure 3.3
This adult-oriented Web site offers links to restriction software, including SurfWatch, Net Nanny, and CyberPatrol.

TO BLOCK, OR NOT TO BLOCK?

Not surprisingly, filtering software products have sparked much debate in the educational community. These debates raise some questions that parents might be asking themselves. Do these programs help educators better manage student access and select appropriate materials? Or will schools misuse them, leading to an atmosphere of censorship and distrust? Who decides which sites should be blocked?

Few would argue that hardcore pornography sites should not be blocked. But will some educators or parents use blocking software in a Draconian manner to restrict access to every site that conflicts with personal or religious beliefs? Will sites containing information about birth control be blocked? Will blocking access to *all* sites containing the keyword *sex* also block access to areas containing information about AIDS or teen pregnancy? Probably. You can imagine the kinds of conflicts that will emerge in communities with diverse ethnic and religious backgrounds and moral standards. In some schools, trade-offs will likely be made. Students may be denied access to quality educational materials because the alternative—pulling the plug on Net access—is even less desirable.

Customizing features of filtering software to block access to sites that are "known offenders" is one relatively reasonable

Fantasy Showbar

Delaware Valley's Most Popular Gentlemen's Club
Featuring 42 Young, Beautiful, All-Nude Showgirls
and over
10,000 square feet of the hottest, wildest, adult
entertainment you've ever seen!

710 Black Horse Pike
Mt. Ephraim, NJ 08059
(609) 931-8040

Warning: This site contains material of an adult nature.
You must be age 18 or over to continue. If you find adult material portraying nudity offensive or if you are under age 18, you must exit now.

We support Project X and also strongly endorse the use of WWW monitoring software, such as SurfWatch or Cyber Patrol, which permits parental control over what children are allowed to access on the Internet.

Figure 3.4
Some salacious sites try to dissuade minors from entering by posting strict warnings on their home pages. Others suggest that parents concerned about access to such sites use restriction software.

approach to this difficult issue. Rather than use the shotgun approach and block access to *any* site containing the word *sex*, adults can enter the addresses of sites that everyone would agree should be blocked. School libraries that do not stock their shelves with adult magazines are not expected to provide access to electronic versions of these print publications, so this kind of approach is usually fair.

Each teacher, parent, school district, and community is differ-ent, and no single approach can possibly work in every single environment—except for open dialog and debate about the issue. Educators and parents need to work together to become familiar with one or more of these software products. Knowledge of what these programs can and cannot do can cool a hot debate over censorship by giving all parties involved a safe middle ground.

Parents do not face the community-wide issues that schools must confront when it comes to controlling access to informa-tion. Many parents consider these products an absolute blessing. Parents generally enjoy constitutional backing in regards to con-trolling what their children can or cannot see, hear, or read. The new law requiring V-Chips in televisions to help parents control what children watch is an excellent example. Whether you agree with it or not, parents have the right to restrict access to violent or sexual movies, books, magazines, and television shows. These products simply extend their control into cyberspace.

··

A PARENT WHO SHOULD KNOW . . .

Mike Godwin, staff counsel for the Electronic Frontier Foundation, an Internet advocacy group, offered this written testimony concerning software filtering products before the July 24, 1995, Senate Judiciary Committee Hearing on "cyberporn." As an adult who uses the Internet, a father, and a lawyer, Godwin's testimony indicates the value of filtering software as a way both to protect children from indecent materials and to preserve the tenets of the U.S. Constitution.

I come here not just as a lawyer who is concerned about the First Amendment. I'm also a father. My little girl will be the first person in my family to have grown up with the Internet. As a parent, I'm deeply concerned with protecting Ariel from bad material and from bad people. . . . I want to help ensure that whatever legislation or policy comes from Congress regarding the Internet will help me as a parent in protecting my little girl, while at the same time ensuring that she's able to benefit fully from access to the Net. . . .

I believe that the right role for Congress to play is to encourage the development of software filters that prevent my child and others from being harmed in the first place. Recall that the basic technology we're talking about here is the computer—the most flexible, programmable, "intelligent" technology we build and market. Filtering software enables parents to screen certain language, certain kinds of content, certain people, or certain areas on the networks from their children.

Such an approach does no damage to First Amendment values (it does not, for example, put a nonlawyer hobbyist who operates a tiny computer bulletin board system in the position of having to determine what is "indecent"). . . . Furthermore, since such tools are designed to be customizable, parents are empowered to set their own standards of what is acceptable for their children, rather than relying on what the nonelected officials at the FCC choose to include under the definition of "indecency." For example, even if the FCC determines that detailed information about safe-sex techniques is not indecent, a parent who believes that her children should receive all their sexual information from her and not from the Internet could customize the family computer's "filters" to block that information.

NOTHING IS FOOLPROOF

Keep in mind that, although they are powerful and difficult to "hack," none of these filtering programs is completely foolproof. Installing one on a computer at home or at school does not give adults the freedom to simply forget about the problem of inappropriate material. There is always a chance a youngster will stumble upon an inappropriate site or discover your password. Likewise, you might forget to activate the controls, or make a mistake during set-up.

Of course, these programs do nothing if your son or daughter accesses the Internet from a friend's home, where there may be no protection software. Direct teacher or parent involvement and the kinds of common sense protection methods that we discussed earlier are still required. These filtering programs provide *additional*, not absolute, protection and peace of mind.

Even if you do not own blocking software or subscribe to one of the software filtering services, you can still send these companies the addresses of inappropriate sites you find online. That way, other parents and teachers can benefit from your discoveries and even more children will be protected. The Web sites for these products contain information on submitting addresses for inclusion or exclusion. If your email software offers mailing list or distribution list features, you can enter all of the email addresses ahead of time so that you can quickly send an alert to all the companies at once when you find an objectionable site.

INTERNET ACCESS CONTROL AND FILTERING OPTIONS

CyberPatrol

By most standards, CyberPatrol is the premier product of its kind. It incorporates the most desirable features of the other security software products. Adults can customize CyberPatrol's restrictions to reflect school, community, and personal standards. Any Internet World Wide Web, gopher, ftp, Usenet news, or Internet Relay Chat (IRC) site and resource can be filtered.

Figure 3.5
CyberPatrol is best-known for its extensive filtering capabilities.

Figure 3.6
A child would see this message if he or she tried to access a site blocked by CyberPatrol.

You can block access during certain times of the day, restrict the total hours of Internet use per day or week, control access to programs and games stored on your hard drive, and much more. Sites that are specifically blocked by either the special CyberNOT list or your own customized list of unapproved sites will not appear on the screen when users attempt to access them. Instead, they will see a CyberPatrol intercept message on the screen rather than the site's contents (Figure 3.6).

It also includes comprehensive time- and budget-management functions to help you manage your family's online habits and budget.

According to Microsystems (CyberPatrol's publisher), CyberPatrol is the first Internet filter that works with *all* Web browsers, including 32-bit browsers such as Microsoft's Internet Explorer.

The CyberPatrol Home Edition, which offers the basic Internet filtering component of the full CyberPatrol product, is available free to home users. CyberPatrol is backed by an informative Web site where users can find software updates, FAQ (frequently asked questions) files, tips for navigating the Net with children, and links to related resources.

••••••••••••

SurfWatch

SurfWatch was one of the first Internet filtering programs on the market. As such, it received a lot of media attention when the cyberporn issue broke. SurfWatch does not offer quite as many features as the others, but it is simpler to use since it is

Figure 3.7
Although
SurfWatch does
not offer as many
features as other
blocking
software, many
users report that it
is the easiest to
use.

either "on" or "off" and requires little configuration or ongoing maintenance. (See Figure 3.7.) The program works in the background to:

- Screen for newsgroups likely to contain sexually explicit material.
- Keep users from accessing specified World Wide Web, ftp, gopher, IRC, and other sites.
- Automatically update the blocked sites list.

SurfWatch does not work with America Online, Prodigy, or the Microsoft Network. A custom version has been developed exclusively with CompuServe and is distributed through the *Internet In a Box for Kids* product. It is compatible with Windows, Windows 95, and Macintosh. The basic cost is $49.95. Subscriptions to the blocked-site database go for $5.95 per month.

You will find a free version of the SurfWatch software on the CD-ROM included at the end of this book! More information and instructions for the software can be found on the CD-ROM.

. . . .

CyberSitter
CyberSitter (Figure 3.8) offers many of the same features as CyberPatrol, including access control for Web pages, online chat, and newsgroups. One distinguishing feature of the program is its phrase filtering function. According to information on CyberSitter's Web site, "Rather than block single words or predefined phrases, CyberSitter actually looks at how the word or phrase is used in context. Not only does this provide an

Figure 3.8
CyberSitter can define how some words are used. This eliminates the possibility of inadvertently blocking words with double meanings.

excellent blocking method for objectionable text, but it eliminates the possibility that words with double meanings will be
inadvertently blocked."

The program can also prevent access to specific programs
and personal files. CyberSitter keeps a comprehensive log of
all Internet activity, including attempts to access restricted
sites. CyberSitter is available for Windows or Windows 95; no
version is available for Macintosh. CyberSitter requires a
winsock.dll for compatibility. It works with CompuServe and
Prodigy. America Online users can install the optional winsock
file (keyword: winsock) to make it compatible. CyberSitter
costs $39.95. There is no charge for the blocked site database
subscription.

Kinderguard

Kinderguard (Figure 3.9.) is part of an integrated package from
TeacherSoft, Inc., called InterGo. The InterGo package offers

Figure 3.9
Kinderguard allows parents and teachers to assign age and maturity-specific ratings to sites.

Internet access tools, including Web browser, email, and FTP software, as well as an integrated encyclopedia, dictionary, and thesaurus. Kinderguard operates on an age-specific ratings basis. The software is configured for each individual user based on interests, age, and maturity level. Parents or teachers can then assess a site's content and give it an age rating, or use the ratings for sites assigned by the company.

According to TeacherSoft, "When you use InterGo to find and show sites, it only shows those appropriate for the assigned age. For example, a 14-year-old cannot see sites rated 17+ or 21+, and an adult who is assigned an age of 17+ does not see sites rated 21+." The $69.95 software package is currently available only for Windows 95 users. Versions for Windows 3.11 and Macintosh are in the works.

· · · · · · · · · · · · · ·
Net Nanny

Judging from information on Net Nanny's home page, this access control program strives to encompass all the features of its competitors and also provide educators and parents with a single, easy-to-use tool for computer software, hardware, *and* Internet administration. "Net Nanny is the only software program that allows YOU to monitor, screen and block access to anything residing on, or running in, out or through your PC, online or off."

The program includes controls for Web sites, newsgroups, Internet Relay Chat, ftp sites, email, and bulletin board systems. It also controls outgoing phrases and words such as home phone numbers or credit card information. Net Nanny can block access to all images of a particular type like GIFs or JPEGs (popular graphic file formats). Users can also control access to local files and drives, and even restrict loading of unauthorized diskettes and CD-ROMs. Net Nanny works with all of the major commercial online services and is available for Windows, Windows 95, and DOS.

· ·
Bess, the Internet Retriever

Bess combines Internet filtering software and a ratings system with customized Internet access to protect children and others from the sexually explicit and adult-oriented material on the Internet. Bess is more than a software package—it is an Internet access service that offers a point-and-click environment families can use to explore thousands of educational online sites. Unwanted material is blocked at Bess's main site. See Figure 3.10.

Subscribers simply dial into Bess and use the Netscape browser to guide them through the World Wide Web. The company's staff continually searches the Internet for undesirable material and immediately blocks it. Parents and school officials do not have to update software packages or subscribe to any services other than Bess. "Put simply, Bess is designed to provide parents, educators and children with a safer and easier way to use the Internet."

Here is a brief list of some of Bess' features:

- Certain domains (entire computers) containing large amounts of inappropriate material are blocked completely.
- Specific Web sites are blocked individually.
- Newsgroups and open chat areas, the parts of the Net most likely to contain explicit material, are not accessible to Bess users.
- Inappropriate language on otherwise acceptable sites is "X"ed out.
- Email—outgoing and incoming—is not delivered if it contains inappropriate language.

Bess also provides menus and an email interface with colorful icons to make navigating the Web easier for children. Teenagers and adults who do not want to use the Bess menus can access a simpler home page and still get all the protection of Bess's filtering system. Subscribers will need a Macintosh computer with

Figure 3.10
Bess offers more than blocking software. It's actually an Internet access service that provides links to thousands of safe educational locations. Undesirable material is blocked at Bess' main site, which is continually maintained.

System 7.5 or higher or an IBM-compatible computer (386 minimum) running Windows. Costs include a $30 activation fee and $29.95 monthly access fee for up to 30 hours of online use.

. . . .

Net Shepherd

Net Shepherd is unique in that it is the only shareware Internet filtering product. NetShepherd "does not require monthly subscriptions or updating of blacklists . . . no time limits, no ongoing fees, no 'friendly' please pay reminders, just download, install, and use!"

This software lets parents create individual, password-protected accounts that restrict Web access based on site ratings. All individual accounts and ratings are controlled through a supervisor account. Supervisors can freely surf the Internet and assign ratings to any Web site. Net Shepherd also gives a supervisor the option to subscribe to the company's own ratings service.

Each time your Web browser is launched, Net Shepherd asks the user for a password. Once logged in, children can visit only those sites that meet the rating criteria assigned by the supervisor. If a child tries to access a site rated as inappropriate, Net Shepherd will deny access. If neither the personal rating database or Net Shepherd's rating service database has a listing for the requested site, then access will be denied.

Another aspect that sets Net Shepherd apart is their effort to collect ratings preferences and form Internet community standards for site content ratings. According to the publisher:

> With your permission, the personal rating database you develop can be uploaded to a rating service. NetShepherd tallies your ratings, along with others, in a democratic process to derive ratings that reflect the majority of a service's users.

Versions for Windows and Windows 95 are available. Macintosh versions will be available shortly. You can download a copy at http://www.netshepherd.com.

. . . .

Specs for Kids

Specs for Kids from NewView is one of the newest filtering and access control programs. It's targeted mainly at the consumer market and provides access to its own selection of Internet sites, called SafeSites, rather than just filtering out bad ones.

Specs for Kids takes an inclusive approach and allows access only to SafeSites while not allowing sites that have not yet been rated. The company's large staff of experienced raters keeps its site-rating database current and comprehensive, freeing customers from this burden.

Specs for Kids claims that they have the largest database of family-friendly sites ("50,000 high quality sites—chosen for popularity and orientation toward children, families and education") to go along with its filtering software, which allows parents to customize access profiles for each user. (See Figure 3.11.) The filtering software offers most of the standard features of other such products, including:

- Filtering of Web, BBS, Internet Relay Chat, email, ftp, newsgroup, telnet, and graphics activities.
- Time controls and four levels of tampering security.
- Customized profiles for each user's ID and password.
- Automatic maintenance and updating.
- Comprehensive rating categories, with fifteen categories comprising up to five levels of filters.

Even if you don't subscribe to Specs for Kids, you can still access its ratings look-up service by going to the following URL:

http://www.newview.com/demo/rpticp.html

Simply enter a URL to see if Specs for Kids has rated a site. It actually rates individual documents and directories under a particular URL, as well as the entire site. If the database does not have a rating for the site you enter, you can submit one. (See Figure 3.12.)

Figure 3.11
Rather than just filtering questionable material, Specs for Kids, from NewView, provides access to its own selection of Internet SafeSites. NewView claims the largest database of family-friendly sites.

Figure 3.12
Specs for Kids!
rates individual
documents and
directories, as
well as entire
sites.

Site Information on http://www.whitehouse.gov

Following is a list of all rated URL's *under* the site requested. If the site itself
has a rating, it will be indicated with asterisks and larger print.

http://www.whitehouse.gov/: Rated & Indexed

http://www.whitehouse.gov/White_House/EOP/First_Lady/html/holidays-out.html:
Rated & Indexed

http://www.whitehouse.gov/White_House/EOP/First_Lady/html/holidays-in.html: Rated
& Indexed

http://www.whitehouse.gov/White_House/EOP/First_Lady/images/raw/christmas_tree.gif:
Rated & Indexed

A version is currently available for Windows 3.11. Both
Windows 95 and Macintosh versions are scheduled for release.
Beta versions of Specs for Kids are currently available free. The
full release will cost $39.95 per year.

REFERENCES

"Computer Pornography: What Can Schools Do?" National
Council of Educational Technology. [Online] Available
http://www.ncet.csv.warwick.ac.uk/WWW/gen-sheets/porn/index.html, March 3,
1996.

Godwin, Mike. "Testimony from July 24, 1995 Senate Judiciary
Committee Hearing on Cyberporn." [Online] Available
http://www.cdt.org/policy/freespeech/godwin724.html, February 2, 1996.

Jespen, Dee. "Testimony from July 24, 1995 Senate Judiciary
Committee Hearing on Cyberporn." [Online] Available
http://http://www.cdt.org/policy/freespeech/724list.html, February 3, 1996.

Magid, Larry. "Child Safety on the Information Highway."
[Online] Available http://www.larry's world.com.

Savitzky, Steven. "Interesting Places for Parents." [Online]
Available http://www.crc.ricoh.com/people/steve/parents.html, March 4, 1996.

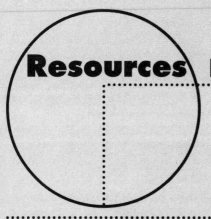

Resources LEARN MORE ABOUT IT!

Related Internet Sites—Safety

- **NCET—National Council for Educational Technology**
  URL: http://ncet.csv.warwick.ac.uk/

- **OUDPS—Kid Safety**
  URL: http://www.uoknor.edu/oupd/kidsafe/start.htm

- **Schools and the Internet: The Management of Student Access to Controversial Material**
  URL: http://teloz.latrobe.edu.au/circit/schome.html

- **Protecting our Children from the Internet (and the World)**
  URL: http://www.pacificrim.net/~mckenzie/fnojune95.html

- **Educational Access Issues from NCSA**
  URL: http://www.ncsa.uiuc.edu/Edu/ILM/CAUM/CAUM.html

- **Steven Savitzky's Notes, Advice, and Warnings**
  URL: http://www.crc.ricoh.com/people/steve/warn-kids.html

- **SAFE-T-CHILD Online**
  URL: http://yellodino.safe-t-child.com:80/

- **Kids and Parents on the Web**
  URL: http://www.halcyon.com:80/ResPress/kids.htm

Related Internet Sites—Software

- **The Internet Filter**
  URL: http://www.xmission.com/~seer/jdksoftware/

▣ **WebTrack**
URL: http://www.webster.com/

▣ **Internet In a Box for Kids**
URL: http://www.spry.com/products/kidbox.html

▣ **Parental Internet Control (reviews and links to software)**
URL: http://www.iinet.com/re/miscinfo/censor1.html

▣ **Pitsco Launch to Safe Internet Access**
URL: http://www.usa.net/~pitsco/pitsco/safe.html

▣ **Internet Access Management Software Reviews**
URL: http://www.mindspring.com/~safesurf/filters.html

▣ **Yahoo's Listing of Filtering and Blocking Software and Companies**
URL: http://www.yahoo.com/Business_and_Economy/Companies/Computers/Software/Internet/Blocking_and_Filtering/

·································

Other Helpful Resources

▣ **Bess.Net**
206-971-1400
URL: http://bess.net
Email to: bess@bess.net

▣ **CyberPatrol**
Microsystems Software, Inc.
600 Worchester Road
Framingham Massachusetts 01701
508-879-9000
Email to: info@microsys.com

▣ **CyberSitter**
Solid Oak Software, Inc.
PO Box 6826
Santa Barbara, California 93160
800-388-2761
Email to: info@solidoak.com
URL: http://www.rain.org/~solidoak/cybersit.htm

□ **Kinderguard**
TeacherSoft, Inc.
903 East 18th Street, Suite 230
Plano, Texas 75074
800-285-2662
Email to: TeacherSoft@teachersoft.com
URL: http://www.teachersoft.com

□ **Net Nanny**
Email to: netnanny@netnanny.com
URL: http://www.netnanny.com/netnanny/

□ **Specs for Kids**
NewView, Inc.
558 Brewster Avenue
Redwood City CA 94063
415-299-9016 extension 110
Email to: ccc@newview.com
URL: http://www.newview.com/

□ **SurfWatch**
SurfWatch Software, Inc.
175 South San Antonio Road, Suite 102
Los Altos, California 94022
800-458-6600
Email to: info@surfwatch.com
URL: http://www.surfwatch.com

> **Special discount available through**
> ***Classroom Connect !***
> Email to: connect @classroom.net
> URL: http://www.classroom.net/cyberpatrol

□ **The National Center for Missing and
Exploited Children**
2101 Wilson Boulevard, Suite 550
Arlington, Virginia 22201-3052
Phone: 800-THE-LOST
Email to: 74431.177@compuserve.com
URL: http://www.isa.net/isa

□ **WebWhacker**
Forefront Group, Inc.
1360 Post Oak Boulevard, Suite 1660
Houston, Texas 77056
Phone: 800-867-1101
Email to: jelder@ffg.com
URL: http://www.ffg.com

4 Chapter

NETIQUETTE

Without a set of manners, anarchy would reign supreme over the Internet. Surprisingly, this is not the case, which is why it's important to teach youngsters about "Netiquette" and personal responsibility when using the Internet. This chapter will help you do that.

Netiquette is a system of manners for the Internet, a set of generally agreed-upon conventions and guidelines for interacting with other people online.

HELPING US ALL GET ALONG IN CYBERSPACE

Manners may be in decline in the "real world," but the Internet world could not function without them. Parents and institutions can easily set rules for Internet use and expect students to behave appropriately. But it's another issue entirely for each individual in the Internet community to behave in a consistent, organized fashion that enables civilized online communication. This civility is the result of Netiquette.

A combination of the words "net" and "etiquette," Netiquette is a system of manners for the Internet, a set of generally agreed-upon conventions and guidelines for interacting with other people online. The only enforcers of Netiquette are, by and large, other users, which is why it is so important to teach young Internet users about personal responsibility and Netiquette.

The Internet is—for the most part—an open, friendly, conversational place. This is no accident, though, especially considering the huge number of people from different cultures and backgrounds who go online every day. If a sizable portion of Internet users did not adhere to Netiquette, this massive conglomeration might quickly become too chaotic, unfriendly, or disorganized to be of any value—like a modern day Tower of Babel.

As you may remember, the Internet is really just the sum of all the *people* who use its resources. And just as we need norms for behaving and interacting with others in shopping malls, stadiums, schools, and parks in the real world, we need standards in the online world. Most Netiquette rules exist for two general but essential purposes: to promote basic civility and to encourage wise use and sharing of limited network resources.

A CIVILIZED NET OR NO NET AT ALL

The alternative to having guidelines for online courtesy and respect is an Internet "free-for-all." Those who scream the loudest or come up with the nastiest messages would drown out the voices of those trying to hold meaningful discussions. The "signal-to-noise" ratio would change for the worse—there would be much more noise and less content or interaction. Instead of discussing issues that are important, for example, newsgroup readers would spend most of their time dealing with abusive, ignorant, and rude users. Fortunately, most Internet users agree to follow Netiquette.

AN INTERNET WE CAN ALL USE

You may have noticed the phrase "limited network resources" a paragraph or two ago. And you may be asking: "Isn't the Internet an unlimited, global Information Superhighway?" It is, but only up to a point. The wires and computers that transmit and store data—which could be a single email message, a huge zipped file, or real-time video transmission—can only handle a certain amount. As a result, Netiquette is often related to how much and how often users send or request information.

Needlessly clogging up the Internet's "pipes," which are already getting pretty congested, is not fair to other users. It might seem as if your online activities are too small in themselves to be of much effect, but each user really *does* affect the entire network. If you worked out the math, you would discover that every byte of every email message transmitted has some monetary value associated with it—including costs associated with time, transmission, and storage. This is why sending "junk email" or repeatedly posting the same message is considered poor Netiquette.

NETIQUETTE AND INTERNET SAFETY

What does Netiquette have to do with Internet safety? Plenty, if you, your child, or your student seriously violates Netiquette! Internet justice can be harsh on users who break the rules of Netiquette, and the results can be distressing to a young person.

Users who break the online rules can be:

- *Flamed.* They receive many nasty email messages condemning their online actions. The messages can include derogatory, vulgar language and even threats.
- *Flooded or mail bombed.* They receive so many messages or files at once that their system or their provider's system is overwhelmed and crashes.

- *Banned from mailing lists or newsgroups.* Moderators who tire of repeated Netiquette violations can shut the offender out of online discussion groups.
- *Dropped by their ISP.* The ISP can cancel their account if they find the offenses are serious and frequent enough that other users complain.
- *Banned from using an Internet connection.* School and companies will take action if the rules in an acceptable-use policy (AUP) are violated.
- *Sued.* If they make libelous, racist, or misleading statements that hurt or offend, the offended party may pursue litigation.

Each type of Internet tool or resource, such as email, has its own particular points of Netiquette. We will address the most important points to get you started. There are many other more subtle guidelines or nuances that you can learn only by actually surfing for a while.

Created at the Computer Ethics Institute, the Ten Commandments of Computer Ethics are an excellent way to start teaching young people about appropriate online behavior. A word of advice: Don't take it upon yourself to become the Internet Netiquette Enforcer, rather *educate* people about Netiquette and be forgiving of their mistakes. Don't jump down someone's throat for a minor violation. We were all new users at some point, and everybody has violated Netiquette at least once.

TEN COMMANDMENTS OF COMPUTER ETHICS
1. Thou shalt not use a computer to harm other people.
2. Thou shalt not interfere with other people's computer work.
3. Thou shalt not snoop around in other people's files.
4. Thou shalt not use a computer to steal.
5. Thou shalt not use a computer to bear false witness.
6. Thou shalt not use or copy copyrighted software for which you have not paid.
7. Thou shalt not use other people's computer resources without authorization.
8. Thou shalt not appropriate other people's intellectual output.
9. Thou shalt think about the social consequences of the program you write and the messages you post.
10. Thou shalt use a computer in ways that show consideration and respect.

EMAIL NETIQUETTE

Email is one of the most widely used Internet tools—and for good reason. Electronic mail is an excellent way to communicate: fast, simple, efficient, permanent, yet immediate. Often, it is one of the first Internet tools children use. Email's power and flexibility, however, require Internauts to be careful about how they use email. If your company or school has a private, internal email system, you may already be familiar with some of these caveats.

- Email is easily stored and forwarded, so be careful what you write. As they say on the Net: "Never put anything in an email message you wouldn't mind seeing on the six o'clock news."
- Electronic mail may seem ethereal, but is more permanent than many people realize. Any email message can be printed on paper or saved to a hard disk. Also, email messages are often forwarded to mailing lists or newsgroups—without the author's realization—where they can live forever. This is because archives of nearly all newsgroups are kept at various locations on the Internet and those archives are keyword searchable. If you write something inflammatory or stupid, it could come back to haunt you. Imagine if presidential candidates had used electronic mail when they were younger—reporters would be searching Usenet archives all day!
- Use informative subject lines in your email messages. Many people get hundreds of messages each day, and few things are more annoying than not having at least a small idea of what the message is about before actually reading it. Some Internauts will not even read mail without subject lines. Do not, however, use bogus subject lines such as "Emergency—you must read this NOW" just to get attention.
- Make sure you try to preserve the context of conversations. When responding to someone else's email message, for example, do not extract one sentence and respond out of context. Include text of the original message in your reply. Most email programs will automatically put the text of the original message, surrounded by carats or brackets, into your reply. This is called the "message thread." So much email can go back and forth in a day that we could easily lose track of who said what if we did not use threads.

- Do not, however, include text in your reply and thread if it is not essential to your reply. Use just the portion of the message that is necessary to preserve the flow of the conversation. Pretend you are an editor, scanning for the most important and relevant details to include in your reply.

- Never post someone's email message to a newsgroup, mailing list, Web site, or other online area without the author's written permission. It could be illegal and is always disrespectful.

- Be sure to respect copyright notices and license agreements. Cite all quotes, references, and sources. Pretend you are writing a research paper—you would not simply include information without citing where it came from or giving others credit for their ideas. Since email allows you to send graphics or programs as part of your message, be sure not to forward copyrighted items such as logos, Disney characters, or games.

- Never, *ever* pretend you are another person when sending email messages. It is not funny and is not tolerated. Doing so could easily lead to a lawsuit, depending on the situation. For example, if you pose as someone else and post a libelous or defamatory message about a third party, you could be sued by the defamed person, as well as by the person that you impersonated.

- Keep messages short and to the point. Focus on one subject per message. Remember, the more words in your message, the more bandwidth and hard drive space it consumes—and the longer it takes for someone else to download.

- Always include a brief signature file with your email messages. A signature file is the email equivalent of letterhead stationery or a business card. Without a "sig file," those who receive your message may not realize who the message is from, especially if their email programs do not display or print all the typical header information. Figure 4.1 provides an example of a signature file.

  If you are using email at work or school, you should be sure that information in your sig is in keeping with your organization's communications guidelines. Children should not include identifying information such as their address and telephone number. They should be cautious about including their full name.

- Check your email daily—Internauts appreciate a quick reply. Also, since email can quickly accumulate and consume lots of hard drive space or RAM when email programs are running (Eudora, for example, keeps copies of all your incoming, outgoing, and trashed mail—requiring more RAM for operation), be sure to keep up with your computer housekeeping by deleting unwanted messages.

- Turn the other cheek when it comes to flame messages. Responding to a flame with an even harsher flame will only cause a *flame war*. Make conversation, not war.

- Be careful using sarcasm or attempting humor in your messages. Without face-to-face communication and the benefit of body language, an email joke may be misinterpreted.

- If you would like to convey a certain emotion but still want to maintain an economy of words, use smileys or emoticons. Smileys are expressions meant to look like little faces. (Smileys are discussed further later in this chapter.)

- DON'T TYPE IN ALL CAPS, UNLESS YOU WANT TO SHOUT YOUR ENTIRE MESSAGE! Typing in all caps is an easy way to *really* annoy your message recipients.

- You would think that since email is a purely written form of communication, it would be natural for people to check their message. For grammar and punctuation. But they ain't always maybe going to. :-) To make a good impression, spell-check your documents, check punctuation, and make sure everything is grammatically sound. Many email programs have integrated spell checkers. If yours does not, you can always copy the text into a word processor, run a spell-checker, and paste the corrected document back into your email message.

```
<-=-=-=-==-=-=-=-=-=-=-=-=-=-=-=-=-=o
Vince DiStefano
Classroom Connect: vinced@classroom.net
http://www.classroom.net
Private: vince@networkings.com
o-=-=-=-=-=-=-=-=-=-=-=-=-=-=-=-=-=->
```

Figure 4.1
Signature files placed at the end of email messages are best kept to four or five lines.

EMILY POSTNEWS ON SIGNATURE FILES

Emily Postnews, created by Internet veteran Brad Templeton, is a spoof on newspaper columns about manners and etiquette. Emily provides strictly tongue-in-cheek advice that is really the opposite of how Internet users should behave. This is what "she" says about signature files:

Dear Miss Postnews:

How long should my signature be?

Signed: verbose@noisy

Dear Verbose:

Please try and make your signature as long as you can. It's much more important than your article, of course, so try and have more lines of signature than actual text. Try and include a large graphic made of ASCII characters, plus lots of cute quotes and slogans. People will never tire of reading these pearls of wisdom again and again, and you will soon become personally associated with the joy each reader feels at seeing yet another delightful repeat of your signature.

Aside from your reply address, include your full name, company, and organization. It's just common courtesy—after all, in some newsreaders people have to type an entire keystroke to go back to the top of your article to see this information in the header.
By all means include your phone number and street address in every single article. People are always responding to Usenet articles with phone calls and letters. It would be silly to go to the extra trouble of including this information only in articles that need a response by conventional channels!

Signed: Miss Postnews

- Likewise, formatting your message is important. Use double line breaks to indicate new paragraphs and set your column width to 80 rather than 85. That way, people with email readers that display 80 characters will not have to suffer through messages with broken lines and paragraphs.
- Refrain from using email as a substitute for transferring files. You can attach massive documents or binary files such as programs to your email messages, but doing so could crash your service provider's email server or slow down access for other users. Use ftp programs or exchange removable media with floppy diskettes, zip disks, or SyQuest cartridges.

MAILING LIST NETIQUETTE

Like email, Internet mailing lists are an excellent way to communicate online—and also provide more opportunities for violating Netiquette. Using email, members of a list on a particular topic—The Fly Fishing Mailing List, for example—post messages to a central email address. Then, the message is forwarded to all the other people signed onto the list. These worldwide discussion lists are a wonderful way for people with similar interests and hobbies to correspond and share ideas, but care must be taken to follow the guidelines so that everyone can fully benefit from the list.

Since the medium for mailing lists is email, many of the same Netiquette guidelines apply. There are, however, some points of Netiquette specific to mailing lists.

INFO BYTE

Spice up your email with these common "smileys."

:-)   Smiling
;-)   Winking—an inside joke or coy statement
:-(Frowning, displeasure
:-O   Surprise, astonishment (can be sarcastic)

A smiley "dictionary" is shown in Figure 4.2.

URL: http://www.olympe.polytechnique.fr/~violet/Smileys/

Figure 4.2
You can consult
this online smiley
dictionary to
spice up your
email and
confuse your
friends!

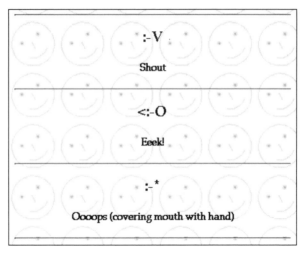

:-V

Shout

<:-O

Eeek!

:-*

Ooooops (covering mouth with hand)

◑ Learn about the focus and purpose of the mailing list before
  signing on, or "subscribing." Mailing lists require somebody,
  somewhere, to spend time and money keeping the list going.
  Joining lists you do not really want to be on is wasteful.

◑ Follow the correct procedure for joining a given list—their
  procedures often vary—and save the FAQ or list participa-
  tion guidelines in case you are unsure about what posts are
  appropriate. If the list is moderated, save the moderator's
  email address in case you have questions later. Most moderators are more than willing to work with you, rather than let
  you frustrate other participants with inappropriate messages.

◑ Make sure your posts fit the focus and topic of the list. Do not
  join a Windows 95 mailing list and then post messages about
  Macintosh or DOS computing. There are about 15,000 different lists on every topic imaginable, so you are sure to find the
  appropriate lists for your interests. If you cannot find a list but
  you absolutely *must* be heard, create your own list. And don't
  let anyone on your list post off-topic messages.

◑ Save copies of the instructions for getting off the list. If you
  do not, you could end up sending your "subscribe" or
  "unsubscribe" messages to all of the members of the list
  instead of the list administrator. People are not interested in
  reading "Please remove me from the mailing list" a hundred
  times per day. That is perhaps one of the single most aggra-
  vating violations of Netiquette. It often causes people to
  leave lists or moderators to shut lists down.

- When you first join a list, hang out or "lurk" for a few days before posting your own messages. Get a feel for the atmosphere and tone before jumping in and possibly stepping on people's toes right away. Also, you might find information about the topic without having to waste other people's time with questions that have already been exhaustively covered.

- Keep in mind that mailing lists are global, so people from different cultures or countries may be on the list. Do not assume they will understand your culture-specific slang or jargon. Will your references to *Seinfeld* characters be understood or appreciated? Not everyone knows who Kramer is!

- When responding to someone's question on the list, consider sending email directly to that person rather than to the list so all can read it. This is especially advisable when the answer is likely to be echoed by all the other members of the list. Who wants to read 50 identical responses to the same question? Before posting any response on a list, ask yourself "Will most readers of this discussion list appreciate or care to see the reply?"

- By the same token, when you post a question that is likely to receive many responses, ask that people email you directly with their answers. And offer to provide a summary of responses to the list. This is not required, but if you do not do it, you will be *taking* from the Internet and the list members without *giving* anything back—a violation of the Net's spirit of sharing! Receiving replies by private email helps minimize list traffic and gives everyone a chance to hear what others on the list are saying.

Keep email brief with the help of some common Internet abbreviations. BTW, there are hundreds!

INFO BYTE

BTW	by the way
IMHO	in my humble opinion
IOW	in other words
RTM	read the manual!

Visit this site for Internet acronyms, abbreviations, and definitions:

http://www.umiacs.umd.edu/staff/amato/AC/main.html

- Do not, however, simply paste all the replies in their entirety into a single message and then forward that message to the list. Instead, put on your editor's cap again and provide a brief but informative summary of responses. People on the list will appreciate your efforts.
- Don't subscribe to mailing lists using shared email accounts or temporary accounts, such as an America Online trial account. If your email address disappears, the software that handles these lists will not know it and will keep trying to send you posts. The list administrator will have to deal with the resulting error messages. If you *must* sign on with a temporary account, at least be considerate enough to unsubscribe from the list before your email address expires.

USENET NETIQUETTE

Some of the same Netiquette points, such as keeping messages brief and to-the-point and including signature files, that apply to email and mailing lists also apply to Usenet newsgroup communication. Be sure to "lurk" awhile before posting your own message. Then, follow the same rules for responding to individuals or asking questions as you would follow for mailing lists. Here are a few specific guidelines for participating in Usenet newsgroups.

- Keep in mind that Usenet is the most open public forum for communicating online, so mistakes made here are mistakes made in front of millions of people. And Usenet can be a volatile place, a fertile breeding ground for personality clashes and heated arguments.
- Almost all newsgroups have a charter that group administrators make available to all interested Internet citizens. Read the charter before participating. For FAQ (frequently asked questions) or help files on virtually all the Usenet newsgroups, go to the following ftp site. You will find a huge list of groups organized by name and hierarchy, plus documents on how to create your own newsgroup or vote on developing newsgroups. To reach the FAQ Archive,

    ftp to: **rtfm.mit.edu**

Select the pub/usenet subdirectory

- Do not "spam"—that is, post advertisements to groups that do not accept them. A few newsgroups are designed especially for posting want ads or for-sale notices. Use them instead.
- Don't post "testing—please ignore" messages to newsgroups just because you are not sure if your posts actually make it to a particular newsgroup. Some groups are set up especially for test messages, such as alt.test.
- Do not flame-bait, that is, post messages that you know will cause a flame war. Do not, for example, post antiabortion messages in prochoice newsgroups. These groups are for people who are, by and large, *already* decided on such issues. It is unlikely that your post will change anyone's mind one way or the other. Be careful about posting articles of a religious nature, especially if you attempt to push your own morality on others. Like mailing lists, there are enough Usenet groups out there that you should be able to find one in which your posts are both accepted and appreciated.
- Avoid starting one of those "Which one is better—Mac or Windows?" wars in Usenet. Most Internauts are extremely tired of this topic.

FTP NETIQUETTE

On the surface, violating ftp Netiquette might seem to be a "victimless crime" since no other people are involved. Wrong: ftp sites—computers that store documents and shareware programs and make them accessible to the public—have limited resources. Only a certain number of people can be logged into the computer at once. And ftp servers can only process so many requests at once. Follow these guidelines to ensure you will not irritate an ftp site administrator, who could cut off your access to the site as punishment for repeated violations.

- Most ftp sites provide a list of usage guidelines, which you should follow as much as possible. For instance, if a system administrator requests that you refrain from logging in until after 5 P.M., it is probably for good reason. Some organizations use their ftp computers for internal purposes, and lots of users connecting during business hours will slow down their system.

- Instead of wandering around an ftp site and guessing which file you need, look for README.TXT or INDEX.TXT files first. They contain information about the site's holdings and point you to the directory where the files are stored.
- Keep your ftp sessions as short as possible so that others can connect to the site. Don't download just for the sake of downloading—take only what you need.
- Don't forget to log off of an ftp site when you are finished downloading files. Users often forget to disconnect and then move on to something else or leave their work stations, thus needlessly tying up the ftp server.
- If you upload or transfer a shareware program from your computer to the ftp site, make sure you have checked the program for viruses and included a description of the file. Some sites have restrictions on uploading. Contact the system administrator first for details.
- Don't contact the site administrator with questions about the software on the site. They usually do not have the time or propensity to help you figure out software they do not use or did not create.

TELNET NETIQUETTE

Telnet use is waning, but you may discover some invaluable resource that can *only* be accessed via telnet . . . we think. Many of the same rules that apply to ftp also apply to telnet, but here are a few telnet-specific considerations.

- Be sure to read the messages from the site or system operator that appear when you first begin your session.
- Whenever possible, exit or quit a telnet session in the manner indicated on the screen (usually E[X]it or [Q]uit) rather than merely shutting off your modem connection or resetting your computer. Like Windows, DOS, or Mac operating systems, telnet computers function best when exited properly.

WEB NETIQUETTE

Not many Netiquette rules associated with *visiting* Web pages have evolved. But you should follow some general guidelines if you decide to *create* a site.

- Don't steal other people's graphical buttons, horizontal rules, or other Web page navigational graphics. You'd be surprised how much time and effort often goes into designing simple little 3D buttons. Buy your own graphics software and learn how to use it. Or visit one of the many sites that offer freely downloadable icons, rules, and buttons. You will be much more satisfied when your Web site is really *your* Web site.

- Keep graphics to a minimum on your home page, or give users the option of being able to select high-speed or low-speed. A majority of Internauts still have somewhat slow modem connections, so superfluous graphics can be time-wasting annoyances. Consider interlacing your GIFs so that they progressively display. Use ALT tags that provide text alternatives for graphics in case users stop loading or turn the graphics off in their Web browsers.

- Pay attention to copyright restrictions when adding graphics or photos to your Web pages. Often it is easy to figure out what constitutes a violation and what is legitimate. Putting *Simpsons* cartoons on your home page would definitely be an infringement. But other cases are not as obvious. (See Chapter 7 for more on copyrights and related issues.)

- Never copy someone else's pages wholesale to include on your site unless you obtain permission. Use hyperlinks instead.

- If you are going to include a lot of hyperlinks to someone else's site and your site gets lots of traffic, it is common courtesy to ask the Web site's owner for permission first. Most will be eager to accommodate you, since they want lots of Internauts linking to their pages. Others, however, may not have adequate servers or may soon change their server address and therefore will want to keep the traffic to their sites restricted.

- Do not pirate someone else's Web page counter or email form for your use. It's a little tricky to carry off, but it is possible to put visitor counters or forms on your page that are processed on someone else's server.

- When visiting Web sites, do not abuse interactive email forms by sending prank messages. Those forms are put in place to gather feedback from legitimate users, not to collect messages from "Jacques Strappe" whose interests include "supporting athletes."

Resources LEARN MORE ABOUT IT!

Related Internet Sites

◻ **The Net: User Guidelines and Netiquette by Arlene H. Rinaldi**
   URL: http://www.fau.edu/rinaldi/netiquette.html

◻ **Netiquette: The Mailing List**
   Email to: netiquette-request@albion.com
   Type **subscribe <your name>** in the subject line

◻ **The Netiquette Home Page**
   URL: http://bookfair.com/Services/Albion/nqhome.html

◻ **Dear Emily Postnews**
   URL: http://www.clari.net/brad/emily.html

◻ **PolitenessMan's Guide to Netiquette (commercial)**
   URL: http://www.organic.com/1800collect/Netiquette/index.html

◻ **The Netiquette Netisodes**
   URL: http://www.carbon.concom.com/~d

ACCEPTABLE
USE POLICIES

An AUP is a written agreement
signed by students, parents,
teachers, and possibly
administrators or technology
coordinators. The agreement
outlines the terms and conditions
of Internet use within a school.
This chapter will give educators
plenty of details about AUPs and
how to make them work in your
school community. Parents will
find ideas for setting rules of
Internet use in the home.

SPELLING OUT GUIDELINES FOR BEHAVIOR

You are now more familiar than you would probably like to be with the dark side of the Net and are keenly aware of how important it is to structure Internet use at home or at school. The Internet is a vast, mostly disorganized ocean of information and people. Just as you wouldn't toss someone in the real ocean if you hadn't first taught them how to swim, so responsible adults should not allow young people to enter Internet waters without teaching them the rules of online behavior (Netiquette) and setting rules for Internet use in general.

Have you heard of an AUP, or acceptable-use policy? If your child is using any type of online service at school, you probably already know about AUPs or will soon. An AUP is a written agreement signed by students, parents, teachers, and possibly administrators or technology coordinators. The agreement outlines the terms and conditions of Internet use within a school.

If you are an educator, this chapter will give you plenty of details about AUPs and how you can make them work in your school community. If you are a parent, you might find ideas for how you want to set the rules of Internet use in your home. You will also find a section at the end of the chapter that covers home AUPs.

An AUP builds the foundation for Internet use in the school community. It applies to students and, increasingly, to staff. Most AUPs answer questions such as these:

- How will students be supervised as they surf the Net?
- Who can have access and to what degree? Do teachers get full accounts or email only? Does each student get his or her own email account or will the whole class share an email address? Can students access their school account from home?
- Will access be prescribed according to student age or grade?
- What online areas or resources are acceptable for students and faculty to visit?
- What online areas or resources are off-limits?
- If the school has a Web site, what are the guidelines for creating pages?

- How should students and teachers behave when interacting with others on the Internet?
- What constitutes an acceptable use of email? Can Internet services not directly related to school assignments ever be used?
- Which computers in the school can be used to get online, during what times can they be used, and to what degree can they be used (i.e., terminals for email access only, full access, etc.)?
- What kind of software can be uploaded or downloaded?
- Can students bring in their own Internet programs from home?
- What happens when someone breaks the rules?
- Who is responsible for enforcing the AUP?

AUPs are so new—about two years old—that standards for them are still evolving. On one hand, some in the K–12 education community do not think AUPs can possibly anticipate every Internet issue and do not rely on them as heavily as others do to regulate Net use. On the other hand, the concept of using an AUP to set guidelines for Net use is being adopted by many businesses and even some parents. This chapter will give you details about the most common structure of school AUPs. Appendix A contains several examples of real-world AUPs used by specific schools and districts.

THE MAJOR SECTIONS OF AN AUP

1. *Brief explanation of the Internet.* This provides a definition of the Net, how students and teachers will access it, and how it will be used in the classroom. Schools cannot assume that parents know what the Internet is or why it is valuable to schools. By avoiding "technobabble," the explanation brings them up to speed before going into the specifics.
2. *Overview of online dangers.* This includes the potential of accessing "objectionable materials" and student responsibility for "doing the right thing" online. Also included are details about protection software (such as CyberPatrol or SurfWatch) the school uses and practical steps teachers and administrators take to keep kids safe online, such as monitoring and supervision.

3. *List of acceptable and unacceptable activities or resources.* This section is the "meat" of the AUP in that it contains all of the specifics about what is acceptable and what is not. Language is generally broad, since the document cannot cover all specific illegitimate uses or possibilities for abuse.

4. *Information on netiquette.* Details about how students are expected to behave when interacting with others on the Internet, including guidelines for using email, ftp, and Usenet newsgroups. (Chapter 4 in this book covers netiquette.)

5. *Consequences of violations.* This section makes it clear that using the Internet at school is a privilege, not a right, and that violations will be quickly dealt with. Penalties need to be stated specifically and usually range from a written warning and phone call to parents for first or minor offenses to loss of access privileges for more serious or repeated violations.

6. *Signatures.* The most well-crafted, detailed AUP will not account to much if students, teachers, and parents do not sign it! Anyone using the school's Internet connection—including faculty and staff—should be required to sign before launching even one piece of Internet software. There are rarely any arguable cases for exemption. Parents need to read and sign the school's AUP to verify that they are aware of the potential dangers of the Internet and that they permit their children access under the conditions set forth in the AUP.

An AUP should always pass through school boards for approval and should probably be reviewed by school district lawyers. It should be kept on file as a legal, binding document to help protect teachers and schools from liability problems. If your son or daughter uses the Internet or a commercial online service at school, but you have never signed, seen, or even heard of an AUP, consider contacting the administration to find out if some kind of policy is in place.

Many AUPs also include sections that apply to staff and visitor use of the Internet. Again, these documents are only now evolving into a standard form and answers to the question of how to regulate staff use of the Net are only now surfacing. Check Appendix A to see how some schools handle this issue in their AUPs.

INCLUDE WEB PUBLISHING GUIDELINES IN YOUR AUP

One increasingly popular aspect of school Internet use is online publishing by students or teachers. Schools are not using the Net merely to download information—they are publishing student papers, the results of Internet projects, and more—all for the rest of the world to see. Web "server-in-a-box" products make it easier than ever for schools or districts to put up their own World Wide Web home pages—complete with school logos, pictures, newspapers, community pointers, and so on.

Web publishing gives students a great creative outlet, enables them to learn to actively use Internet technology, and broadens their communication to a truly global scale. Schools can collaborate on projects, publish fiction or poetry, or put scientific experiment results online for peers to review. At some schools, students and teachers are much more concerned about maintaining their Web servers and putting content on the Internet than they are about surfing other sites!

But what information is appropriate to put on a school's Web site? While the conclusions of a research paper might be acceptable, a photo from *Playboy* or *Playgirl* would not. A school has to be careful about becoming a censor of ideas, but it should also include in its AUP details about who is allowed to post information on Web pages. It should include a subsection outlining a specific approval process for adding content to the Web site, as well as guidelines for how pages are to be organized, structured, and so forth.

Are students allowed to publish personal information, and if so, what kind? Will photos of students or school activities be permitted? What restrictions need to be put into place to protect the school's Web server and connection? For example, huge graphic files could slow the server down for other classes trying to use the connection. Will students be able to log-in from home to upload pages? Who will maintain the server and software? Take a look at your school's policy concerning other student publications, such as newspapers or yearbooks, for guidance. A school's Internet AUP should be compatible with existing publishing guidelines.

CASE STUDY: PAUL KIM'S "UNOFFICIAL SCHOOL HOME PAGE"

The Paul Kim case demonstrates what can happen if schools do not have acceptable-use policies that cover Web publishing, or if they do not have an AUP at all. In 1995, Kim, a 17-year-old student at Newport High School in Bellevue, Washington, created a Web page called "The Unofficial Newport High School Home Page." The page—which Kim reportedly created on his own computer on his own time—was apparently meant as a spoof or parody of his high school. It contained a section called "Favorite Subjects of Newport High School Students." One of the links included pointers to *Playboy* and articles about masturbation and oral sex. A school administrator allegedly discovered the page, which Kim had entered into the popular Yahoo directory of Internet sites, and complained that Kim was improperly using the school's name.

That launched a series of events—the most significant being that the school principal revoked the school's endorsement of Kim as a National Merit finalist, precluding him from winning a National Merit Scholarship. The principal contacted the colleges Kim applied to, informing them that the endorsement had been withdrawn and that the school could no longer recommend Kim for enrollment.

The Washington ACLU stepped in as Kim's defense. One of the major points it made—and a point that may have hurt the school's case considerably—was that Kim was denied his right to due process since the school did not have guidelines covering such actions. In addition, "high schools certainly may not exercise more control over off-campus behavior than on-campus conduct," attorneys for the ACLU wrote in a letter to the district's superintendent, "and such control must be based on the standard of 'substantial interference with the normal operations of the school.'" The ACLU asked the school district to submit a written apology to Kim, write an explanatory letter to the seven colleges the principal contacted, and compensate Kim for the lost National Merit Scholarship opportunity.

It is not clear whether a policy specifically addressing activities like Kim's would have changed things, but the affair does stress the need for schools not only to cover all the bases when designing and implementing AUPs. They should also, however, write AUPs that do not violate the established constitutional rights of students. A well-crafted AUP, reviewed by a lawyer for constitutional soundness, might have shown Kim more clearly the possible ramifications of his Web publishing behavior and helped the school avoid negative media coverage and criticism for its actions.

EDUCATORS TALK ABOUT THE PROS AND CONS OF AUPs

AUPs are now commonplace in many schools, so it is easy to network with them to see what they have done and avoid rein-venting the wheel. However, it is generally not a good idea to assume that an AUP used in one school will also work in yours. In fact, some schools do not use formal AUPs at all. They take a different approach to prescribing appropriate and inappropriate uses of computer networks. Instead of having each student or teacher sign a contract, some recommend that each district's school board put together system-wide guidelines that cover all users. Here's a post from the K–12 Acceptable Use Policy mail-ing list that explains why some districts do not require signed AUPs.

> [The signing of AUP contracts prior to use] is frequent-ly done, but it is probably done more because everyone is doing it rather than the fact that there is a need. The school system should approve guidelines for acceptable use of the district system, and these guidelines should apply to all users. As district employees, teachers are required to follow board policy, so having teachers sign a contract is at best redundant . . . but could be poten-tially confusing if the contract sets forth provisions that are not in accord with the district employee discipli-nary process.

> There really is not a need for students to sign a contract. After all, we expect students to follow the district discipli-nary code but do not have them sign contracts requiring them to do so. But since it is important for parents to specifically approve a student's individual account, and it

never hurts to emphasize to a student that something is serious ;-) a contract for students is probably a good way to go. A signed agreement may also help a district avoid liability.
—Nancy Willard, Eugene, Oregon

Nancy Willard, an information technology consultant and former attorney, has completed an extensive legal and educational analysis of K–12 AUPs in which she discusses some common AUP clauses and wording from a legal perspective. She believes that many school AUPs are flawed in their legal language. As an alternative, Willard has developed a template for a board policy and student AUP. (To find out more about her efforts, visit the Classroom Connect Web site:

URL: http://www.classroom.net/

Some K–12 AUPs can be found at:

URL: http://www.erehwon.com/k12aup

Some schools simply feel that the Internet is such an integral part of the curriculum, no special parental permission is required. Other teachers and schools feel that having to spell out every possible use of the Internet and all its possible ramifications only serves to increase hysteria, fear, or misunderstanding. Parents may begin to question why such detailed legal documents are required and may wonder: "Can't teachers manage a few computers in their classrooms and determine what constitutes an appropriate learning environment?" Parents don't sign consent forms for textbooks used in the classroom or for periodicals offered in the library; they trust that the school board will make wise decisions. Of course, unlike a textbook, the Internet is not a static learning tool—it changes and grows every day, so it can not be "pre-approved" for use all year long.

Regardless of the way your school handles AUPs, be sure that all elements are carefully developed before anyone signs anything. If you spell out severe punishments for misuse, will you be able to administer them? Does the AUP put teachers at undue risk? Having a "sponsoring teacher" sign the form may seem fine on the surface, but will it put teachers in the position of possibly having to defend themselves in court?

Does the AUP have any loopholes—or, at the other extreme, is it so uncompromising that it discourages people from using the Internet? Does your AUP cover guests who use the Net at your school? What about foreign exchange students, substitute teachers, or support staff such as secretaries or custodial workers? If you are going to put an AUP in place, the more thorough and inclusive it is the better. Be sure to read Dave Kinnamin's excellent editorial, "Critiquing acceptable-use policies" at the GNN Education Center Internet site. It provides good coverage of all these questions and issues.

Note that, in cases where minors access the school's Internet connection from home, parents must usually assume full responsibility for their children's online activity. You may want to consider using a parental or home AUP.

A LIBRARIAN'S VIEW OF AUPs

It is worth noting that AUPs may require modifications or compromise concerning Internet access in school libraries. In an article titled "Free Access to Libraries for Minors: An Interpretation of the Library Bill of Rights," the American Library Association (ALA) makes these assertions concerning policies that restrict access to information, including information on the Internet, based on age:

> Library policies and procedures which effectively deny minors equal access to all library resources available to other users violate the Library Bill of Rights. The American Library Association opposes all attempts to restrict access to library services, materials, and facilities based on the age of library users.

INFO BYTE

We currently don't want to require parental permission for Internet use, as we feel network access is inherently connected with our curriculum—we might as well be asking for permission to show a video in teaching current events.

—Don Detweiler post to K12-AUP mailing list

Library policies and procedures which effectively deny minors equal access to all library resources available to other users violate the Library Bill of Rights.
—*American Library Association*

Article V of the Library Bill of Rights states, "A person's right to use a library should not be denied or abridged because of origin, age, background, or views." The "right to use a library" includes free access to, and unrestricted use of, all the services, materials, and facilities the library has to offer. Every restriction on access to, and use of, library resources, based solely on the chronological age, educational level, or legal emancipation of users violates Article V.

Librarians have a professional commitment to ensure that all members of the community they serve have free and equal access to the entire range of library resources regardless of content, approach, format, or amount of detail. This principle of library service applies equally to all users, minors as well as adults. Librarians and governing bodies must uphold this principle in order to provide adequate and effective service to minors.

It is important to make sure your school AUP is compatible with the Library Bill or Rights

PARENTAL OR HOME AUPS

Schools are well on their way to dealing with the issues of balancing responsible control with freedom of Net use. But what about Net use at home? How should parents who want to allow their children to use the Net set the rules?

Some parents find it useful to formulate an acceptable-use policy for children using the Internet at home. AUPs for the home are similar to contracts teenagers sign with parents promising that they will call if they are ever in a situation where they have had a few drinks at a party and need a ride home. Parents sign the same AUP, showing their commitment to "doing the right thing" and embracing the same principles they ask their children to embrace. They are more like informal agreements between parents and children, not contracts per se.

You do not have to view implementing an AUP in the home as an overbearing, distrustful move toward absolute control over your children—unless you decide to make it that way. Rather, home AUPs can help crystallize in your child's mind the importance of following the rules, and it can help families avoid any confusion about those rules. Keeping a copy of the AUP near the computer or posting it on a bulletin board in your home will serve as a reminder that the privilege of going online for fun or learning also carries with it some responsibilities, just like driving the family car or going to the movies.

Explain to your kids that having an AUP for home Internet use does not mean you don't trust them—it just means that they have to take on an adult responsibility—a responsibility that you are confident they can handle. Point out that they will probably have to sign more AUPs in the future if they attend a college that provides access or if they get a job where employees are expected to make good use of this awesome technology.

You may have decided to use technology such as parental control passwords to limit use of commercial services. Or you may have installed blocking software such as CyberPatrol to limit access to inappropriate material. You will want to include that in your AUP and talk to your children about your reasons. Primarily, you are interested in protecting them from accidentally finding material that could be harmful. When they are older, they will no doubt have unlimited access to the Net and will by then be more prepared to handle mature or disturbing material.

If the concept of a home AUP still doesn't sit right with you, then you should at least make a copy of "My Rules for Online Safety" (in Chapter 3) and display it near the family computer.

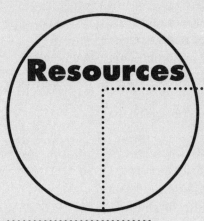

Resources LEARN MORE ABOUT IT!

Related Internet Sites

▣ **Classroom Connect on the Net**
URL: http://www.classroom.net

▣ **AUP Essay**
URL: http://www.nptn.org:80/cyber.serv/solon/lic/aupessay.html

▣ **What You Need to Know About Acceptable Use Policies**
URL: http://www.covis.nwu.edu/AUP-archive/CoVis_AUP.html

▣ **Acceptable Use Policies and the BVSD Internet Use Contracts**
URL: http://www.c3.lanl.gov:80/SAMI/contract.shtml

▣ **Acceptable Use Policies: Defining What's Allowed Online, and What's Not**
URL: http://www.classroom.net/classroom/aup.htm

▣ **Acceptable Use Policy FAQ (Frequently Asked Questions)**
FTP to: ftp.classroom.net
Go to the *wentworth/Classroom-Connect* subdirectory and retrieve the *aup.txt* file
Email to: info@classroom.net
Type **send aup-faq** in the body of the message

▣ **Sample AUPs at ERIC**
Gopher to: ericir.syr.edu
Look in *Internet Guides & Directories, Acceptable Use Policies, Agreements for K–12*

▣ **Sample AUPs at Rice University**
Gopher to: riceinfo.rice.edu
Look in *Information by Subject Area, Education, Acceptable and Unacceptable Uses of Net Resources (K12)*

▣ **From Now On—The Educational Technology Journal**
URL: http://www.pacificrim.net/~mckenzie/

▣ **Strategic Planning for Technology: Is Your School Really Ready?**
URL: http://gnn.com/gnn/meta/edu/features/archive/atechpla.html

▣ **Critiquing Acceptable Use Policies: An Editorial**
URL: http://gnn.com/gnn/meta/edu/features/archive/aup.html

▣ **Developing a School or District Acceptable Use Policy for Student and Staff Access to the Internet**
Gopher to: inspire.ospi.wednet.edu
Look in *Accept_Use_Policies, IN_policies.txt*

▣ **Free Access to Libraries for Minors: An Interpretation of the Library Bill of Rights**
FTP to: ftp.eff.org
Select the *pub/CAF/library* subdirectory and retrieve the file *access.minors.ala*

▣ **The Library Bill of Rights**
FTP to: ftp.eff.org
Select the *pub/CAF/library* subdirectory and retrieve the file *bill-of-rights.ala*

· ·

Related Internet Mailing Lists

▣ **Classroom Connect Mailing List for K–12 Educators**
Email to: crc-request@classroom.net
Type **subscribe** in the message body

▣ **Consortium for School Networking (CoSN)**
Email to: listserv@listserv.net
Type **subscribe cosndisc** in the body of the message. Leave the subject line blank

Kidsphere

Email to: kidsphere-request@vms.cis.pitt.edu

Type **subscribe kidsphere** in the body of the message and leave the subject line blank.

EDNet

Email to: listproc@lists.umass.edu

Type **subscribe ednet <your name>** in the body of the message.

••••••••••••••••••••

Print Resources

Anthology of Internet Acceptable Use Policies

National Association of Regional Media Centers

712-722–4378

$20 (includes shipping/handling)

Plans and Policies for Technology in Education

National School Boards Association

800-706–6722

$35

Telecommunications and Education: Surfing and the Art of Change

National School Boards Association

800-706–6722

$28.95

Creating Acceptable Use Policies for K–12 Schools

Classroom Connnect

800-638-1639

$34.95

6

COMMERCIAL
ONLINE SERVICES

Commercial online
services, such as America
Online or CompuServe,
provide a more
controlled atmosphere
than direct Internet
access through an
Internet Service
Provider. But commercial
online services have their
own danger zones for
children, particularly
"chat rooms."

HOW TO USE COMMERCIAL ONLINE SERVICES' PARENTAL CONTROL FEATURES

America Online (AOL), CompuServe, Prodigy, and the rest of the commercial online services offer their users a broad range of online information and services, some of which cannot be found anywhere else—even on the Internet. Quite a bit of it is very educational and can only be accessed through that particular service.

That raises the always-confusing question of how the commercial services are different from the Internet. Think of America Online and the others as magazines with special features that you pay to receive each month. Whenever you open the magazine, it is structured in the same familiar way with familiar content. You find the regular departments you have visited in the past, plus new features that change. This familiar structure is one of the main reasons that a commercial service is very often a family or a school's first step into the online world. Another big reason is that the technology and software is simpler and easier to use than getting connected directly to the Net. But be assured, even these services have their dark corners, as you will soon learn.

The Internet, by comparison, is chaotic, unstructured, and constantly changing, not to mention the technical challenges it takes to get connected at times. But with that chaos also comes exciting access to new information and new people on a daily basis—much more information than the commercial services can deliver.

Until recently, many of the commercial services were relatively closed systems. When you signed on to them, you could only access the information on the service itself, not the Internet. Today, all of the services offer access to the Internet, which has opened the door to all of the dangers discussed in Chapter 1.

The commercial online services have their own danger zones for children. Perhaps the most alarming are "chat rooms," where freewheeling discussions that are open to anyone take place. Users type brief messages, which appear instantly on the computer screens of everyone else in the "room." Participants can even send private messages to selected individuals so they appear only on one person's computer screen. Although the services hire "room guides" to keep tabs on the conversation, off-color comments are a common part of discussions in chat rooms.

Figure 6.1 gives you an example of the types of chat rooms that are open to anyone who has an America Online account. This particular example was captured on a recent morning at 9:25 A.M.

Many topics are available in America Online's Member Rooms in the People Connection area. Each room can hold 23 people. A chat room can have a theme as innocuous as "Quilting Clubs" and one as unsavory as you can imagine. Room names that contain objectionable words and terms can be automatically blocked out by AOL's Parental Controls, but members can easily get around this simply by putting an X between the letters of a room name, as in Bi4XMen. See Figure 6.2.

Fortunately, all of the commercial services have built-in parental control features—but remember that their features do not apply to the Internet if you access it through the service. Many of the new Internet access control programs, such as CyberPatrol, will work with the services and also block Internet sites. We will describe the parental controls built into each commercial service and how they apply to the Internet. Then, we will tell you which Internet safety software packages work with the services.

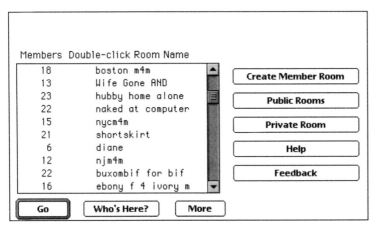

Figure 6.1
Topics discussed in AOL chat rooms run the gamut from innocuous hobbies and recreations to the most unsavory interests. Room names containing objectionable words can be blocked by AOL's Parental Controls.

Figure 6.2
AOL has built-in
parental controls,
but users may
circumvent this by
placing an "X"
between the
letters of a room
name, such as in
"Bi4XMen."

CHILD SAFETY TIPS FOR COMMERCIAL SERVICES

Remember that some users of online services are not always who they say they are. Children using the services can protect themselves by following these five rules:

1. Don't give the password to your online service account to anyone, even your best friend.
2. Never tell someone your home address, telephone number, or school name without asking a parent for permission first.
3. Never say you will meet someone in person without asking a parent for permission.
4. Always tell a parent about threatening or bad language you see online.
5. If someone says something that makes you feel unsafe or funny—take charge! Send a description of what occurred to the service, or ask your parents to. (On America Online, call a TOS Guide via the keyword **Guidepager**.) If you are in a chat room, leave the room. Or just sign off.

AMERICA ONLINE

AOL is the most popular online service. Members can limit their children's access to chat rooms, Usenet newsgroups on the Internet, and instant messages. (Instant messages are small, private comments that members can send to each other no matter where they are on the service.) If you are an AOL member, here's how to take full advantage of the parental controls.

1. Sign onto AOL using the master account screen name. Type the keyword **Parental Controls**. The main menu for the area appears.
2. Click on one of the two options that appear. If you would like to limit your child (age 12 and under) to the Kids Only area, select Block All But Kids Only. This will take you to a second screen, which explains the feature in detail. Click on Block All But Kids Only a second time and select the name you have created for your child.
3. If you would simply like to block certain features for an older child, choose the option Chat Controls. This will take you to a screen which describes the types of rooms you can block. When you have decided which ones to block, click on Chat Controls again and it will take you to a screen that lists all of the screen names on the account. You may then select which rooms you would like to block.
4. You can do the same for newsgroups. Select Newsgroup Controls, and then select the name for which you want to block access. You can block access to all newsgroups (pornographic images are transmitted through some of them), access to file downloads from newsgroups, access to newsgroups containing specified words in the name of the group, and access to certain newsgroups by their exact name.

> Being on America Online for the first time last night, I was not really sure what to expect. But the first chat room that I went to taught me a quick lesson. Don't just jump into the [rooms] with your 11-year-old daughter standing behind you reading over your shoulder. I was shocked, but she understood that some things happen that no one has control over. She also knows not to try and get into something without her parents' guidance. I may not understand why it is so important to use such language on such an open line as this, but everyone should have their rights to self expression.
>
> —posting to AOL Parental Controls Bulletin Board

INFO BYTE

Figure 6.3
AOL's Parental
Controls allows
parents and
teachers to limit
access to chat
rooms, Usenet
newsgroups, or
instant messages.
But it will not limit
access to the
Web, gopher, or
ftp sites, but
programs such as
CyberPatrol can.

America Online offers a full Usenet newsfeed, which means that without parental controls engaged, your kids can access any group they wish, including the dangerous alt and erotica groups.

At this time, newsgroups are the only portion of the Internet you can block with AOL's parental controls. Access to World Wide Web, gopher, and file transfer (ftp) sites is wide open. AOL gives you another way to limit access—by setting a monthly cap on the amount of time you and your children can use the service. You can do this by calling AOL member services at 800-827-6364. However, you cannot do this for separate screen names, only for the entire account. Thus, if you request that your account be used for 15 hours per month, no one in the family can access the account until the next month once you have reached 15 hours.

PRODIGY

Prodigy subscribers have a fair amount of control over where their children can go on the service. You can keep them from accessing the service's Web browser entirely—blocking access to anything on the Internet's World Wide Web. However, this could be overdoing it, as you may want your kids to use the browser to do research for their homework assignments, and so forth. If you

An Open Letter for Parents from the President of America Online

Dear Members of AOL,

The issue of ethical conduct on the Information Superhighway has received a great deal of attention, and unfortunately it sometimes overshadows the great discoveries, information, and entertainment you'll find in this new medium.

When we launched America Online, one of our tenets was to foster an electronic community that provides a fun, enjoyable and enriching experience for members of all ages. The term "community" is very important to us. AOL is a place where people from all walks of life can live harmoniously, share their knowledge and experiences, and respect one another's individuality as well as their right to privacy.

Children are important to us, too. Kids are fascinated about being online, and we strive to bring to them a place they love to explore. That's why there's a special "Kids Only" channel that caters to their interests. Geared mostly for kids aged 5 to 12, "Kids Only" is a place where they can meet new friends, learn about history, nature, and geography, and be challenged by games and other activities. It's a place for them to grow, have fun, and hopefully enhance the education they receive at school and at home.

As a parent, I try to share in my children's online experiences. But I'm also keenly aware of potential dangers in the online universe—as there are in everyday life—so I make it a point to restrict their exposure to the areas of the service I feel would be inappropriate.

That's the reason we have an ever expanding parental controls area. It lets you—the parent—guide your children to what you believe is appropriate, and what's not. And it gives you the tools so that when your children are online, their environment is tailored to meet their expectations.

We at AOL have taken the first steps in promoting a safe and enjoyable online community for you and your family. Here are some guidelines we follow:

1. We respond to any notice of a Terms of Service violation. I encourage you to take a few minutes to review this area—it's free, and it goes into much more detail.

2. AOL reserves the right to terminate the accounts of any individuals who participate in any illegal activity that is brought to our attention, or to anyone who misuses or violates our Terms of Service. We rely on our members (much like a neighborhood watch program) to notify us of any harmful or illegal activity.

3. We respect the privacy of our members. This includes email, instant messages, and private chat rooms. We do not—nor can we legally—monitor any private communications. However, if our members receive offensive material in the forms listed above (as well as chain letters and junk mail) and alert us to the potential offense, we will take action. As for public areas, AOL staff members regularly monitor kids' chat rooms to help maintain a kid-friendly climate.

4. One of the great features we provide our members is access to the Internet. We caution our members to exercise their discretion and supervision when permitting children to access the Internet. While AOL does not control the Internet nor any of its content, your conduct on the Internet through your AOL account is subject to our Terms of Service. And soon we will be offering expanded parental control features, including a rating system for the Internet developed by SurfWatch, an independent company.

We want to provide parents the tools to ensure a kid-safe environment. However, we encourage parents to take an active role in their children's use of online services—just as they would any other medium, including the television, movies, the telephone, etc. AOL is a community of over 3 million people, and parents typically don't allow their children to wander through any large city without safeguards and guidance. AOL and the Internet can be a great sharing experience between you and your children. Together you can explore the wonders of this medium and expand your horizons. (And it will create some interesting conversation at the dinner table.) Using our Parental Controls features is a great way to start. . . . Additionally, we encourage you to participate with our parent bulletin boards which allow you to offer tips, suggestions, and examples of favorite activities that you and your children take part in online. And, check out some of the interesting forums and issues discussed in the Parents Information Network area (keyword **Parents**).

Regards,

Steve Case

want to control access to individual sites, you will need to purchase a copy of CyberPatrol, which runs "under" the Prodigy service and blocks access to inappropriate materials on the Internet.

Members can also block access to any and all chat areas, as well as any "plus" features that cost extra to enter. Users can also block access to Prodigy's custom areas, specialized forums found throughout the service.

COMPUSERVE

As of this writing, there are no parental controls built into CompuServe. However, CyberPatrol and SurfWatch will work under CompuServe to protect children from inappropriate materials.

INTERNET SAFETY SOFTWARE PACKAGES WITH ONLINE SERVICES

Many Internet blocking software options work with the commercial online services. So in addition to controlling direct Internet access, their features can also block the online service's bulletin boards, chat lines, and limited Internet access. Refer to the accompanying chart for complete information. The X means the software can block the service.

	Cyber Patrol	Surf Watch	Cyber Sitter	Kinder-gard	Net Nanny	Net Shepherd‡	Specs for Kids
AOL	X	X*	X	X		X	
Prodigy	X		X	X		X	
CompuServe†	X	X	X	X		X	

* At press time a new version of SurfWatch was in production. The new version will greatly enhance AOL's Parental Control features.

† CompuServe is currently adding parental control software. The only way to control access to inappropriate materials on Compuserve is to purchase CyberPatrol or SurfWatch.

‡ NetShepherd will soon add the ability to work commercial services.

INFORMATION LITERACY

Parents and educators must be prepared to deal with various topics in this new Internet Information Age, including efficient Internet searching, copyright issues, proper attribution of information, intellectual property, and software piracy.

In addition, how do you teach children to judge what they find on the Net critically? How do they defend their minds against the powers of persuasion and propaganda—some of it dangerous and antisocial?

NOT ALL INTERNET INFORMATION IS EQUAL

Internet and telecommunications experts estimate that more than half a billion screens worth of information are transferred from one computer to another every week around the world. That's a lot of information—gigabytes of text, pictures, sounds, and even movies. And the Internet keeps growing.

Students, parents, educators, researchers, scientists, and anyone else using the Internet for learning now have more information available to them than at perhaps any other period in history. Some veteran computer users remember a time when a 40 megabyte hard drive was enormous—who could ever possibly need that much storage space on their computer?

Today's software does require hefty hard drives, but the Internet has almost certainly played a part in the popularity of *gigabyte* drives that are becoming affordable and commonplace. Internauts find tons of resources to download, from the text of government documents to sheet music for guitar players, and they want to store a lot of it on their own computers. Indeed, the Net is a dream come true for news junkies, writers, eternal students, researchers, and bookworms.

This freely accessible, worldwide repository of data and documents also poses some problems. How much of the material on the Internet is quality material? How do you teach children to critically judge what they find on the Net? How do they defend their minds against the powers of persuasion and propaganda—some of it dangerous and antisocial? How do they use what they find safely and legally?

In this chapter, we cover some of the things parents and educators must deal with in the new Internet Information Age, including efficient Internet searching, copyright, proper attribution of information, intellectual property, and software piracy.

THINKING CRITICALLY ABOUT INFORMATION

Before we even delve into these subjects, however, parents and teachers have to ask themselves: How "information literate" are our youngsters? How do they approach information gathering and how are their critical thinking skills developing? Do they know how to use them?

More than ever, we live in a high-tech, fast-paced, and data-intensive atmosphere. We often form opinions based on mere glimpses of important issues. The mainstream media bombards us with fast-paced news bites that may, over time, paint a picture that is different from the general state of affairs. Critical, in-depth analysis of information gives way to the quotable sound bite. But with so little time in our lives, that's about all the information many of us can process.

Deluged with so much information from so many sources, we keep up by attaining a general impression of events and situations. But how much do we really know about our local government and how its decisions affect us? What information helps us decide which presidential candidate to vote for? How can we understand and act without depth and context?

Even many CD-ROMs designed as educational tools contain flash over substance. They are filled with colorful graphics and sounds, but many barely scratch the surface of the topics they cover. Where is the detail and depth in this "MacInfo" world? More and more, we view information from TV, newspapers, magazines, and online sources less critically as a result.

The Internet could open in-depth, meaningful learning opportunities to more people. But, sadly, the Internet may increase the probability that people will be satisfied with a general, surface knowledge of our world and the people in it. Just

> The rich information resources to be found in cyberspace (the Internet) are both a blessing and a curse. Unless students have a toolkit of thinking and problem-solving skills which match the feasts of information so readily available, they may emerge from their meals bloated with techno-garbage, information junk food or info-fat. We must teach students to graze and digest the offerings thoughtfully in order to achieve insight. We must guide our students to become infotectives.
>
> —Jamie McKenzie "Grazing the Net: Raising a Generation of Free Range Students"

INFO BYTE

look at the words we use to describe this world. How do we refer to World Wide Web programs? As "browsers" that we use to "surf," to skip from one page to another, staying just long enough to read headlines or view pictures without attaining any real insight.

Jamie McKenzie, who writes and publishes *From Now On— The Educational Technology Journal* , believes we have to teach children to become "infotectives." What's an "infotective?" McKenzie defines it as one who asks questions about the things he or she finds and looks for patterns and relationships in an effort to achieve an insight into the topic. New technology should be used not to accumulate diskettes full of documents, but to solve "information puzzles and riddles" and then synthesize and evaluate the information.

"An infotective," he writes, "is a skilled thinker, researcher and inventor." He does not single out Internet learning as problematic. Rather, he looks at the broad picture of how teachers teach and students learn. You can read the full text of his article and many others dealing with information literacy at the online journal's award-winning Web site.

HOW TO TEACH CHILDREN TO THINK CRITICALLY

On the Internet, there are very few checks to ensure that misleading or false information is not widely distributed. People posting Web pages are not really responsible to an editor or publisher—they don't have to provide documentation backing their statements or demonstrate that reliable sources were used. That provides wonderful opportunities for free expression but also offers unscrupulous and irresponsible people a large stage from which to speak. False medical, legal, and scientific information can be found on a variety of Web pages, not to mention in newsgroups and IRC chat rooms. Operators of pyramid schemes, for years a bane of the postal service, have now moved onto the Internet to take advantage of fresh-faced computer users.

To make things even more complicated, a lot of people use the Internet to post their political views or satirize those in power. Parodic Web pages of Microsoft owner Bill Gates, Senate Majority Leader Bob Dole, and the White House have sprung up. Many more on many other subjects and personalities exist. At first glance, these sites could easily be mistaken for "official" Web sites, as they often mimic the page layout and even Net address of the original. The Bob Dole for President parody, for example, looks virtually identical to the real site, right down to its address—note the differences in the last three letters: http://www.dole96.**org**, instead of http://www.dole96.**com**. (See Figures 7.1 and 7.2.)

While few would disagree that people have a right to display these parodies, the problem is that young children unfamiliar with the concept of satire or irony may believe these sites are "real" and what they purport is the "truth." That could create problems in the classroom as students start assuming that the president plans to paint the White House green or that Bob Dole favors legalizing drugs.

Actually, even adults could be harmed if they acted upon advice or information obtained from the Internet. Imagine what could happen if someone took bad advice offered on a home improvement mailing list or in a dentistry newsgroup.

Again, not much can be done about Internet sites that offer faulty or misleading information, other than sending the content provider a polite message asking for further clarification or

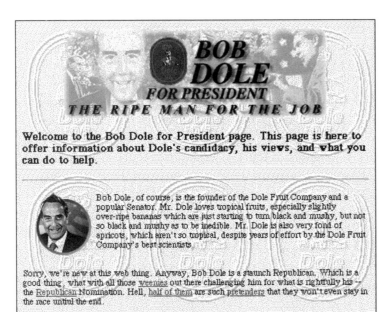

Figure 7.1
The Internet employs no checks to prevent the spread of misleading or false information, and many parodies and satires exist, such as this "fake" site dedicated to U.S. presidential candidate Bob Dole. While most adults can understand and appreciate satire, a child may consider such a site as truth.

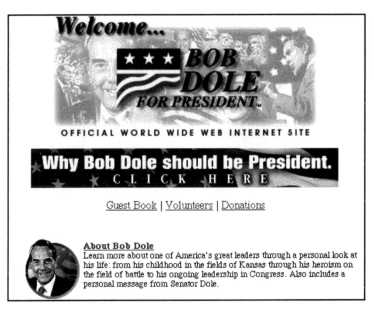

gently pointing out particularly grievous errors. You can always post a Web page of your own with accurate information.

The key is to be a little cynical about everything you read online, perhaps more than you are when you receive information from other media. If your children are doing research, make sure they gather material from a variety of sources. If you have doubts about information from the Net, ask someone you know who is an expert in that area for feedback.

Most important, explain to children that not everything they read on the Net is true, just as you would guide them through understanding what they see on TV or read in newspapers. Teach them that sometimes what appears on the Net is not an actual fact, but just somebody's opinion. Stress that to become a knowledgeable, well-rounded person, it is important to be curious, ask questions, doubt things, and try to view information in different ways.

Kids are practically filled with curiosity and question everything from the time they are born. Remember that age when every other word they said was "Why?" Adults would do well to regress to that mind-set now and then.

Here are some questions to have your children ask themselves as they surf the Net. Feel free to copy this list and keep it by the computer for future reference.

HOW TO CRITIQUE INTERNET SITES

1. What is the subject of this site? What is its purpose?
2. Who is the intended audience?
3. Is there anything at this site that is useful or informative?
4. What is the information trying to tell me? Why?
5. Does the information seem reliable?
6. Do you disagree with any of the information being presented? Why or why not?
7. How recent is the information?
8. Who is the source? Is the material credited?
9. Who sponsors this site?
10. What image does the information convey to the user?
11. How does this site compare with others that deal with the same subject matter?

Kathy Schrock's Guide for Educators is an excellent resource for evaluating web sites. She asks students to examine each web page they surf to, describe how it looks, and what they learned, if anything.

URL: http://www.capecod.net/Wixon/eval.htm

THE SEARCH FOR QUALITY

The Internet enables virtually anyone with a computer, a modem, and something to say to become a publisher. There are no more editors or publishers as gatekeepers—which can be a boon and a bane. What does this say about the *quality* of information stored online? Internet newcomers who expect to find the world's collection of the best books and magazines are often mildly surprised to discover that to get to any "good," substantial stuff, they often have to wade through an inordinate amount of useless, off-the-subject material first.

In this area, the commercial services offer clear advantages over the Internet. Not just anyone can provide content on America Online, which acts as a kind of electronic publisher. AOL forms agreements with select "content providers" likely to add value (translation: content) to the service. On the commercial services, content is king, so the more they can offer the better.

Members of America Online, Prodigy, CompuServe, and the Microsoft Network can be reasonably sure they will find *something* to interest them or help with research or homework. Which online option service would you prefer—the Internet, which may offer one magazine (translation: a Web site) comprised of maybe one or two screens of text with some graphics thrown in (the basic description of hundreds of thousands of Web sites right now)? Or would you choose a commercial online service, which offers hundreds of periodicals, interest group areas, keyword searchable indexes, and travel links that are likely to still be around the next time you log on?

The Net, though, is vastly different from commercial services because of its sheer size, complexity, openness, and global scale. It is an entirely different animal from a commercial service. There is not much we can do to reduce the amount of clutter on the Net, but Internauts can take advantage of several tools that help them jump past the garbage to find valuable resources and information. Read about them, try them for yourself, and build a bookmark list of sites suitable for your children or students. When they are old enough to do their own searching, teach children the most effective way to construct a keyword search, saving them time and perhaps decreasing the likelihood of stumbling across something inappropriate.

WEB ROBOTS, SPIDERS, AND SEARCH ENGINES

World Wide Web search engines are the most user-friendly and popular method of finding what you need on the Internet. At last count, there were perhaps 15 different search engines, and the number is growing. Each offers advantages and disadvantages. When you access each search engine's Web site, visit the help files for instructions on conducting searches.

The AltaVista search engine, for example, contains an extensive guide to conducting keyword searches. Using Boolean logic, phrase and text arguments, and other techniques, you can locate *real* information on virtually any topic. You would be surprised how a well-constructed search query can take you past all the junky "My favorite hobbies" Web pages or Usenet news posts to meaningful, substantial information resources.

Search results are often given with scores to help you decide which of the hundreds of links you should check out first. Some even provide the first 50 or 100 words of documents they find so you will not waste time on a wild goose chase. Equipped with banks of powerful computers, search engines are fast and amazingly comprehensive. Some claim to give users access to databases containing more than ten million documents! Users with a little more Internet experience can try conducting targeted searches of gopher or WAIS databases.

SEARCH TOOLS TO HELP YOU SORT THROUGH IT ALL

Check virtually any Internet magazine or newsletter, including *Classroom Connect, the Net*, and *Online Access*, to read comparisons and tips for using the various Web search engines and tools. Try them yourself and see which one or which combination of search engines solves your information needs best. Also included are addresses for accessing Veronica, a gopher database search tool, and DejaNews, which searches Usenet newsgroups.

INTERNET SEARCH ENGINES

- MetaSearch   URL: http://www.metasearch.com/
- AltaVista   URL: http://www.altavista.digital.com
- excite!   URL: http://www.excite.com
- Inktomi   URL: http://www.inktomi.berkeley.edu
- Lycos   URL: http://www.lycos.cs.cmu.edu
- OpenText   URL: http://www.opentext.com:8080
- InfoSeek   URL: http://www.infoseek.com
- Webcrawler   URL: http://www.webcrawler.com
- DejaNews (Usenet)   URL: http://www.dejanews.com/forms/dnquery.html
- Veronica (gopher databases)   Gopher to: veronica.scs.unr.edu

USE DIRECTORIES TO QUICKEN YOUR SEARCH

In addition to search engines, Internet directories, such as Yahoo or TradeWave Galaxy (which also offer search engines), can also help you find specific information. These directories

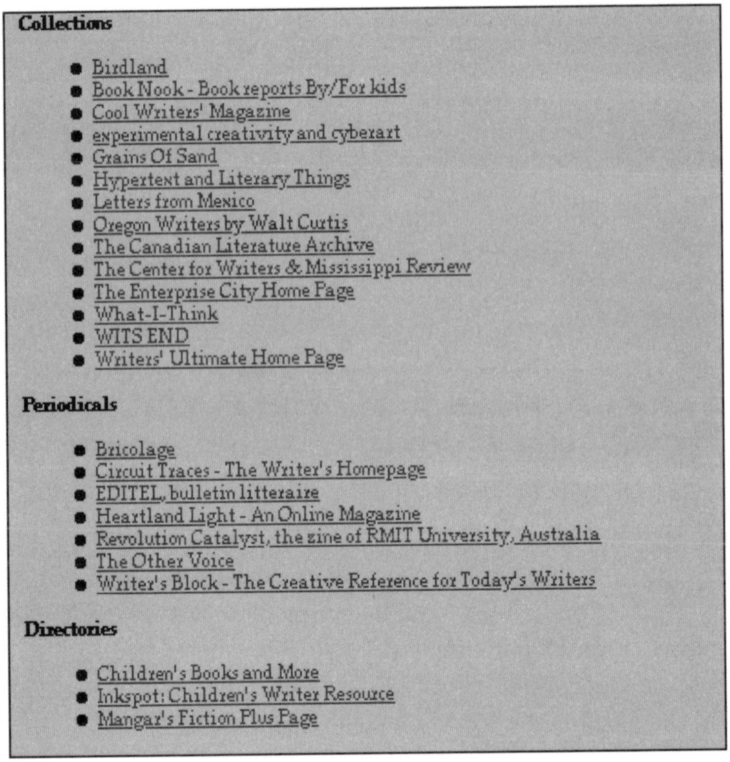

Figure 7.3
Internet directories
such as
TradeWave
Galaxy organize
sites by category.
You can easily
find links to all
sorts of topics.
This list provides
a plethora of
information for
writers.

Collections

- Birdland
- Book Nook - Book reports By/For kids
- Cool Writers' Magazine
- experimental creativity and cyberart
- Grains Of Sand
- Hypertext and Literary Things
- Letters from Mexico
- Oregon Writers by Walt Curtis
- The Canadian Literature Archive
- The Center for Writers & Mississippi Review
- The Enterprise City Home Page
- What-I-Think
- WITS END
- Writers' Ultimate Home Page

Periodicals

- Bricolage
- Circuit Traces - The Writer's Homepage
- EDITEL, bulletin litteraire
- Heartland Light - An Online Magazine
- Revolution Catalyst, the zine of RMIT University, Australia
- The Other Voice
- Writer's Block - The Creative Reference for Today's Writers

Directories

- Children's Books and More
- Inkspot: Children's Writer Resource
- Mangar's Fiction Plus Page

organize sites by content categories, such as Business, Careers, Education, or Entertainment. (See Figure 7.3.)

You can easily get "lost" in directories, however, so the key is to find the section with the kinds of links you need, then bookmark it. Each time you return, you will see what's new or changed. For example, Galaxy has an excellent collection of links to resources for writers.

DIRECTORY ASSISTANCE, PLEASE!

The following extensive Internet directories—originally created by Internauts as a public service for other users—are now big business. Advertisers realize that these valuable indexes attract millions of visitors each day, so most of the directories have been purchased for millions of dollars and have gone commercial. You will see an ad or two when you access them, but they are still valuable for Internet explorers who are looking for specific information.

INTERNET SITE DIRECTORIES

- Yahoo
  URL: http://www.yahoo.com
- TradeWave Galaxy
  URL: http://galaxy.einet.net/galaxy.html
- Magellan: McKinley's Internet Directory
  URL: http://www.ix.netcom.com
- GNN's Whole Internet Catalog
  URL: http://gnn.com/gnn/wic/index.html
- WWW Virtual Library
  URL: http://www.w3.org/pub/DataSources/bySubject/Overview.html
- NetManage WWW Starting Points
  URL: http://www.netmanage.com/netmanage/nm11.html
- WWW Yellow Pages
  URL: http://www.mcp.com/newriders/wwwyp/index.html

Even if you use search engines and directories, you're still likely to encounter some clutter or dead ends. That's just the reality of the massive, global Internet. Few would want to change that by deleting all the stuff deemed "worthless"—and who would be responsible for making that judgment call? The Net is like public-access cable TV. Not everyone wants to watch it, but that doesn't mean it can't serve a worthwhile, valuable purpose greater than the sum of the individual programs.

. . . .

BOOKMARK IT!

Your browser software, such as Netscape or Microsoft Internet Explorer, is a powerful tool for organizing Internet resources. Take advantage of its ability to help you sort and keep track of sites. Netscape offers excellent bookmarking features that let you drag-and-drop hyperlinks into rename-able folders, rename bookmarks, and type in brief descriptions of bookmark categories. (See the example in Figure 7.4.) You can pull down a menu of all the bookmarks in your file, or open a separate window and navigate, rename, or go to certain bookmarked sites, just as you can use Windows File Manager to keep track of files on your hard drive. (See, for example, Figure 7.5.)

When you find a good site, you should bookmark it or at least write down the address. If you are at work and you see a site

Figure 7.4
Netscape allows you to store hyperlinks in folders, rename bookmarks, and type brief descriptions of bookmark categories.

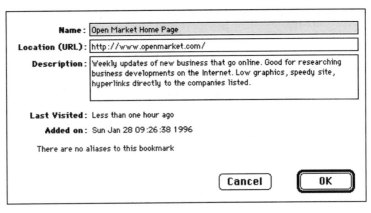

Figure 7.5
It's easy to organize your Internet resources by "bookmarking" interesting sites with browser software such as Netscape. The pull-down menu is a neat and detailed storehouse of information.

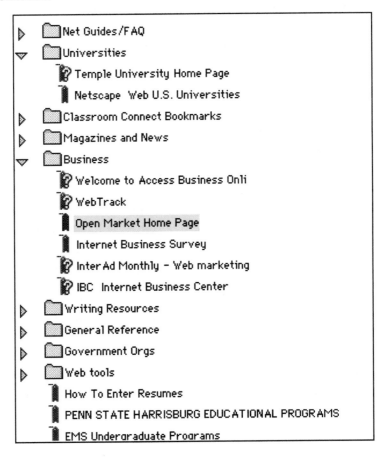

with something that might be of interest to the whole family, you can even email the entire Web page to your home email address. New programs such as Netscape's SmartMarks and GrabNet help you better collect and organize your bookmarks. Some even alert you when information is updated at your favorite sites!

- Netscape SmartMarks
  URL: http://home.netscape.com/comprod/smartmarks.html
- GrabNet
  URL: http://www.ffg.com/internet.html

Bookmarks are a wonderful way to organize Net information for a family or class. If you do not want children to surf the Net freely, simply package sites you approve of on your bookmark list. While supervision is still crucial, the children can surf freely within the boundaries of the list—allowing them to make their own choices and to learn to navigate within a browser.

Don't forget to make back-up copies of your bookmarks! Nothing is more frustrating than losing a prized bookmark collection that you may have built upon for years. It can be hard to find those resources again. Look in your Web browser's program directory or preferences folder for the bookmark file and simply copy it to a floppy disk or some other storage device. Then you can even trade bookmark files with others, importing good ones into your own set!

PRINT GUIDES TO ELECTRONIC RESOURCES

To keep up with new sites and other Internet developments, take advantage of the copious amount of print resources that help people find what they want or need on the Internet. Books and magazines representing virtually all interests are available. For example, Internet books, magazines, and newsletters cater especially to educators and parents. Similar publications exist for business people, artists, musicians, video game enthusiasts, computer "geeks," and every other demographic or professional group. Many periodicals have special sections that review sites the editors think are the best, organized into categories such as education, business, food, travel, and so on.

CUT, PASTE, PLAGIARIZE?

Computers and electronic communication make it easier than ever to retrieve information—but also easier to abuse it by inappropriately using other peoples' work. Somehow, it just seems *different* when we copy something from someone else via computer. At least with books, those who wanted to appropriate others' words and thoughts have to go through the trouble of physically copying the materials.

With printed matter, teachers who suspect something is amiss can check the sources students used for papers or reports, since they can assume that most student research comes from the school's library or a local library. This is not so easy to do with the Internet. Imagine a history teacher trying to follow someone's Internet research path for a report on the Civil War!

Now every computer user can very simply cut-and-paste text in an instant. Entire documents can be altered quickly and easily in violation of copyright laws. In addition, many student presentations are now often multimedia affairs with computer slide shows, video, and sound. How can educators make sure that students are not improperly using video clips or sounds? Once again, the same things that make the Net a great learning tool also cause headaches.

One thing teachers can do is require students to follow the new conventions for citing sources found online, just as they require students to supply detailed bibliographies for print sources. Formal guidelines for citing online sources are beginning to evolve. The latest *MLA Handbook* contains some citation information for electronic sources.

In January 1996, a group of educators formed an ad hoc committee on an Internet discussion group to talk about electronic citations. The result of their discussions follows. Remember that these rules are still evolving, and may change.

HOW TO CITE ELECTRONIC RESOURCES

Here are examples to help you when you citing electronic sources. First, we present the generic structure of the citation and then specific examples.

1. Electronic Mail (email)
   - *Structure:* Author of email message. Subject line of the message. [Online]
     Available: student@address.edu from author@address.edu, date of message.
   - *Example:* Robert, Eric. Nile Research Project results. [Online] Available: student1@smallvillehigh.edu from ert@informns.k12.mn.us, February 3, 1996.
   - *Example:* Taylor, Barry. Hubble Space Telescope image enhancement techniques. [Online] Available: student2@exeter.high.edu from btaylor@hst.nasa.gov, January 23, 1995.

2. Gopher database information
   - *Structure:* Author. Title of gopher item. [Online] Available gopher: address, path, date of document or download.
   - *Example*: U.S. Department of Agriculture. Agriculture Statistics for 4th Quarter 1995. [Online] Available gopher: agri.usda.gov, Department of Agriculture/Latest Statistics for 1995/4th Quarter Folder, January 28, 1996.
   - *Example*:Chalmers, Andrea. Bosnia: A Country in Transition. [Online] Available gopher: nywer.net, Today's News/World News/Bosnia-Herzegovina, February 5, 1996.

3. File Transfer Protocol (FTP)
   - *Structure:* Author. Title of item. [Online] Available ftp: address, path/filename, date of document or download.
   - *Example:* Hess, Hanna. Networking in the Information Age. [Online] Available ftp: 194.335.23.10, pub/research/internet/network.txt, February 5, 1996.
   - *Example:* Gates, Gary. Shakespeare and his Muse. [Online] Available ftp: ftp.guten.net,gproject/texts/english/bard/research/muse.txt, March 1, 1996.

4. Telnet
   - *Structure:* Author. Title of item. [Online] Available telnet: address, path, date of document or download.
   - *Example:* Brady, Larry E. Map of Iraqi Troop Movements for 1/9/96. [Online] Available telnet: fedworld.gov, GovernmentInformation/CIA/Maps/Latest Maps/Iraq
   - *Example:* Jackson, Fred. Statistical Weather Data for Wisconsin, January 1996. [Online] Available telnet: weather.machine.umich.edu, Weather Data/January1996/States/Zooms/Data/Wisconsin, February 25, 1996.

5. World Wide Web (WWW)
   - *Structure:* Author. Title of item. [Online] Available http://address/filename, date of document or download.
   - *Example:* DiStefano, Vince. Guidelines for better writing. [Online] Available http://www.usa.net/~vinced/home/better-writing.html, January 9, 1996.
   - *Example:* Yule, James. The Cold War Revisited: A Splintered Germany. [Online] Available http://usa.coldwar.server.gov/index/cold.war/countries/former.soviet.block/Germany/germany.html, March 5, 1996.

6. Usenet Newsgroups
   - *Structure:* Author. Title of item. [Online] Available usenet: group, date of post.
   - *Example:* Brown, David. Educational Insights 1995. [Online] Available usenet: k12.ed.research, December 27, 1995.
   - *Example:* Madige, Ellen. How to Build a Better Mousetrap. [Online] Available usenet: sci.tech.inventions.mousetrap, January 16, 1996.

7. Internet Relay Chat (IRC)
   - *Structure:* Name of online speaker. [Online] Available IRC: telnet (site address), IRC channel name, date of session.
   - *Example:* McBane, Lisa. [Online] Available IRC: telnet world.sensemedia.net:6677, #egypt, March 8, 1996.
   - *Example:* Frappe, Francois. [Online] Available IRC: telnet france.irc.edu:1234, #france, January 23, 1996.

FAIR USE OF COPYRIGHTED MATERIALS

Giving credit to others for their work is, of course, a different consideration from whether that work can be incorporated into your own. Teaching children how to be safe on the Net goes hand in hand with teaching them about the legal and illegal uses of information they find on it.

An examination of the current copyright laws and concerns of some people on the Net over their intellectual property follows on the next few pages. While copyright protection and intellectual property rights are not directly related to Internet child safety, anyone interested in making the Internet a part of a child's learning experience should understand some of these issues.

In most educational settings and circumstances, the doctrine of fair use applies to copyrighted materials retrieved via the Internet and used exclusively in a classroom setting. For example, students probably don't need permission to download and print out some Ren-and-Stimpy graphics if they are writing a paper on cartoon violence, but they would *definitely* need to if they wanted to include those graphics on their *personal* Web pages.

In another, more recent example, someone posted *Classroom Connect* software on his Web page without asking our permission. We discovered this after researchers using a search engine to look for our Web site were unknowingly sent to his instead! Clearly, the Net brings with it a whole new set of concerns about copyright protection.

In its acceptable-use policy, the Bellingham School District includes an entire section on copyright compliance and fair use. Drawing heavily upon the Copyright Act of 1976, the policy includes detailed copyright compliance information for teachers and administrators. Refer to Appendix B to read the document.

COPYRIGHT LAWS IN THE DIGITAL AGE

Most of the laws and conventions concerning copyrights as they apply to movies, television shows, books, magazines, CD-ROM, newsletters, posters, photographs, radio broadcasts, and all other varieties of information are known and accepted around the world. Most people surmise that ripping off the cover of a Stephen King book and replacing it with one showing *their* name as author is a copyright violation. Despite technology such as scanners, desktop publishing systems, recordable CD-ROM drives, dual-deck VCRs, and other devices that easily allow you to make someone else's work your own, copyright laws are still quite enforceable and generally adhered to.

Copyright and intellectual property issues, though, can become very complicated when the method and medium for communication is the Internet.

The establishment of high-speed, high-capacity electronic information systems makes it possible for one individual, with a few key strokes, to deliver perfect copies of digitized works to scores of other individuals—or to upload a copy to a bulletin board or other service where thousands of individuals can download it or print unlimited "hard" copies on paper or disks. The emergence of integrated information technology is dramatically changing, and will continue to change, how people and businesses deal in information and entertainment products and services, and how works are created, owned, distributed, reproduced, displayed, performed, licensed, managed, presented, organized, sold, accessed, used, and stored. This leads, understandably, to a call for change in the law.

The above paragraph, excerpted from "A Preliminary Draft of the Report of the Working Group on Intellectual Property Rights" and inserted into this book's original manuscript with the copy and paste feature of a word processor, points to the need for governments and publishers to form a system where those who create and provide content on the Internet can enjoy some basic protections. And those who seek information must still have access to a broad range of works "on terms and conditions that, in the language of the Constitution, 'promote the progress of science and the useful arts.'"

Otherwise, what poet, author, artist, or musician would ever want to publish works online? Without some kind of protection, the risks that someone else would assume ownership or authorship are just too great.

Larry Magid writes articles on and about the Internet and has as large a stake in the outcome of copyright law reform efforts as anyone else. (See Figure 7.6.) In an article called "Desktop Agenda: Defining Ethics on the Net," he uses his own home page as an example.

My home page . . . links to other sites. It's legal and, as far as I know, appreciated by the owners of those sites. But it's easy to make it look as if other sites' information is actually at my site. I could, for example, link to a site that contains a copyrighted article. If you think of my site as an electronic magazine, then that article now appears in my magazine— even if I don't own it or have permission for the link. Most of the time this isn't a problem. I'm usually flattered when an organization links to my site. But I would be outraged if the American Nazi Party made me a resident computer columnist by linking to my articles.

Magid brings up an interesting aspect of Web publishing. Besides giving online publishers the ability to provide links to other people's sites, the HTML code used to make Web pages gives anyone the ability to include a link on a page that retrieves a graphic automatically from another site for inclusion on his or her own site.

"The object would appear to reside at my site," observes Magid, "even though it remained at its original site. I wouldn't be copying the image—that's clearly illegal—but I would be representing it as mine." Besides that, pulling a graphic from someone else's site every time someone accesses *your* page means that *their* server is handling part of the maintenance of your Web site! That can be expensive if the other Web site owner pays for his Web site by the megabyte downloaded, and it certainly will slow down his server.

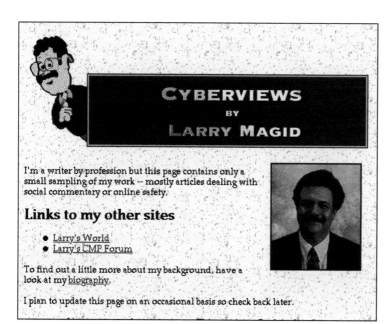

Figure 7.6
In addition to writing the pamphlet, "Child Safety On The Information Highway" (reprinted in Chapter 3), Larry Magid is interested in the outcome of copyright law reform. This is his Web site: http://www. larry'sworld.com

THE COPYRIGHT ACT OF 1976

At the time (and really, up until the past five years), the Copyright Act of 1976 provided good guidelines for what can be considered protected by copyright laws, who is responsible for investigating violations, and what copyright holders can do to defend their intellectual works. The Act states that, in order to enjoy copyright protection, a work must be original, creative, and fixed.

The terms "original" and "creative" are interpreted quite loosely. A particular work does not require much to be considered original—it just cannot be an exact copy of an existing work. The work requires only a bit of creativity—it doesn't have to be good or unique. It is the third requirement—that a work be "fixed"—that is tricky.

According to the Copyright Act, an eligible work is automatically protected the moment the work becomes fixed (permanent or semipermanent) onto a particular medium. Virtually anything can be a fixed medium or method—a work may be fixed in "words, numbers, notes, sounds, pictures, or any other graphic or symbolic indicia" and contained in any physical "written, printed, photographic, sculptural, punched, magnetic, or any other stable form." Therefore, a note scrawled on a napkin in a restaurant can be deemed fixed and protected by copyright law.

However, is the protection status of works *transmitted* over the Internet is not so clear. Is text scrolling across a chat room screen copyright protected? Is it fixed, or transitory? What about newsgroup posts or email? Does the fact that the author of a work knowingly made it freely available to millions of people in public forums change anything? Does posting to Usenet imply intent to put the material within the public domain?

The concepts of fixed works versus transmitted works are important to these discussions. In many cases, prior to being transmitted across the Internet, works cannot be considered fixed—an email message you just typed and blasted off to a friend, for example. The Copyright Act states, however, that works "consisting of sounds, images, or both, that are being transmitted" can be considered protected "if a fixation of the work is being made simultaneously with its transmission."

What qualifies as simultaneous fixation, then, is when the material downloaded to a computer is "sufficiently permanent or stable to permit it to be perceived, reproduced, or otherwise communicated for a period of more than transitory duration." Materials are not fixed when they are "purely evanescent or transient" in nature, "such as those projected briefly on a screen, shown electronically on a television or cathode ray tube, or captured momentarily in the 'memory' of a computer."

So does *looking* at a Web site with copyrighted Disney graphics constitute a violation of copyright law? Probably not—it is really no different from watching Mickey Mouse on the Disney Channel. Disney put those graphics there because they want people to visit and view the information. Copyright violations occur when images or text from that Web page are downloaded, saved, and redistributed—or when movies or programs are taped and distributed. "Carol's Unofficial Disney Fan Club Page," for example, may generate additional exposure for Disney. It may even be of better quality than Disney's—and she doesn't charge anything for accessing it. But only Disney, as owners of those copyrighted characters, can put forth a Web page for the public.

This is a pretty clear-cut example, but there are other instances in which computer technology can make this very confusing. For example, items "captured momentarily" in RAM can in fact be made permanent, depending on the program you use. (We're going to get techie, so skip ahead if you like.) Works viewed in Netscape, for example, are stored in cache memory—but that memory is user-defined. Items within it can be easily made permanent. You can "temporarily" store 300 MB of pages and graphics if you have hard drive space. That material is cleared only when the allotted space has filled up or when the user decides to erase those cached pages from memory.

Lines of IRC chat seem transient on the surface, except for the fact that you can log sessions to a hard drive. There's just no easy way to lay out all the variables—hundreds of different programs with different features are used in countless ways by people all over the world. One user may have a Web browser that never caches visited pages, or at least makes that cache inaccessible, while another may use a browser that saves everything it sees forever.

Realize that our intent is only to present to you some of the larger issues that have surfaced as a result of the world's love affair with high technology and our propensity to use information as currency. Most of us don't know the inner workings of copyright law, and we can get by without it. If you need to know about copyright law as it applies to the Internet before you use or publish certain information, consult your lawyer or your school's legal counsel.

The only thing we can say for sure is that, unless you receive express written permission from the owner of copyrighted material, you would be breaking the law by putting text or graphics from your favorite TV show, movie, rock band, or cartoon on your Web site. Hundreds of thousands of people do it all the time, and few are ever punished—the possible repercussions are not really all that severe—but it is unethical, nonetheless.

For a less-technical look at copyright issues from a perspective that most people can relate to, you should check out Brad Templeton's article "10 Big Myths About Copyright Explained" on the next page. Templeton is a publisher at ClariNet, the Internet's largest electronic newspaper with over a million paid subscribers (he also started the Net's most widely read newsgroup, **rec.humor.funny**). He provides some key information about copyrights that most Internet users will find fascinating and useful.

Did you know that almost all material is copyrighted the moment it is created, even if it has no copyright notice? Or that copyrights can still be violated even if you don't charge money for materials? Or, perhaps most importantly, that articles posted to Usenet or mailing lists are *not* considered public domain works and therefore cannot be forwarded or reprinted without permission?

INFORMATION WANTS TO BE FREE!

That's the popular battle cry of Internauts worldwide. For those who adopt it, the phrase means that all information should be freely available. Some even take it to mean that all copyright laws should be eliminated in the digital world. Before you adopt this slogan, however, be sure to check out the interview with Bruce Lehman in the November/December 1995 *Educom,* called "Royalties, Fair Use, and Copyright in the Electronic Age (Or Why We Could Call this Article Forrest Gump and Not Get in Trouble)."

Lehman is the chair of the Working Group on Intellectual Property Rights, Assistant Secretary of Commerce, and Commissioner of Patents and Trademarks. He provides valuable insight into why copyright laws must remain intact, and how much information would suddenly disappear if all information truly was free. Lehman discusses some controversies surrounding the working group's new take on the Copyright Act, including whether materials exchanged over the Internet qualify as public performances or copies, the legal differences between print and electronic versions of works, and whether there should even be a copyright system for the digital world.

Here is the short version of *Brad Templeton's 10 Big Myths About Copyright.* Visit the Web site to learn why each item is incorrect.

INFO BYTE

1. If it doesn't have a copyright notice, it's not copyrighted.
2. If I don't charge for it, it's not a violation.
3. If it's posted to Usenet it's in the public domain.
4. My posting was just fair use!
5. If you don't defend your copyright you lose it.
6. Somebody has that name copyrighted!
7. They can't get me; defendants in court have powerful rights!
8. Oh, so copyright violation isn't a crime or anything?
9. It doesn't hurt anybody—in fact it's free advertising.
10. They emailed me a copy, so I can post it.

DON'T COPY THAT FLOPPY!

One of the biggest reasons for the popularity of the Internet is that users can find and download shareware (freely distributed software that they can try out before deciding whether or not keep it and to pay for it). Yet this privilege is abused by many Inernet users who download games or other shareware programs and use themm without ever registering or paying for them.

Whether you buy your software or download it from an online source, understanding the basics of copyright law as it applies to computer software can prevent costly trouble. We discussed the dangers of software piracy and "warez" trading in Chapter 2. That's why the Bellingham School District's copyright policy contains a whole section on software, with very specific details about bringing software from home into school, installing multiple copies, or running programs on a network.

As a rule, think of all computer media in this way: treat each program or document as a single copy of a book that only one person can read at a time. Similarly, only one computer can access the software or document at one time, that is, you can't use it on two computers at the same time. For example, your child can't take a copy of a program in to school and use it while you use the same program at home.

All computer files fall into one of five categories, each with different rules of use and distribution: commercial, shareware, postcardware, freeware, and public domain. It is important that you understand the differences and can guide your children when they begin downloading programs. You want them to "do the right thing" by the software maker. And they should also understand that downloading or copying software from an unknown or questionable source can put your computer at risk from viruses or other problems.

Commercial Programs

Commercial software has the most restrictions. Software an individual or school purchases and puts on its computers cannot be copied or redistributed without the author's or publisher's permission. Be careful not to allow multiple-user network access to a single copy of the program. If the software is copied, the offender and school could face a civil suit and more than $100,000 in fines.

Making a backup copy in case the original is lost or damaged is usually permitted. Schools can purchase site licenses or lab or bulk packs that allow copying software to more than one computer. Before making copies of software or installing it on multiple computers, check the software license agreement that comes with it. Some are more restrictive than others.

........·····

Shareware

Authors of shareware programs don't initially charge for the software. They generally ask for a donation or registration fee if you like the program and plan to use it. If you pay the fee, you will usually receive printed documentation and notice of updates or enhancements. If you don't pay, you can still use the software. But most programs will continue to display a welcome screen announcing that the software is copyrighted by the author and can be freely redistributed but not sold.

····........·

Postcardware

Some of the software on the Internet is postcardware. The programmers want you to send them a postcard as "payment" for the program so they can track who is using their software and where. In most cases, the authors retain full copyright, allow anyone to make copies, and ask that it not be sold without their consent.

···.......··

Freeware

Freeware is software that can be freely used and distributed. The author retains the copyright, but strongly advocates freely copying and distributing the program at no cost.

····.........

Public Domain

Many software authors dedicate some of their work to the public domain. These programs are not subject to any copyright restrictions and can be freely copied and redistributed. If you have any specific questions about whether a particular piece of software can be duplicated, contact the software publisher. For other copyright law questions, contact the Software Publishers Association (SPA) for free literature.

OTHER INFORMATION

Microsoft—one of the world's largest software publishers—also offers lots of information about software copyrights and piracy. In its International Report on Software Piracy, the company states that:

> [F]or every authorized copy of personal computer software in use, at least one unauthorized copy is made. . . . [I]n 1994 it cost the software industry in excess of US$15 billion. Software piracy harms all software companies and, ultimately, the end user. Piracy results in higher prices for honest users, reduced levels of support and delays in funding and development of new products, causing the overall breadth and quality of software to suffer.

It's certainly something to think about the next time you're tempted.

REFERENCES

Lehman, Bruce A. and Ronald H. Brown. "A Preliminary Draft of the Report of the Working Group on Intellectual Property Rights." [Online] Available http://cirrus.mit.edu/met_links/iitf_draft.html, March 16, 1996.

Magid, Larry. "Desktop Agenda: Defining Ethics on the Net." [Online] Available http://techweb.cmp.com:80/techweb/iw/547/47uwlm.htm, March 12, 1996.

McKenzie, Jamie. "Grazing the Net: Raising a Generation of Free Range Students." [Online] Available http://www.pacificrim.net/~mckenzie/grazing1.html, March 16, 1996.

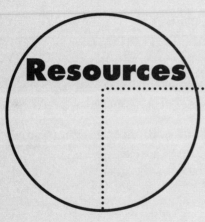

Resources LEARN MORE ABOUT IT!

Related Internet Sites

▣ **Copyright FAQ**
URL: http://www.cis.ohio-state.edu/hypertext/faq/usenet/Copyright-FAQ/top.html

▣ **Brad Templeton's 10 Big Myths about Copyright Explained**
URL: http://www.clarinet.com:80/brad/copymyths.html

▣ **From Now On**
URL: http://www.pacificrim.net/~mckenzie/

▣ **Library of Congress—U.S. Copyright Office**
Gopher to: marvel.loc.gov
Look in *Copyright*

▣ **Intellectual Property Rights**
URL: http://www.isa.net/project-open/proprights.html

▣ **MLA Citation Guide**
URL: http://www.cas.usf.edu/english/walker/mla.html

▣ **Educom**
URL: http://www.educom.edu/educom.review/review.95/nov.dec/lehman.html

▣ **Educom: Transforming Education through Technology**
URL: http://www.educom.edu/

▣ **Citing Computer Documents**
URL: http://www.neal.ctstateu.edu/history/cite.html

▣ **Williams College Library Web**
URL: http://www.williams.edu:803/library/library.www/cite.html

▣ **A Preliminary Draft of the Report of the Working Group on Intellectual Property Rights**
URL: http://www.cirrus.mit.edu/met_links/iitf_draft.html

▣ **Parenting for an Age of Information: Preparing Your Daughter or Son for the Next Century**
URL: http://www.pacificrim.net/~mckenzie/parenting/outline.html

....

Other Resources

▣ **Microsoft**
Email to: piracy@microsoft.com
URL: http://www.microsoft.com/Piracy/

▣ **Software Publishers Association**
1730 M St. NW, Suite 700
Washington, DC 20036
202-452–6100
URL: http://www.spa.org/

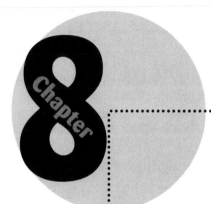

INTERNET TOWN WATCH

For various reasons, many Internet special interest groups, individuals, and software companies want to keep the Internet free of government regulation, yet they realize the importance of shielding children from potentially damaging online material.

In order to achieve this, members of the online community are forming organizations to address the child safety issue. These include grassroots, ad hoc parent-teacher groups in local communities, large nationwide associations like SafeSurf, and major alliances between corporations, such as Netscape and America Online.

THE GROWING KID-SAFE INTERNET MOVEMENT

It's happening all over the Internet—about as quickly as software companies write programs to help parents protect their children from objectionable materials online, thousands of Internet users are working to create ways for the Internet to regulate itself before government does.

These companies are developing databases of sites unsafe for kids and directories of sites that *are* kid-safe, as well as formulating Web content ratings systems that Web publishers agree upon. They are proposing ways to build protection features and parental controls into new versions of popular Web browser programs. In general, they are doing whatever they can to keep the Internet world self-regulated.

WHAT'S DRIVING THE KID-SAFE INTERNET MOVEMENT?

Why try to keep the government from regulating the Internet? Internet special-interest groups provide some good reasons. The financial ramifications of mandatory, government-imposed Internet regulations could be tremendous. For example, ISPs or commercial online services would face serious problems if they were required to monitor every piece of information that flows to and from their services. For users, the costs of these services would probably grow. Yet whatever efforts the companies make to comply with broad legislation and protect themselves from liability could easily be subverted. This is the nature of the Internet.

Larger providers might stay afloat, but smaller providers, unable to accommodate burdensome legislation, could go out of business, leaving some areas without affordable local access to the Internet.

Besides having to pay more for your access because of regulation, you might also have to pay more in taxes to fund the new bureaucracy needed to keep tabs on the millions of people using the Internet. And what about the international nature of the Net? Will world regulatory organizations be formed and have any input in how the Internet is regulated?

How will government agencies enforce new laws? First Amendment and privacy issues come into play. If the government begins monitoring and regulating online services, the feared "chilling effect" could set in, threatening the very thing democracies around the world share—the freedom of citizens to openly and publicly speak their minds without fear of government retribution.

Rather than wait for other people to answer these questions—people who might not have even *used* the Internet or understand its potential—members of the online community are putting their heads together. When it comes to protecting children from inappropriate materials, they are working to find common ground that all Internet users can stand upon. People of all backgrounds are involved—businesspeople, scholars, lawyers, programmers, parents, educators, publishers, students, and artists.

In some cases, major companies with stakes in the online world are joining individuals and forming organizations that range from grassroots, ad hoc parent-teacher groups working in local communities to larger, nationwide associations such as SafeSurf, and major alliances between corporations such as Netscape, America Online, and Sun Microsystems. A new breed of special-interest group and lobbyist has emerged to try to keep the Internet in the hands of its users. Whatever unfolds from debate and the outcome of legal battles will likely have long-lasting, far-reaching implications for the future of the Internet.

What do these groups say about their missions? Let's look at two excellent position statements that demonstrate why parents, teachers, and anyone interested in making the Net safe for kids while preserving its freedom should consider getting involved.

The first is from an informal proposal and Internet RFC (request for comments) called "A Proposal: Voluntary Self-Rating System for Internet Resources" by Alex Stewart.

The Net interprets censorship as damage, and routes around it.

—John Gilmore, Net pioneer

INFO BYTE

We, as a community of informed, responsible people have a duty not only to the rest of the world but to ourselves to show that our community can be responsible and responsive to the concerns of parents, teachers, and others of the larger world in which we also live, and we have a responsibility to children and those who care about them to provide ways in which they can take advantage of the great resources of this environment without a (prohibitive) requirement of constant monitoring or risking exposure to inappropriate or even emotionally or psychologically damaging materials. We also have a responsibility, to ourselves and the world, to ensure that these measures can be undertaken and used, effectively and appropriately, in a way which does not destroy the free flow of information which has made this environment such a valuable resource to begin with, and to demonstrate the way in which this should be done.

The Voluntary Self Rating System for Internet Resources site is:

URL: www.crl.com/~riche/IVSR/proposal.html

The second statement comes from the home page of an organization called SafeSurf, which we will describe shortly.

The Internet has grown by leaps and bounds in recent years because mass consensus has been reached on implementing many standards such as the World Wide Web and the HTML programming language. However, in order to keep the Internet from being consumed by the very information it provides, a consensus must be reached on how this information will be shared. Unless we actively make decisions now as a responsible group, the right to make these decisions will be forever taken from us by our government.

HERE'S WHAT INDIVIDUALS CAN DO NOW

Every responsible Net user can aid the campaign to keep the Net free and safe. The first thing a parent or educator can do is try to spread the word about Internet safety on a personal level. Use speaking opportunities at school board or city council meetings to promote responsible use, safety awareness, and a free

Internet. Write a letter to the editor of your local paper. Or, if you have become your community's "online expert," offer to write a technology column on Internet safety, great places for kids online, or things families can do together on the Internet.

You can also write local, state, and/or federal government officials about your position on government regulation of the Net. If you have found the Internet to be an invaluable parenting or teaching resource, tell people about it! For every negative report about the Internet's dangers, there are hundreds of thousands of positive things happening online that are unreported. You can email most members of the Congress or Senate. Visit the Library of Congress' directory of email addresses.

Gopher: marvel.loc.gov
Look in *U.S. Congress, Congressional Directories*

Remember the blocking software, such as SurfWatch, that we mentioned earlier? You can notify the various companies that produce filtering software of inappropriate sites you find. This is especially important if you find an objectionable site while using one of those products. With your input, the companies can build more comprehensive databases to block sites that fall through the cracks.

Many Internet users take a somewhat different, more active approach to Internet safety and censorship by actively discouraging people from putting inappropriate material on the Internet—and others from accessing it. They post antipornography messages to newsgroups and mailing lists, email individuals posting objectionable materials, and contact Internet Service Providers and lobby them to close down porn sites.

In general, they do whatever they can to hamper or at least discourage people from putting materials online that are unsafe for kids. Some even put fake pornography pages on the Web that act as decoys. A visitor who accesses such a site is admonished about the harm pornography causes. Many of these sites threaten to collect visitor email addresses and forward them to newsgroups so that other Internauts can send flames or mail bombs. They even threaten to send messages to authorities or family members—a course of action that is certainly questionable. Remember that porn page we found after searching for feminism resources in Chapter 1? It was a decoy page. (See Figure 8.1.)

Figure 8.1
Some groups opposed to pornography on the Net set up fake sites to lure porn-seekers. When the sites are accessed, the viewer is admonished. Remember the porn page we found after searching for feminism resources in Chapter 1? This is what we found after clicking on the link: It was a decoy page.

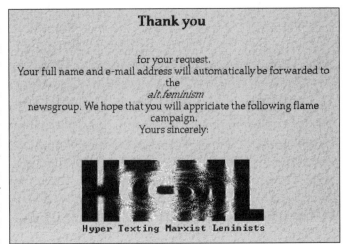

Thank you

for your request.
Your full name and e-mail address will automatically be forwarded to the
alt.feminism
newsgroup. We hope that you will appriciate the following flame campaign.
Yours sincerely:

HT-ML

Hyper Texting Marxist Leninists

GROUPS FIGHTING TO KEEP THE NET FREE AND SAFE

Internet safety and freedom is a new, rapidly developing advocacy movement. Many of the Internet site ratings groups and advocacy organizations will likely merge over the next year or so. Here is just an overview of some of the more press-worthy groups and efforts, plus pointers to online sites with up-to-date information or contact information about how to get involved. With all the hype about cyberporn, it is reassuring to know that people are joining together to try to make the Internet safer for kids.

The Center for Democracy and Technology and the Citizens Internet Empowerment Coalition

We have referred to the CDT several times in this book. If you surf the Net at all, you will surely encounter many links to this nonprofit, Washington, D.C.–based organization. The CDT is a highly visible public policy group interested in all issues surrounding technology, including the Internet, as they relate to free speech, privacy, and other personal liberties and democratic values. The organization's main battle of late has been waged against the Communications Decency Act (CDA). Its weapons have included petitions, public hearings, studies, educational campaigns, and debates. (See Figure 8.2.) The CDT's organizational overview, entitled "Democratic Values for a Digital Age:

1995 Activities of the Center for Democracy and Technology" gives a good idea of the nature and scope of the CDT.

The CDT also coordinated the formation of a coalition of Internet users and content providers, including libraries, publishers, advertisers, civil libertarians, service providers such as America Online, the American Library Association, and many others. This group, called the Citizens Internet Empowerment Coalition (CIEC), recently filed a federal lawsuit seeking to overturn the Communications Decency Act. The CDT's main argument against much of the proposed or enacted legislation is that the Internet, since it is a very different form of communication with many properties not found in traditional media such as print or broadcast, cannot possibly be legislated the same way. Specifically, the group argues that:

- The Internet is a unique communications medium that deserves First Amendment protection at least as broad as that afforded to print media.
- Individual users and parents, not the federal government, should determine for themselves and their children what material comes into their homes based on their own tastes and values.
- The CDA will be ineffective at protecting children from "indecent" or "patently" offensive material online.

To date, over 30,000 Internet users have visited the CDT and CIEC Web page and signed petitions (via Web forms) that will be used in the case.

Figure 8.2
The CDT opposes the Communications Decency Act because it believes the Internet cannot be legislated in the same manner as traditional media, due to its broad, unusual scope. It also believes the act won't effectively protect children from indecent material.

If you are interested in learning more, be sure to visit the CDT and CIEC Web sites. You will find hundreds of links to related online resources, including the latest news, full text of legislation, position papers, transcripts of Congressional hearings, tips on how to set up meetings with congressional staff, and much more. You can find out how to join or lend a hand to the CDT/CIEC or sign up for one of several Internet mailing lists.

•••••••••••••••••••••••••••••••••••••••

Electronic Frontier Foundation

The Electronic Frontier Foundation (EFF) is another nonprofit, civil liberties group "working in the public interest to protect privacy, free expression, and access to online resources and information." Those little "Free Speech Online" blue ribbons you may have seen on the Web come from the EFF. You can download blue ribbons from the EFF home page to use on your own site. (See Figure 8.3.)

Founded in 1990 to "ensure that the principles embodied in the Constitution and Bill of Rights are protected as new communications technologies emerge," the EFF engages in a variety of activities in the interest of protecting Internet citizens, preserving free speech, and making the Internet safer for all. Detailed information from the EFF home page about its mission and work is provided in Appendix C.

The EFF disseminates information all over the Internet. It provides an ftp, gopher, and Web site, newsgroups, and forums on CompuServe, the WELL, America Online, GEnie, and Women's Wire. The EFF also offers a free newsletter called

Figure 8.3 The EFF started the "Free Speech Online" blue ribbon campaign. You've probably noticed the ribbons on Web sites.

EFFector, which provides official EFF position papers, updates on current legislation and cases, news briefs, information on upcoming events and conferences, and more. Visit an EFF site for more information about its history, members, achievements, agenda, current and back issues of *EFFector*, and details on how to join or support EFF efforts.

∙∙∙∙∙∙∙∙∙∙∙

SafeSurf

SafeSurf is "an organization dedicated to making the Internet safe for your children without censorship." (See Figure 8.4.) It was founded by Wendy Simpson and Ray Soular, who were concerned primarily with the dangers of children accessing potentially harmful adult material, but they were also concerned about government censorship.

The system SafeSurf has developed—which includes following an Internet Rating Standard and marking "kid-friendly" sites with the SafeSurf Wave logo—has gained wide acceptance from individual users, service providers, publishers, and Internet developers. According to the organization, over 20,000 Internet sites support the SafeSurf Internet Rating System. Microsoft and Netscape are two of the most notable companies endorsing or involved with SafeSurf. Other supporters of the SafeSurf Internet Rating Standard include Net Nanny, Ltd. (publishers of Net Nanny), Microsystems (CyberPatrol), Teachersoft (InterGO), and SolidOak (CyberSitter). The organization's ultimate goal is to have *all* sites comply with the system, but it

Figure 8.4
SafeSurf is one of the most active and vocal groups lobbying for child safety and free speech on the Net. It has devised an Internet rating standard and marks "kid-friendly" sites with its logo.

believes that, if it can get at least 10 percent to comply, then competition and user pressure will compel the other online information providers to follow suit.

The SafeSurf ratings system focuses entirely on classifying online material for parents and teachers who want to protect their children. This classification serves many of the same purposes as filtering software by allowing adults to choose the type of information children will receive *before* it hits the screen. Adults will still be free to access what they want.

SafeSurf is one of the most active and vocal organizations lobbying for Net safety and freedom. Its members—including "Online Mothers" as well as SafeSurf founders, lawyers, and members of software filtering companies—developed their own declaration of Internet independence on July 4, 1995 (reprinted on the next page). It cleverly called forth the imagery and spirit of the men who drafted and signed the original.

How the SafeSurf Ratings System works

The SafeSurf classification system consists of two-part codes. One part is called a *type* and the other a *number*. The type would indicate the general nature of a site's content, such as sexual or violent, while the number would represent the degree to which a site is sexual or violent. "The higher the number," the proposal states, "the more caution parents should exercise in permitting children to access this information."

Here's an example from the SafeSurf Web site of how the ratings system would operate.

> The computer will interpret the code of ss~0001 as "General Information (the first two zeros) with No Adult Themes (the third "0") with the mildest degree of 1." This is 100% child safe for young children. If the site would contain an occasional mild expletive such as "crap" it would be rated as ss~0011, which the computer would translate as "General Information with No Adult Themes includes Profanity with a degree of 1." We stress that these codes are designed to be interpreted by the computer as they are encoded. By using the computer to do the translating, we can build a very complex system utilizing the computer that is simple to understand by users.

SafeSurf's Declaration of an Independent Internet July 4, 1995

We hold these truths to be self-evident, that all information is created equal, that information is endowed by its creator with certain inalienable rights, that among these is the right to be distributed via the Internet without governmental censorship. That whenever any legislation becomes destructive of these ends, it is the duty of the members of the Internet to oppose it, and to institute self-regulation with parental control, laying its foundation on such principles and organizing its powers in such form, as to them shall seem most likely to effect the safety of children and the sanctity of distribution.

Prudence, indeed, will dictate that regulations long established should not be changed for light and transient causes; and accordingly all experience hath shewn, that mankind are more disposed to accept censorship where none is required, than to right things by opposing such censorship. But when an unnecessary attempt at censorship, pursuing centralized control, evidences a design to place information under absolute Despotism, it is the right of the members of the Internet, it is their duty, to oppose such legislation, and to promote self-regulation with parental control.

We therefore, Parents and Representatives of the Online World, in cooperation, appealing to concerned parents everywhere for the rectitude of our intentions, do, in the Name, and by the authority of the Internet Community, solemnly publish and declare, that the Internet is and of Right ought to be self-regulated with parental control and free from governmental censorship. And for the support of this Declaration, with a firm reliance on the protection of Divine Providence, We mutually pledge to each other and to our children, our Lives, our Fortunes, and our sacred Honor.

For complete details on the ratings system, go to SafeSurf's official Internet Ratings and Classifications System proposal at

URL: http://www.safesurf.com/ssplan.html

....

SafeSurf Kids' Wave

SafeSurf has also developed a special area on its Web site called Kids' Wave. This approach—concentrating on directing kids and families to the good stuff on the Internet instead of focusing on building blacklists—is becoming popular with many Internet content providers. Areas on the kid-friendly Web page include Elementary Ages, Older Kids/Parents, and Space Stuff. SafeSurf also offers a monthly newsletter with reviews on the latest kids' sites, tips for using the Internet, and posts about development of its rating systems. SafeSurf has also developed SERF (SafeSurf's Educational Resource Files), a special Web page "in appreciation of all educators."

If you want to join SafeSurf, find out how to help with the classification system, recommend sites for Kid's Wave, or get the newsletter, gp to the SafeSurf Feedback Page at:

URL: http://www.safesurf.com/ssregis.html

If you run a Web site, you can fill out an online form (Figure 8.5) at SafeSurf that will classify your site automatically. Enter your site address and email address and select one of the options for Recommended Age and Adult Themes. Pressing the "Create Rating" button generates your customized classification at the top of your Web page and automatically forward rating information to your email address. After SafeSurf reviews your site, you will be provided with a certification agreement and a special logo to display on your page. The form is available at:

URL: http://www.safesurf.com/classify/index.html

....

Platform for Internet Content Selection (PICS)

Soon after SafeSurf introduced its Internet ratings system, the World Wide Web Consortium (W3) and the Information Highway Parental Empowerment Group (IHPEG) proposed PICS (Platform for Internet Content Selection), which is a similar standard for labeling content on the Internet. (See Figure 8.6.)

PICS was partially designed to deter Congress from imposing Internet legislation and goes beyond merely classifying sites. It provides a universal protocol and set of HTML tags that software publishers can incorporate into new versions of Web browsers and other Internet programs. The idea is that tools to help parents set access limits will be built into Web browsers and Web sites. Parents, teachers, or organizations would easily be able to apply ratings or descriptive labels to virtually any online resource, including newsgroups and gopher sites. Though not quite as dramatic as SafeSurf's Declaration, the PICS Statement of Principles (see the following page) provides a good overview of the organization's focus and mission.

PICS does not rate or classify sites but simply provides the labeling format anyone can use for classification. Content providers would insert "hidden" information on Web sites to be read by PICS-compliant Web browsers. If a parent sets their browser to disallow access to gambling sites, for instance, access would be denied much as it is with the blocking and filtering software products like CyberPatrol. Again, the key to success for such a proposal is convincing large numbers of Internet content providers and software developers to buy in.

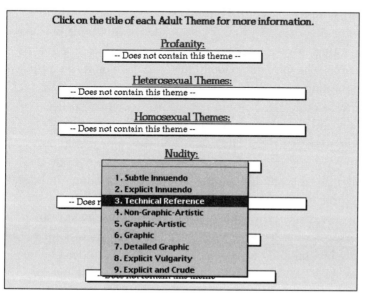

Figure 8.5
You can classify your site automatically with SafeSurf. It will provide a certification agreement and a logo to display on your Web page.

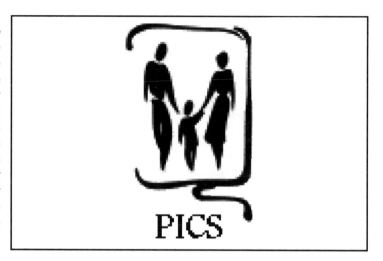

You might wonder what keeps content providers from rating an erotic site as appropriate for minors. The Consortium is betting that most will embrace the PICS system and adhere to guidelines for two reasons: to protect themselves from liability, and to better ensure that the people visiting their sites are the people they *want* to visit their sites. Adult video retailers probably would rather that 12-year-olds not access their sites and tie up the servers, since they are not potential paying customers. A major goal of PICS is to make the system virtually effortless for content providers so that more and more of them will use the ratings systems.

Some Net experts predict that dozens or hundreds of third-party ratings services will emerge, catering to different groups of people. The Christian Coalition could develop its own PICS configuration for members, as could the Gay and Lesbian Alliance. Local organizations could also customize access. Schools and churches could choose PICS configurations specific to their needs. The same Web site, then, could have different ratings depending on who accessed it—not one universal, inflexible rating that may not reflect the values and tastes of all groups.

To date, many powerful corporations, technology industry leaders, Internet Service Providers, and publishers support PICS and are lending their expertise. These include America Online, Apple, AT&T, the Center for Democracy and Technology,

PICS Statement of Principles

PICS is a cross-industry working group whose goal is to facilitate the development of technologies to give users of interactive media, such as the Internet, control over the kinds of material to which they and their children have access. PICS members believe that individuals, groups and businesses should have easy access to the widest possible range of content selection products, and a diversity of voluntary rating systems.

In order to advance its goals, PICS will devise a set of standards that facilitate the following:

Self-rating: enable content providers to voluntarily label the content they create and distribute.

Third-party rating: enable multiple, independent labeling services to associate additional labels with content created and distributed by others. Services may devise their own labeling systems, and the same content may receive different labels from different services.

Ease-of-use: enable parents and teachers to use ratings and labels from a diversity of sources to control the information that children under their supervision receive.

PICS members believe that an open labeling platform which incorporates these features provides the best way to preserve and enhance the vibrancy and diversity of the Internet. Easy access to technology which enables first- and third-party rating of content will give users maximum control over the content they receive without requiring new restrictions on content providers.

Membership in PICS includes a broad cross section of companies from the computer, communications, and content industries, as well as trade associations and public interest groups. PICS member will deploy products and services based on these standards.

CompuServe, Delphi, the Interactive Services Association, MCI, Microsoft, MIT, O'Reilley and Associates, Prodigy, Progressive Networks, SafeSurf, Spyglass, Time Warner, Viacom, and numerous others.

For more information, including a detailed explanation of how PICS coding works, visit the PICS Web site. PICS also maintains several mailing lists and email addresses you can use to learn more about their efforts. The PICS-info list is used for distributing public announcements about the PICS project.

Email to: **PICS-info-request@w3.org**

Type **subscribe** in the subject line. If you have a specific question about PICS or ratings systems, use the following address.

Email to: **PICS-ask@w3.org**

Recreational Software Advisory Council

The Recreational Software Advisory Council (RSAC) is another organization involved with universal Internet content labeling. Originally dedicated to providing content labeling to help parents and educators choose age-appropriate software, the mission of this independent, nonprofit organization is to "empower the public, especially parents, to make informed decisions about electronic media by means of an open, objective content advisory system." (See Figure 8.7.) As a natural extension to its software labeling activities, the RSAC now also focuses on the same issues as SafeSurf and PICS with a new division called RSACi (the "i" is for Internet). Here's a description of the RSAC's rating system, taken from the organization's home page.

> The RSACi rating system is a fully automated, paperless system that relies on a quick, easy-to-use questionnaire that the Web master completes at RSAC's home page for free. The questionnaire runs through a series of highly specific questions about the level, nature and intensity of the sex, nudity, violence, offensive language (vulgar or hate-motivated) found within the Web master's site. Once completed, the questionnaire is then submitted electronically to the RSAC Web Server, which tabulates the results and produces the HTML advisory tags that the Web master then places on their Web

site/page. A standard Internet browser, or blocking device that has been configured to read the RSACi system, can recognize these tags, enabling parents who use the browser to either allow or restrict their children's access to any single rating or combination of ratings.

The RSACi system, according to executive director Stephen Balkam, offers improvements over current systems. "Rather than simply authorizing an advisory for a web site, the RSACi system offers the ability to go into a Web site and rate new 'pages' as well as separate pages within that site, to account for the infinite variation of information located within any given home page. Thus, the high school student would be able to gain access to the Jimmy Carter interview conducted by *Playboy* in 1976 at Playboy.com, but not the February Playmate of the month."

The RSACi system is said to be compliant with PICS standards. The organization is currently working with Microsoft on incorporating parental controls into the company's Internet Explorer Web browser. RSAC's system is even being evaluated as a possible solution to the current debate over television programming content disclosure and the V-chip.

··

Information Highway Parental Empowerment Group

PICS was partially formed by the Information Highway Parental Empowerment Group (IHPEG). IHPEG is an industry-wide effort led by Microsoft, Netscape, and Progressive Networks (creator of RealAudio) that coexists with other groups to create and implement standards to help parents, educators, and others

Figure 8.7
Through its objective content advisory system, RSAC wants to help people make informed decisions about what they access on the Internet.

block youth access to objectionable materials online. The system is designed to meet the following goals:

- Enable parents to make sure that their children cannot purposefully or accidentally access objectionable materials online.
- Make it easy for content providers and third-party rating services to characterize Internet content.
- Through its efficiency, become a standard part of Internet access systems.

The group met at the end of 1995 to devise viable ways of incorporating parental controls for all Internet access software. At the beginning of 1996 the companies in IHPEG started the process of incorporating those ideas into their software product lines. As of this writing, IHPEG has no official Web page, but you can get a press release about IHPEG activities from the Netscape public relations area.

URL: http://home.netscape.com/newsref/pr/index.html

• • • • • • • • • • • • • • • •
CyberAngels

CyberAngels is an all-volunteer Internet patrol and monitoring project started by senior members of the famous International Alliance of Guardian Angels, whose headquarters are in New York City. Their motto is "The Internet Is Our Neighborhood—Let's Look After It!" Their mission is analogous to the mission of Guardian Angels—to be a Cyberspace "Neighborhood Watch." (See Figure 8.8.)

According to the CyberAngels home page, when Guardian Angels founder and president Curtis Sliwa announced his email address on his radio show on WABC in New York, his email box was flooded with stories of Internet dangers. They included online harassment, hate mail, and pedophiles trying to seduce children. Parents also wrote him saying they were outraged by the ease with which children could access pornography. Soon after, CyberAngels was born.

> We sat down and discussed what we the Guardian Angels could do to help reassure parents and to make the Net a safer place for kids and others. The answer was simple—we should do what we do in the streets. The Internet is like a vast city: there are some rough neighborhoods in it, including "red light" areas. Why not patrol the Internet, particularly in these "rough neighborhoods" just like a Neighborhood Watch? Just like our own Guardian Angels Community Safety Patrols. And why not recruit our volunteers from the very people who inhabited this vast world CyberCity? Who better than to cruise the Net watching out for people's safety than members of the Internet community themselves? After all, who else could do it? Never an organization to blame it on or leave it to the government, we decided to do something ourselves.

The goals of the CyberAngels project, as described on their Web site, are to:

- Promote and protect the idea that the same laws of decency and respect for others that apply in the streets should apply also to the Internet.
- Protect children from online abuse.
- Pressure service providers to enforce their terms of service.

Figure 8.8
CyberAngels seeks to keep the Internet free from dangers for children and adults. Volunteers spend a minimum of two hours a week surfing the Internet looking for places believed to harbor illegal or unacceptable activity.

- Give advice and assistance to online victims of hate mail, harassment, and sexual abuse.
- Watch out for users violating terms of service by committing "cybercrimes" and to report them to relevant authorities (system administrators or even police).
- Help to make unnecessary the government legislation by showing that the Internet community takes seriously the safety of children and the well-being of all its members and can police itself.

CyberAngels volunteers spend a minimum of two hours per week surfing the Internet and looking for places they believe could harbor illegal or unacceptable activity, including child abuse, child pornography, sexual harassment, hate crimes, fraudulent financial schemes, software piracy, terrorism, or bombmaking. They then forward email to the CyberAngels headquarters, where staff review the sites and take appropriate action, possibly even notifying law-enforcement agencies.

The CyberAngels home page contains all the additional information you will need about the group, including how to join the group's mailing list and how to report objectionable sites or dangerous individuals,

email to:angels@wavenet.com

or

URL: http://www.safesurf.com/cyberangels/

• •

Children Accessing Controversial Information

Children Accessing Controversial Information (CACI) is an Internet mailing list for those interested in discussing issues involved with preventing children from accessing undesirable or controversial materials online. Topics include censorship, parent-child communication, acceptable use, community standards, software filtering, and more. The list generates a fairly large amount of traffic, with lots of heated but healthy debate.

email to: caci-request@cygnus.com.

Type **subscribe** in the body of the message; the subject line is ignored.

URL: http://www.zen.org/~brendan/caci.html

....
Project OPEN

Project OPEN (Online Public Education Network) is a partnership of the Interactive Services Association, the National Consumers League, and leading online and Internet companies. Its goal is to help consumers "get the most out of going online." (See Figure 8.9.)

Their mission includes a new consumer education program that is designed to give the public the information they need in order to use the Internet responsibly. At their Web site, you will find information about parental empowerment, intellectual property rights, online consumer fraud, and privacy. It also provides plenty of good information about child safety and Netiquette, and there is even a glossary of Internet terms for new users!

Project OPEN is launching a public service announcement campaign that is designed to help people learn how to use online and Internet services in an informed and responsible manner. Some of the supporting Internet corporations include America Online, AT&T, Netcom, Prodigy, Microsoft, and CompuServe.

Project OPEN™
The Online Public Education Network

Making the NetWork For You™

Figure 8.9
Project OPEN's mission is to help consumers "get the most out of going online." It's a great place for new Internauts to visit.

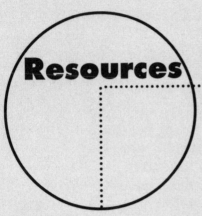

Resources LEARN MORE ABOUT IT!

Related Internet Sites

☐ **Democratic Values for a Digital Age: 1995 Activities of the Center for Democracy and Technology**
URL: http://www.cdt.org/cdtovrvw.html#1

☐ **History of a Child Safe Internet**
URL: http://www.safesurf.com/time.htm

☐ **ACLU: Why We Are Challenging the Communications Decency Act of the Telecommunications Reform Act of 1996**
URL: http://www.aclu.org/news/n020896b.html

☐ **EFF "Rating, Filtering and Labeling of Online Content" Archive**
URL: http://www.ilf.net/eff/Censorship/Ratings_filters_labelling/

☐ **The Debate: Government Control or Individual Responsibility**
URL: http://www.thehub.com.au/%7Erene/liberty/debate.html

☐ **Internet Parental Control Frequently Asked Questions (FAQ) Provided by the Voters Telecommunications Watch (VTW)**
URL: http://www.vtw.org/ipcfaq

☐ **Parental Empowerment, Child Protection, & Free Speech**
URL: http://www.cdt.org/iwg/IWGrept.html

☐ **Mediascope—Media relations, Issue Management, and Advocacy Campaigns**
URL: http://vvv.com/mii/

▣ **Interactive Services Association**
URL: http://www.isa.net/

▣ **SafeSurfing, Inc.**
URL: http://www.mindspring.com/~safesurf/safesurf.html

....

Usenet Newsgroups

k12.chat.teacher
alt.parenting-solutions
alt.society.futures
alt.politics.datahighway
alt.cyberspace
comp.infosystems
comp.infosystems.www.advocacy
comp.internet.net-happenings
alt.internet.media-coverage
misc.news.internet.announce
misc.news.internet.discuss

....

Organizations

▣ **Center for Democracy and Technology**
1634 Eye Street NW, Suite 1100
Washington, DC 20006
202-637–9800
Email to: info@cdt.org
URL: http://www.cdt.org

▣ **Citizens Internet Empowerment Coalition**
Email to: ciec@cdt.org
URL: http://www.cdt.org/ciec/index.html

▣ **Electronic Frontier Foundation (EFF)**
550 Bryant Street, Suite 725
San Francisco CA 94117
415-436–9333
Email to: ask@eff.org
Ftp to: ftp.eff.org
Gopher to: gopher.eff.org
News: comp.org.eff.talk, comp.org.eff.news
URL: http://www.eff.org/

Platform for Internet Content and Selection (PICS)
MIT Lab for Computer Science
545 Technology Square
Cambridge, MA 02139
URL: http://www.w3.org/pub/WWW/PICS/

Project Open
800–466-OPEN
Email to: project-open@isa.net
URL: http://www.isa.net/project-open

Recreational Software Advisory Council
067 Massachusetts Avenue, Fourth Floor
Cambridge, MA 02140
617-864–5612
Email to: info@rsac.org
URL: http://www.rsac.org/rsaci.htm

SafeSurf
16032 Sherman Way, Suite 58
Van Nuys, CA 91406
Email to: SafeSurf@aol.com
URL: http://www.safesurf.com

9

BECOME A COMPUTER DETECTIVE

No matter how hard you try to protect your children from obscene or disturbing online material, situations may arise that you can't control.

Curiosity is a strong urge in youngsters, and some may feel compelled to seek out the type of material you want them to avoid. You need to know enough about your computer and the Internet and to think like a hacker in order to recognize signs of inappropriate use.

THE CHAPTER YOU DON'T WANT YOUR KIDS TO READ!

So, you now have an AUP at home or school (see Chapter 5), and you have discussed some of the dangers of the Internet with your kids and provided guidance on how to avoid them. You copied My Rules of Online Safety (see Chapter 3), posted them next to the computer, try to be present when your children go online, and get involved in their telecommunications activities.

But no matter how much you do, you cannot always protect them or make sure they do the right thing—just like in the real world. Circumstances will develop and situations will arise that are beyond your control. Some young people may try to find pornography or other materials that you object to, probably out of curiosity. Others may try to download inappropriate materials just to see if they *can* or maybe because they want to gain peer acceptance. Maybe they just want to prove that they can thwart your efforts to control their Internet access.

The point is, young people may do things online or with their computer that they shouldn't. As a parent or teacher, it is important that you know enough to be an Internet or computer "detective" and recognize the signs of inappropriate use. They say that to catch a hacker, you have to think like a hacker. Iin light of this, this chapter will cover the following:

- The warning signs that can tip you off to inappropriate activity.
- What you should know about your operating system.
- File formats and the applications you need to view them.
- Commercial and shareware administration and utility programs and how they can be used or abused.
- The ins-and-outs of removable storage devices.
- Features of Internet software that can help you be a Net detective.
- How to spot pirated software.
- The risks of your children using the computer at a friend's house.

We will focus mainly on how to sniff around for trouble in your family or school computer. But isn't this like spying on your children? No. Remember that in a home setting, the family computer should be communal, not private. So you are not spying on anyone or digging around through personal property. Make it clear at the outset that the computer is for the whole family to use and enjoy, but that you will administrate its content and use. But try not to act like too much like the "computer police;" expect and hope for the best from your children.

In school settings, students cannot expect to have total computer privacy. The computers and software are school property, and technology coordinators or administrators have the right to make sure everything is normal on the systems for which they are responsible.

RECOGNIZE CHANGES IN BEHAVIOR

If you notice a few changes in a child's attitude or behavior or in computer-using habits, this should alert you to potential problems. Does the child often appear uneasy when he or she is using the computer and you're in the area? Do weird things seem to happen when he or she uses the computer that *don't* happen to you?

For instance, if a teenager is using the computer unattended, does it always seem to "crash" and need to be restarted the moment you walk into the room? They may deliberately shutting down the computer to hide what they are accessing—it's a classic trick. If it happens consistently, ask the youngster about the application causing the crash. After all, you want the computer to function properly. See if you can recreate the circumstances which led to the crash, so that you can troubleshoot and correct the "problem."

Look for any changes in behavior that occur soon after a child starts really getting into computing. Does he or she hang out with different friends as a result of computer use? Does your child prefer online friends to real ones? Does your child spend too much time online to the detriment of school work, other hobbies, or even personal hygiene? Do you sense any emotional or attitudinal change that might stem from unhealthy online activities?

Of course, you may notice more concrete signs, too. Typical are mysterious long-distance charges that you can't account for—indicating private bulletin board access (home to many pornography purveyors)—or floppy diskettes stashed in a hiding place. Most of the time, though, inappropriate computer use will not be that obvious when it comes to a young person's behavior. A better strategy is to keep a watchful eye for things that don't seem right with your computer, just as you would monitor the status of the family car or charge card bills.

KEEP YOUR COMPUTER ACCESSIBLE

Have you ever tried to launch a specific program on your computer or to access a specific directory, only to be confronted with an "Enter Password" screen? This is a bad sign. The very *worst* thing you can do is let children password protect areas of the computer. Few children could really present legitimate reasons for needing to password protect computers or directories.

If they wish to write a private journal or make diary entries, they can use programs like Word Perfect, which lets you password protect single *documents*, not entire directories full of files. Their personal information remains safe, and you retain access to everything on the computer. In a school setting, the issue is moot—only the system administrator should have password privileges, unless students have their own email accounts.

This can't be stressed enough. One of the best ways to avoid problems is *not* to let kids use the computer in a private setting or area where activity can be easily concealed. If the computer is in a private place, they are likely to feel more secure when accessing materials they know they shouldn't. Install your family computer in an open, accessible location. In schools, strategically arrange classrooms so teachers can quickly spot any monkey business.

LEARN ABOUT YOUR OPERATING SYSTEM

It is crucial that you have a good working knowledge of the system software running on your computer, whether it is DOS, OS/2, Windows, Mac, or something else. For most school technology managers, this is not a problem. They receive extensive training on how to configure and maintain computer networks and spot misuse. At home, however, it could be a much different story. Despite the huge number of families purchasing computers every year, many parents still have only a superficial under-standing of how they work. You should know at least as much about your PC as your kids do—but with today's computer-savvy youngsters, that can be quite a challenge!

One of the best ways to get up to speed is to actually *read* the manuals that come with the system software. Even if you don't understand every word, it helps to at least become familiar with some terms. The computer might come with system and other software preinstalled, but manuals or guides should also have been included. Read them or check out their tutorials to learn about:

- File names and their extensions
- How to rename programs or reassign icons.
- Different ways of viewing and searching your hard drive.
- How to track file modification dates and the most recently accessed applications or files.
- The differences between documents, system files, and applications.
- System administration features, including system software protection and locks.
- Setting up different desktops for different family members.
- Password protecting various areas of the computer.

Many computers come preloaded with jazzy multimedia tutorials that guide you through their workings, but look for documents or FAQs that get a little more in-depth. Local colleges or computer clubs offer user groups, which is a great way to network with other parents or teachers and get hands-on tips and strategies for administrating your computer. Check your local bookstore for good family computing magazines or how-to computer books aimed at new users. You can browse or even purchase family computing and Internet book titles at the Web sites in the resource section at the end of this chapter.

KEEP TRACK OF WHAT'S ON YOUR HARD DRIVE

After you have an understanding of your computer and operating system, you will want to set some rules for installing software that everyone in the family should follow. Start keeping track of your hard drive's contents. In schools, AUPs should spell out in detail the rules for installing programs onto school computers.

Figure 9.1
Some programs or system software enable you to see which programs or files were last accessed.

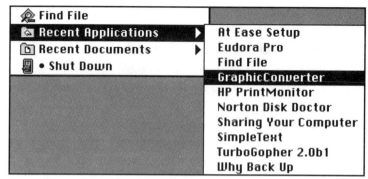

🔍 Find File	
🗂 **Recent Applications** ▶	**At Ease Setup**
🗐 **Recent Documents** ▶	**Eudora Pro**
🖳 • **Shut Down**	**Find File**
	GraphicConverter
	HP PrintMonitor
	Norton Disk Doctor
	Sharing Your Computer
	SimpleText
	TurboGopher 2.0b1
	Why Back Up

Why all the fuss about installing software? Because controlling the programs on your computer is the best way to control *how* the computer is used. The most powerful multimedia machine in the world is only as good as the programs running on it. Here are some tips on software control and maintenance.

☞ If your children buy software with allowance or job money, ask them to clear purchases with you first, just as they might ask permission to rent certain movies. Check your computer workstation for diskettes or manuals for programs that you don't recall buying.

☞ If children are downloading or installing free shareware, the best you can do is frequently scan the computer for programs and see what each one does.

☞ If you find a program with an unfamiliar name, launch it and see what it does. (Programs can be renamed.)

☞ Some programs keep installation logs showing where and when programs were installed. Be sure to check them, too.

The most basic thing you can do, of course, is to just turn on the computer now and then and take a look around, especially if you don't use it much yourself. Use the Finder, File Manager, or DOS directory commands to check out all the files and directories on the computer. Take advantage of any Find or Search Files features or programs. Some programs or system software will let you see which programs or files were last accessed. (See Figure 9.1.)

Downloading computer pornography is one of the most common offenses. Search your hard drive's contents for files with .jpg or .gif extensions—two popular graphic file formats for computer images. File names for pornography are often quite revealing themselves, but a clever young computer user might rename those incriminating files. Periodically launch graphic viewer programs to check out all the menu items available. These programs often have an "Open Latest" feature that lets you select the last file viewed. With other programs, selecting "Open File" will also show the names and locations of the last several graphics loaded.

RESTRICT USE OF HELPER APPLICATIONS

You can even go so far as to restrict access to helper applications such as JPEGView or PaintShop Pro, which enable users to view individual graphics or run slide shows. Consider putting these programs on removable media such as a Zip disk or SyQuest cartridge. Or use another utility to prevent them from being launched.

If you restrict access to these programs, a youngster who downloads a picture won't have any means of *looking* at it—unless he uses a Web browser, of course, which has a built-in graphic viewer. If they want to open a graphic file, they will have to come to you first for the helper applications, which can be an especially effective solution in schools. Depending on how you use the computer, you may be able to get by without using *any* helper applications. For instance, you really won't need them at all if your online activities mainly consist of accessing email, gopher, or commercial online services.

USE SOFTWARE TO TRACK COMPUTER USE

Plenty of easy-to-use commercial programs can help parents, teachers, or other computer system administrators track how their computers are being used. If you own a Macintosh, you should consider using a program called At Ease, which comes with most home computer Mac models such as the Performa series. It enables you to determine which areas of the computer particular users can access. See Figure 9.2.

With At Ease running in the background, you can set up your Mac so that your kids can run only educational software or

Figure 9.2
The At Ease
program lets
you customize
your Mac
desktop for
different users
and enables
you to control
which areas of
the computer
particular users
can access.

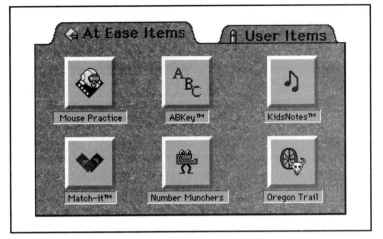

At Ease Items — User Items

Mouse Practice | ABKey™ | KidsNotes™

Match-it™ | Number Munchers | Oregon Trail

games. You can even set up custom desktops for different users.
Your youngest child's desktop might have icons for Mario
Teaches Typing or Tetris. Your teenage son might get access to
ClarisWorks, Myst, or Kaplan's SAT tutor. Mom and Dad's
options might include Excel, MacInTax, and Netscape.

Actually, programs such as At Ease aid in prevention more
than detection. For utilities to help you detect funny business,
check out SolidOak Software's home page. The company, which
makes the CyberSitter filtering and Internet access management program, also produces three Windows/DOS titles parents
or educators might want to check out.

- TattleTale—a Windows 3.1 and 3.11 application designed to
  monitor and restrict computer activity.
- Disk Historian—a Windows 3.1 and 3.11 application for
  monitoring all file activity. Helps you clean up your hard disk
  by providing file usage statistics such as last access, total
  accesses, and more.
- PC-Sentry—a DOS package of utilities that provides security
  and activity monitoring for stand alone PCs and networks.
  URL: http://www.rain.org/~solidoak/

Besides offering filtering capabilities, CyberPatrol gives you
options for controlling and monitoring overall computer use.
You can restrict usage of certain applications or set daily, weekly,
or cumulative time limits. CyberPatrol can also let you view
several charts and graphs to help you track application usage.

Other disk management programs include Norton DiskLock (Symantec), Empower (Magna), DiskGuard, and FileGuard (ASD Software). One particularly powerful program called FolderBolt Pro (Kent Marsh Ltd.) offers several levels of password-protected encryption so that you can protect applications or documents. On a larger, organizational scale, some heavy-duty network management software such as Windows NT is probably in order, if it is not already in place. Check with your local software vendors for system requirements, pricing, and availability.

Numerous programs can help you be a better computer detective, but they were not necessarily designed for that purpose. Norton Utilities gives users the ability to "unerase" files from the hard drive. (See Figure 9.3.) With a special Norton extension working behind the scenes, all files deleted will actually remain in a reserved part of the hard drive so that you can choose to recover them at a later date.

This feature is offered so that you can recover important documents you may have accidentally erased. But it also gives you a very revealing look at what has been happening on your hard drive, showing you items that have been deleted and giving you the option of restoring them. Not all items will be restorable, but you can at least check the filenames or get a better idea of how much activity is occurring on your computer. Huge lists of suspect filenames followed by .gif extensions probably means trouble. Keep on the lookout for other ways you can creatively use software you already own to administrate your computer.

LEARN SOME SHAREWARE SECRETS

Anyone who wants to hide information or activities on computers can choose from hundreds of popular shareware tools. Commercial services such as AOL offer thousands of them in their software and computing areas. Knowing about these programs can help you better trace computer activities and "think like a hacker." Fortunately, most of them don't let users hide the *program* used to hide files, so you can poke around a little with your File Manager or Finder for programs with suspect names. If you find one, don't hesitate to ask your child to explain what the program is or why it is on the family computer.

Figure 9.3
Norton Utilities allows users to "unerase" files deleted from the hard drive. All files actually remain in a reserved part of your computer's memory so you can recover them at a later date.

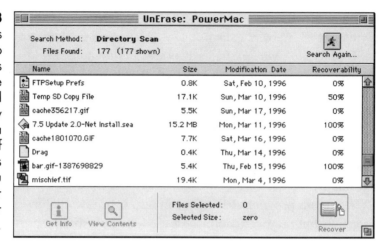

What do these programs do? A little Mac application called Big Secret, for example, turns programs and files stored on hard drives or removable media invisible. Enter a password, select a folder or file, and click "Hide." The folder or file will then be invisible to anyone scanning the hard drive.

Another is called The Big Cheese Key. It enables users to click a single key to instantly replace what is on the screen with a phony spreadsheet or word processor document. Utilities such as Obliterate or FlameFile give users the ability to do such things as make deleted programs unreadable by recovery utilities. Some, such as PowerLock, give users the ability to password protect the entire computer. When the computer starts up, users are given three chances to enter the password before the machine shuts down.

Even seemingly harmless screen saver extensions can be used for illegitimate purposes. Many have features that password-protect the desktop, so that when someone tries to click a key or the mouse to return to computer operations they must first enter a password. In addition to these, there exists a whole separate class of programs and utilities designed not to hide programs and files, but to encrypt them so that only password holders can have access, including MacEncrypt and various PGP (pretty good privacy) encryption utilities.

These kinds of shareware programs are like a double-edged sword. If used properly, parents and teachers can control access to applications and files. AutoLock, for example, lets you quit the Macintosh Finder and lock a single application into the foreground. The flip side is that kids can use these programs to hide unauthorized online activities. So be careful how you use these shareware programs. It is possible to wreck your system by running programs with sloppy programming codes or to forget passwords and have to reformat hard drives. Be warned: These programs can be especially dangerous when used on networks.

Hundreds of shareware security, desktop control, and file utility programs are available for Windows, DOS, and Macintosh computers on numerous ftp sites. The addresses of two of the largest of these software repositories follow. To save time, when you first log in look for documents such as an index or readme file that describe the programs stored in each directory. Print and save these indexes.

- Windows/DOS: **ftp to: oak.oakland.edu.** Select the *SimTel* subdirectory
- Macintosh:**ftp to: mirrors.aol.com.** Select the *pub/mac* subdirectory

MONITOR REMOVABLE MEDIA

Some types of removable media, such as Zip disks or Syquest cartridges, offer cheap and fast storage capabilities that come in handy when your hard drive starts filling up. But they also provide ill-intended youngsters with a place to store graphics or movies. All the special system utilities or protection software in the world won't detect pornographic images stored on a disk that is not *in* the machine. So occasionally scan the contents of any removable devices you own and look for inappropriate materials, just as you would on your hard drive. You might even want to check standard floppies, too, although that can be time consuming.

Some removable storage devices come bundled with special software that lets you password protect entire disks. Review the documentation for programs that come with external drives or removable media to make sure they don't give your youngster the ability to conceal things. Finally, question any requests for more than one or two high-capacity cartridges. What, exactly, is all that storage for?

KEEP INFORMED ABOUT FRIENDS

Your children may have friends who bring computer diskettes or external drives with them when they visit. Or, you may have students who bring disks to school from home. Hooking up one-gigabyte external devices to your computer is not like a Sega Genesis game. Today's storage devices can hold quite a bit of inappropriate material, such as pictures or pirated software. They travel light and install quickly. There is always a risk when a well-meaning but unwise young "computer expert" is hooking up devices that conflict with your hardware when the power is on! Make sure your children and their friends are aware of the house rules of computer use.

On the flip side, you may want to make some rules that your children should follow when using computers or the Internet at a friend's house. Call your child's friend's parents ahead of time and make sure they will be properly supervised as they surf the Net. Make your desires clear to the other parent, as some perceive supervision to mean being in the same building. Find out what programs are on the friend's computer and ask if they have any filtering software.

CHECK FOR ILLEGAL SOFTWARE

One of the easiest things to do is to regularly monitor your computer for illegal software. It is pretty difficult to consistently hide large programs on the family computer *and* conceal their use. (Have you ever heard the *noise* some of these games make?)

Look around on your hard drive, but also check diskette holders for programs that appear to be illegal copies. The popular game Doom does *not* come on five 3M floppy disks with hand-written labels. And there should almost always be an accompanying box with a registration card and user manuals. Watch for friends who bring over glossy Rebel Assault or Microsoft Golf software boxes full of diskettes. It's illegal to install more than one copy of a game or program even temporarily. It is always possible to download pirated software from the Internet or a local bulletin board, so look for massive files with names such as bloodbath.sit.hqx or myst.zip. Also look for directories containing disk images, which are used to get around programs that require installation from the original diskettes by enabling direct desktop mounting.

KNOW THE DIFFERENCE BETWEEN SHAREWARE AND COMMERCIAL PROGRAMS

If you are unsure as to whether a game or program is a legitimate shareware program or a pirated commercial program, launch the application and see if a "Shareware reminder—please pay $10" message pops up. Most shareware programs have them. Almost all of these programs come with several documents or forms you can use to order the full version. Look for these as well.

You can usually tell by the quality and robustness of a game whether or not it is shareware. For instance, if you hear your son getting excited about finishing the 10th level of Dark Forces—but you never *purchased* Dark Forces—it is probably an illegal copy. There are demo copies of such games, but they usually include only one or two levels and/or leave out some functionality, such as cut-scenes, soundtracks, the ability to save games, and so forth.

HOW INTERNET SOFTWARE CAN HELP

The best tools for controlling and monitoring Internet usage are blocking and filtering programs such as SurfWatch and CyberPatrol, which we addressed earlier. However, many Internet programs have some built-in functions that could help you discover if your children are accessing materials that are off-limits—as long as your kids don't figure out how to use those very same functions! We will focus mainly on a few key Web browser, newsreader, and email functions. Always be sure to read the documentation for Internet programs thoroughly. Spend some time using them to learn what they can or cannot do.

WEB BROWSERS AS NET TRACKERS

Netscape and some other Web browsers have features that can help you retrace steps through cyberspace. Most obvious are the

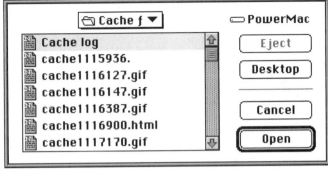

Figure 9.4
You can monitor your child's Internet use by looking into your Web browser's "cache," which saves previously viewed pages. Pages in the cache clear only when they're removed manually or the browser reaches its storage limit.

followed link indicators. Sites that have been visited show up as purple or red hyperlinks. Sites that have not been visited are usually represented by blue links. It's probably not a good idea to rely on that alone, however, since it is pretty easy to reset the links so that they *all* appear to be unfollowed. You can make sure your children know that they cannot reset the links without your permission, and that you will take appropriate action should someone reset them.

A somewhat better approach is to learn how your Web browser "caches," or saves previously viewed pages. Pages you visit on the Web, including text and graphics, are stored in a cache or "holding" directory until you manually clear the cache or until the browser reaches its cache limit. Then it begins writing over cached pages with newly visited pages. Retrieving a page from the cache speeds up page loading, since you don't have to retrieve the same pages from the server each time. By accessing the cache, you can look at the pages viewed over many past sessions. See Figure 9.4.

To open a page stored in Netscape's cache memory, load your browser and select *Open File*. Locate the Netscape folder within your system folder. (In Mac, look in System Folder, Preferences. In Windows, look for a Cache directory in your main Netscape directory.) You can scan a list of files stored in the cache. Double-click on one to view the contents.

You can also open the cache log (Mac) or fat (Windows) file to see a complete text listing of all the pages stored in the cache. This technique lets you see the complete URL of the Web page accessed, along with the date the page was visited and the names of graphics on those pages. As with the followed links feature, unfortunately, it is relatively easy to reset the software so that all information about previous Web access is erased. Again, you can rule that followed links and cached pages cannot be reset. Make it clear that tampering with these files will result in loss of computer or Internet privileges or some other punishment.

To get usage logs that can't be altered by the person operating the browser—and to restrict what realms of the Internet are accessible with your dial-in account—you may want to investigate connecting to the Web through a "network proxy." A network proxy, most often used to access the Internet from behind a firewall, is a conduit between your computer and the Internet. All outgoing requests for information and incoming data are checked by this proxy against a set of predefined access rules. Proxies can be used only with Web, gopher, WAIS, and FTP applications. Ask your Internet Service Provider or school's technology coordinator for more information on using proxy servers.

For complete information about using all of Netscape's features, look at its online handbook by selecting Handbook from the program's Help menu or by using the following address.

http://home.netscape.com/eng/mozilla/2.0/handbook/

MONITOR USE OF USENET NEWSREADERS

You can monitor someone's Usenet newsreading routines in several ways. First, realize that many newsreading programs let users create distinct collections of newsgroups, such as "Brad's sports newsgroups" or "Jane's music groups." To do this, you drag and drop newsgroups from a full group list into a new, blank window, then save that window with a name. Only the main or full group list may show up when you first start your newsreader software, but that doesn't mean that your child hasn't created and hidden a customized collection of groups somewhere else on the computer.

Make sure you understand how the subscribe and unsubscribe function of a newsgroup works—it has its limitations when it comes to controlling access. A teacher or parent can go through the full list of newsgroups, subscribe to the good ones, and unsubscribe to the bad ones. The problem is that, in many cases, the label "subscribed" is misleading.

Often times, subscribed groups are really nothing more than groups that are somehow singled out from the "unsub-scribed" groups, much like the custom newsgroup collections. The unsubscribed groups are available—they just aren't initially *displayed*. Parents or teachers are mistaken if they believe that unsubscribing from an erotica newsgroup means they have blocked access to it. The fact is, with most news-readers any group available from your news server can be accessed, regardless of how you have classified it on your computer with your software preferences. And even if you have taken groups off the list, a user can select a menu item called Rebuild Full Group List to reload all of the groups again.

If you have ever scanned the whole group list thinking that "unsubscribing" to all the nasty groups prevented access to them, think again. The flip side to this is when a young person "subscribes" only to groups you approve, and "unsubscribes" to groups you would frown upon, hoping you will believe that he therefore cannot access the unsubscribed groups. What can you do? Figure out how your newsreader program handles subscribed and unsubscribed groups before you decide that everything is on the up-and-up.

Similarly, recognize that some newsreader programs display read (and unread) articles or subscribed (and unsubscribed) groups in different colors than unread or unsubscribed articles and groups. This is similar to the way Netscape displays follow links in different colors. This feature can also be misused to hide online activity in newsgroups. Users can change the text color of subscribed groups in the full group list to white so that they are not visible to anyone scanning the list—the white text on a white background renders it invisible. Or they can simply mark articles or groups which have been accessed as unread to cover their tracks. Those articles or groups then revert to the color specified for unread articles or groups.

Also like Web browser software, many newsreading programs keep a log of activities. (See Figure 9.5.) Like the Netscape cache, logs show when and how newsreader software is used. Check your particular software to see if it has a Generate Log option. While somewhat cryptic, you can at least see the names of groups accessed. Again, however, the log is similar to the Netscape cache. Since it is just a text file, the log can be easily deleted or altered.

In the end, your best bet for monitoring or controlling access to Usenet newsgroups is to employ a special software filtering program. You can also contact your Internet Service Provider and ask about removing certain groups from its newsfeed. They may not do so if only one or two people ask, but if you can demonstrate that a majority of users would rather do without the alt.sex hierarchy, they may act.

Be aware, though, that even if your provider drops some of the bad groups, there are several news servers that anyone can access, regardless of the newsfeed their provider carries. This is done by simply changing the newsreader's server configuration from your provider's news server address to the address of a public server.

One interesting way to see if your young charges have been in the wrong newsgroups is to run a search through DejaNews. If they have spent any time in a particular group, they may have

Figure 9.5

Like your Web browser's cache, many newsreading programs keep a log of activities.

Figure 9.6
With DejaNews,
you can check if
your child has
participated in
conversations in
any particular
newsgroup by
doing a key word
search.

Deja News Results of Query: Vince DiStefano

16 Hits:

Date	Scr	Subject	Newsgroup	Author
1. 03/13	032	Hard Rock Cafe	**alt.fan.cfny**	DISTEFANO VINCENZO
2. 03/13	032	Re: Rollins in Montreal,	**alt.fan.henry-rollin**	DISTEFANO VINCENZO
3. 03/14	030	Re: Rollins in Montreal,	**alt.fan.henry-rollin**	wwj@execpc.com
4. 01/13	029	Norton Utilities 3.2 wor	**comp.sys.mac.misc**	vince@success.net (V
5. 01/24	027	Adobe Catalog--can it pr	**comp.text.pdf**	vince@godfrey.com (V
6. 01/17	027	Re: EUDORA PRO!	**comp.sys.mac.misc**	vince@godfrey.com (V
7. 01/17	027	Re: **WANTED** converter	**comp.sys.mac.misc**	vince@godfrey.com (V
8. 01/17	027	Re: CPU Speed of PB190	**comp.sys.mac.misc**	vince@godfrey.com (V
9. 02/14	026	K12>...How to Cite I#2/2	**comp.internet.net-ha**	Gleason Sackman <sac
10. 02/13	026	...How to Cite Inter#2/2	**schl.sig.hmnet**	Tim McLain <tmc@CLAS
11. 01/15	026	Re: Norton Utilities 3.2	**comp.sys.mac.misc**	hemiro@pi.net (Henny
12. 01/14	026	Re: Norton Utilities 3.2	**comp.sys.mac.misc**	John Brandwood <jcb@
13. 01/25	025	Re: Adobe Catalog--can i	**comp.text.pdf**	100126.1304@compuser
14. 01/14	025	Re: Norton Utilities 3.2	**comp.sys.mac.misc**	ttha@uhura.cc.roches
15. 01/13	025	Re: Norton Utilities 3.2	**comp.sys.mac.misc**	frankt@qni.com (Fran
16. 02/11	024	Re: Free Public News Ser	**alt.newbie**	a.priest@cowan.edu.a

posted a question or request to the group at some point. Simply type his or her name in as keywords in the search field on the DejaNews Web site. You will get a page of hyperlinks you can click on to read articles in Usenet containing those keywords. See Figure 9.6.

THINK TWICE BEFORE READING EMAIL

Checking up on your child's email habits should really be done only if you suspect that he or she is communicating with a potentially dangerous person or accessing dangerous information about drugs, sex, and the like. Otherwise, reading a child's email is tantamount to listening in on phone calls or opening postal letters. Your ISP probably wouldn't turn over your son's or daughter's email messages to you, even if you are the one paying the monthly bill. If you *must* monitor your youngster's email activities, consider these methods.

- Look for messages stored in the "Sent Mail" and "Deleted Mail" areas as well as the new mail area.
- Set your email program so that it automatically forwards a copy of outgoing messages to any separate email addresses you might have, such as an America Online or Prodigy account.

◌• Configure your email program so that messages are not deleted from the host email server for a certain period of time after they are downloaded. Then you can go back later to retrieve messages even if they are deleted from within your email program. By the way, you can set your software to reject any messages from the server that are over 10K or so. That will at least keep anyone from sending large graphic files or illegal software to your child via email. See Figure 9.7

◌• If you *really* suspect the worst, periodically log on and check email messages as if you were your son or daughter, using his or her password to retrieve new messages from the server. That way you will get a chance to scan messages for dangerous developments before messages can be read and discarded.

OTHER NET TOOLS

We mentioned earlier that we were covering Web browsers, newsreaders, and email programs, but we will quickly mention just a few aspects of ftp, telnet, and IRC use that you can investigate.

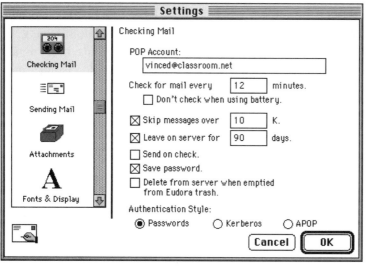

Figure 9.7
The Eudora email program allows you to configure the software to your specifications. For example, you can set the software to reject messages over 10K, which could prevent people from sending questionable graphic files or illegal software to your child.

Track ftp Use via Your Hard Drive

Since ftp programs are used for retrieving documents and programs from remote computers, the best way to find out what's being downloaded is to use the techniques we mentioned to keep tabs on your hard drive.

In addition, some ftp programs offer customizable "shortcuts" or bookmark features that are similar to those in Web browsers. Check ftp addresses or use them to connect to a site and see where you end up and what kinds of files are offered. Also, certain ftp programs may keep logs of past activities—check your software documentation for more information.

Try Logging IRC and Telnet Sessions

In theory at least, it is easy to find out what your kids have been doing during Internet Relay Chat or telnet sessions. But in practice, however, it is a bit more difficult. You can track all Internet Relay Chat or telnet usage by logging all sessions, which means that all sequences, actions, and information viewed during an IRC or telnet session will be stored in a file on your hard drive.

The problem is that logging even short sessions is hard work for computers. Capturing all the session information requires lots of processor power and hard drive space. Fortunately, telnet isn't used too often for covert activities, and IRC is probably the most expendable tool in your Internet software collection. You can probably get by without having an IRC program, since IRC chats often expose children to vulgar and offensive language and their educational value is not yet clear.

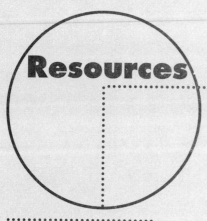

Resources LEARN MORE ABOUT IT!

Related Internet Sites

◻ **Network Management: A System Administrator's Perspective**
URL: http://www.erg.cuhk.hk/~shlam/workshop/

◻ **Software Management Resource Center**
URL: http://www.express-systems.com/default.html

◻ **Steve and Ruth Bennet's Family Surfboard**
URL: http://www.familysurf.com

◻ **FamilyPC on the Web**
URL: http://www.zdnet.com/familypc/

◻ **Computer Life**
URL: http://www.ziff.com/~complife/

Publishers

◻ **Que Publishing Home Page**
URL: http://www.mcp.com/que/

◻ **Ventana Online Book Shop**
URL: http://www.vmedia.com/cat/

◻ **Welcome to Prentice Hall**
URL: http://www.prenhall.com

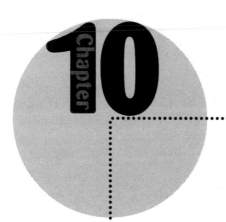

10 POLICE THE NET

By now, you are aware of the possible dangers lurking on the Internet, and are aware that your children may intentionally or inadvertently access something disagreeable.

In the real world you would probably call the police if a strange man was harassing your teenage daughter or sending pornographic images to your young son. But what action do you take in the amorphous online world?

WHAT TO DO IF SOMETHING BAD HAPPENS WHILE ON THE NET

It's only fitting that the last chapter of this book deals with what to do *after* a bad experience on the Internet. By now, you know a good deal about the dangers of the Internet and how to prevent children from having inappropriate experiences. Your children know the rules of behavior in the online world. They are ready to bear the special responsibility that comes with using the world's largest communications network. But you realize, nonetheless, that children may misuse the Internet or they may find something "bad" by accident.

What should you do about that harassing email message your daughter received yesterday—besides change her email address? What should you do about the person who forwarded your son pornographic images—even if your son asked for them—from an America Online chat room?

In the real world, you would probably call the police if your daughter received harassing phone calls or postal letters. The police might contact postal inspectors or the phone company to track the offender. If you found your son with a pornographic magazine or video, you might call the local adult book store or video store and complain to the owner. You could notify authorities that your underage son was able to purchase pornography, and demand that the store be fined or shut down.

But what action can you take in the online world if either of these things happen? How can you track down the people who harass you and then report their activities to some kind of authority? Can you make them pay for their misbehavior, so others are discouraged from engaging in similar activities?

In short, you probably can't expect to achieve the same outcomes as you would in the real world. The anonymous nature of the Internet complicates efforts to make irresponsible Internet users own up to their actions.

HOW CYBERANGELS WOULD MAKE THE NET SAFER

The CyberAngels, an organization begun by the Guardian Angels, offers interesting ideas on how to deal with the inherent difficulty of tracking down online offenders. They compare the Internet to a riot, in which people feel more free to act irresponsibly because of the anonymity afforded. Although some suggestions may seem extreme, they bring attention to the problems of catching cybercriminals. Changes the CyberAngels advocate to bring safety to the Net include:

- Improving user identification, which is currently almost impossible to verify or effectively trace. "The very anonymity of users," the organization states, "is itself causing an increase in rudeness, sexual abuse, flaming, and crimes like pedophile activity. We the Net Users must take responsibility for the problem ourselves. One of our demands is for more accountable User IDs on the Net. When people are anonymous they are also free to be criminals. In a riot you see rioters wearing masks to disguise their true identity. The same thing is happening online. We would like to see User ID much more thoroughly checked by Internet Service Providers."
- Better enforcement of Internet Service Providers' terms-of-service contracts or acceptable-use policies. ISPs must take a more active role in finding and eliminating violations of their user contracts, rather than turning a blind eye.
- Creating a worldwide "blacklist of known cybercriminals, circulated to all providers and regularly updated, so that these people could be denied access to Internet accounts." This is equivalent to the efforts of many communities toward identifying rapists or child molesters who move into their neighborhoods. The constitutionality and feasibility of this is still in question.

> The fact that the Net is impossible to maintain crime-free is no reason for us to do nothing. Each person does their part. If everyone picked up their own trash, there would be no need for garbage collectors. The same could be said of our streets. We are not naively hoping to eliminate crime from the Net, only to play our part in protecting the innocent majority from the violations of the tiny minority.
> —The CyberAngels

INFO BYTE

What to Do if Your Child Accesses Disturbing Material

The issue of child safety on the Internet is an indication of our technologically advancing society. Safety precautions must be updated to reflect the demands of the modern world. As with movies, television, and books, all material available via the Internet is not suitable for children. But you are already aware of this. The question remains:

> What do you if your child accidentally accesses an inappropriate item on the Internet or experiences an unfortunate situation?

Even though you may have employed all of the safety precautions discussed in this book, your child may still confront some illicit or damaging online material. Luckily, most events, such as a child viewing a nude or sexy photo, are not serious, and in many cases just require a discussion and the sharing of parental views. If, as a parent, you feel that your child has seen something more disturbing or serious, you may need to consult professionals such as school guidance counselors or school psychologists. In the worst scenario, serious incidents, like harassment, may necessitate individual counseling, notifying your Internet Service Provider, or alerting law enforcement.

If you feel your child is acting particularly distressed about something witnessed on the Internet, you may want to consult a professional psychologist. But remember that interventions of this type have to be specific to the individual needs of the patient and his or her unique situation. Seeking psychiatric help depends on what the child saw, his or her age/development level, and how the child responds to it. Psychologists believe it would be inappropriate to suggest intervention without knowing all the information and personally evaluating the situation.

For example the majority of children would not have any long term effects from limited exposure to one horrific photo. But if parental discussion doesn't seem to significantly ease the child's anxiety, and he or she is still stressed a week later, professional help may be warranted.

If your youngster is somehow contacted by a harassing adult, he or she should ignore the person's messages or phone calls, and tell you immediately. Depending on your perception of danger in such a case, you may be wise to contact law enforcement. Certainly, the proper authorities would want to know about any direct threats to your child or family.

Although the dangers of the Internet may seem daunting, don't be discouraged. The Net is still a great place for children and adults to learn and have fun. If you employ the safety tips discussed in this book, you decrease the chances of your children encountering unwelcomed situations. With just a little effort, you can really make the Internet safer than a trip to the local library. A whole global classroom is available to you and your children from the comfort of the family home.

—*Peter Borghese*

COLLECTING EVIDENCE OF NET INCIDENTS

As you travel the Net's roads with your family, it's important to have some kind of strategy for collecting evidence should something undesirable happen. Always be sure to record at least the date and time of bad experiences. Write down as specific a description as you can. In school settings, the AUP should provide guidelines for procedures in the wake of an online incident.

You can always save email messages and newsgroup posts, or write down Web site addresses so you can pass them on to an ISP or enforcement agency. (Hint: If you print out a Web page be sure to write the URL on the hard copy since it is usually not included in the Web page text). Make sure you are familiar with all of your software's "Save As" functions, which let you save virtually any document you encounter on the Internet as ASCII text.

Screen capture programs are especially handy in some situations. If you connect to a CU-SeeMe videoconferencing site to chat with some friends, but an unscrupulous individual flashes himself in front of the camera (it has happened), a screen capture utility enables you to quickly press a few keys and save the image to your hard drive. (See Figure 10.1.) Using the information you captured, you could locate the individual's ISP and forward the screen capture. Encourage them to take action.

Plenty of great shareware screen capture programs are available online, most with features that let you draw boxes around areas you wish to capture, select active windows for captures, and save the screen shot to a variety of graphic formats. Here are pointers to two screen capture utilities, ScreenSnap (Macintosh) and PaintShop Pro (Windows). Load your favorite Web search engine and enter "screen capture" for your keywords to find links to dozens of other capture utilities:

- ScreenSnap (Mac)
  ftp to: ftp.classroom.net
  Select the *wentworth/Clip-Art/Utilities/MAC* subdirectory and retrieve *Screen_Snap2.4.sit.*
- PaintShop Pro (Windows)
  ftp to: ftp.classroom.net
  Select the *wentworth/Clip-Art/Utilities/IBM-PC* subdirectory and retrieve *PSP30.zip.*

FIRST, TAKE CARE OF THINGS AT HOME

Before calling someone on their inappropriate behavior online or turning them in for illegal activities, make sure you first understand your child's role in the matter. Determine whether your son or daughter played a part in the objectionable activity, or whether somebody else is completely responsible. Assess the seriousness of any damage that has been done.

Some incidents will require you to give a simple, honest explanation to your child, such as: "Not everyone on the Internet is a nice person." Bad situations can be turned into learning experiences when you help children understand what has happened. If someone sends a child a message containing foul language, explain why the behavior is unacceptable and discuss why a person might be tempted to act in such a manner.

Other cases may require much more follow-up. For example, if someone sent your child pornographic pictures, you will need to do much more than delete the files and tell your child that the person who sent them isn't nice. Child pornography, images of violence and gore, and personal threats need to be taken very seriously. They my warrant the intervention of a family counselor or child psychologist.

Figure 10.1
A CU-SeeMe camera makes videoconferencing easy. Unfortunately, it can also be misused by a prankster who thinks it would be funny to "flash" in front of the camera.

SECOND, ASK THEM TO STOP!

It may seem like an obvious thing to do, but many people never consider simply *asking* someone to stop offensive online behavior. Perhaps they think it will only encourage the individual further or escalate the situation. Or perhaps they think that such a request would just be ignored, which could very well be the case. Whether you respond directly to someone really depends on the situation and severity of the situation. If it is a pretty lightweight offense—perhaps someone sent you an off-color joke or posted a message in a newsgroup with mildly vulgar language, it probably won't hurt to send the person a firm message asking him to stop.

Stephen Bell, a member of the Children Accessing Controversial Information mailing list (see Chapter 8), tells how he encountered a particularly offensive individual while reading a newsgroup with his daughter. They were looking for information on a celebrity who had just tragically died. Somebody in the group posted an insensitive, explicit description of an obscene photo in which this celebrity was supposedly depicted (apparently, there really was no such photo).

"Apart from anything else," he explains, the article heading in the newsgroup "was a gross insult to a recently deceased person. The address of the poster was clearly fictitious, so I posted a message in the group concerned, outlining what had happened and saying it was not appreciated. I got no reply, but I hope the conscience of the poster, and of others, was stung."

Sometimes just telling the offender that you are offended is enough. In fact, it's possible the person didn't realize he was being overly offensive or that his words might hurt others. A reply such as Bell's might make the offender think twice about what he says in the future. In fact, the person posting that particular message could have been someone as young or inexperienced as your own child, unaware of the implications of what he or she was saying or maybe just trying to stir things up a little. A gentle admonition just might work.

If you are ever unsure as to what kind of reception your reproach will receive, it is best to leave the situation alone. Do not get directly involved by stirring up a hornet's nest in a newsgroup or on a mailing list.

ANONYMOUS REMAILERS AID THE IRRESPONSIBLE

People who want to send anonymous email messages can use something called "anonymous remailer services" to make sure their messages can't be traced back to their source. (See Figure 10.2.) A recipient of an anonymous email message can even respond to the message because the remailer forwards replies to the sender. The most famous anonymous forwarding service has almost half a million users sending almost 10,000 messages per day. You can even use this remailer to post messages to newsgroups anonymously.

But the remailer does keep standard database records of all the anonymous addresses and their corresponding real email addresses. It is possible that someone could obtain the database information and discover the true identities of remailers. But most remailers take steps to prevent that from happening by encrypting the user databases: putting the information into codes no one can break. The code protects those sending messages, but

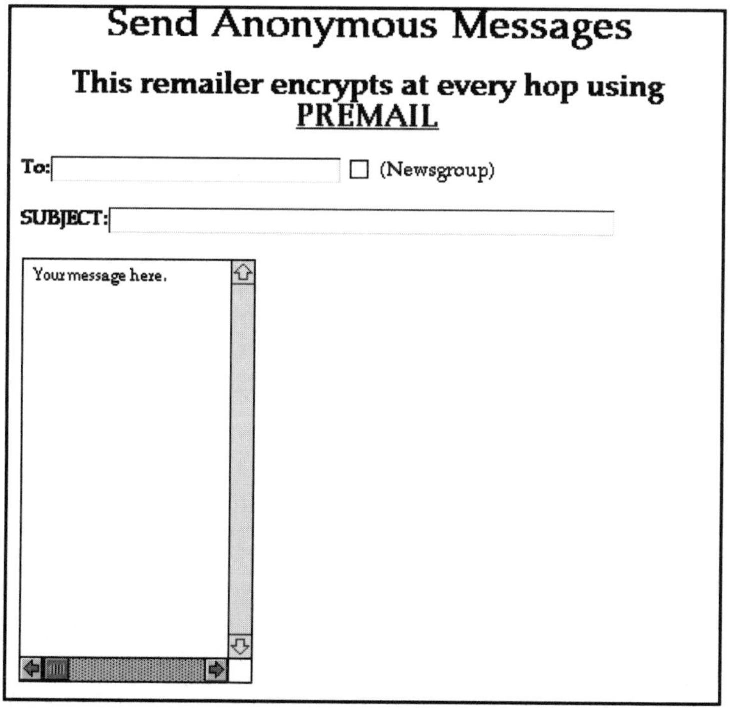

Figure 10.2
An anonymous remailer can send anonymous email messages that can't be traced back to their source. Most pedophiles and others trafficking in illegal activities take advantage of this service.

also makes it impossible for law enforcement agencies to track online pedophiles who take advantage of this service.

With just a little research, even the newest Internet users can figure out how to use these services to send email or post to newsgroups anonymously. In fact, you no longer have to read through lengthy FAQs to figure out how to do it, because many Web-based services make it as easy as point-and-click.

Apart from remailers, the changing nature of the Internet provides many ways for the irresponsible to hide. Email, ftp, and Web addresses can be changed quickly at the first sign that an authority may act. A pornographic image you stumble across on the Web might be here today, somewhere else tomorrow. The Net is an exciting, dynamic place, but as law enforcement officials and "cybercops" know, its constant evolution makes it difficult to hold people accountable and seek justice.

CONTACT THE SYSTEM ADMINISTRATOR, NOT THE CRIMINAL

Sometimes it will be *very* apparent that you shouldn't directly confront an individual. If someone posts threatening messages, or claims to live in your area or know who you are, it is not worth inviting more trouble. CyberAngels provides this guidance for its volunteers:

> We do not encourage our volunteers to identify themselves online. We DO NOT advise our volunteers to challenge cybercriminals directly, neither by arguing in live areas, nor by flaming in emails, nor by counter-postings on message boards or newsgroups. Being a CyberAngel involves no risk or danger. You are volunteering only to be eyes watching the Net. Please follow our advice and DO NOT attempt to challenge cybercriminals directly. Simply report the violations to us . . . and also to the system administrators, or service providers, of the cybercriminal. Email can usually be sent to "postmaster@ . . ." or "sysop@ . . ." or "sysadmin@ . . . ", or find out by writing to or calling the company (the cybercriminal's service provider) and asking them who you contact to report a violation.

This is pretty good advice. Usually, it is a good idea to let the offender's ISP initiate contact or take steps to stop him from doing further harm. They most likely know exactly who to contact in cases of email harassment, child pornography, or online pedophilia. You can use certain software to track down contact information for someone's Internet Service Provider or system administrator.

SOFTWARE TO TRACK DOWN INTERNAUTS

If you have a fair amount of online experience and some free time, you can become an online detective by trying some of the following Internet tools. They help you locate information about other users.

If you are dealing with a specific incident, a more effective route will be to contact your own Internet Service Provider, explain the problem, and ask if they can locate and contact the offender's ISP for further action. For example, if someone named joe@online.service.com has been sending you harassing email, your ISP may be able to quickly locate and notify this user's provider and get results faster—without any risk of retribution to you or your family.

HOW TO USE FINGER

Finger can help you find specific information about an individual based on his or her email address or host computer. You can enter the user name and host-machine name or just the host-machine name in hopes of getting contact information for the system administrator. (You cannot, however, enter just a user name without host information.) Entering just the machine name rarely works with Finger, however. For better results, do a Whois lookup on a domain name to find out who administrates a particular Internet site.

Figure 10.3 provides an example of how you would use a Finger client to find information about a person whose email address is tmc@classroom.net.

Unfortunately, the only information you can expect to get about a particular person is information the person included in their plan or info file, if they have one at all. (Most times, a plan is created automatically when a user gets an account through an

Figure 10. 3
The result of using a Finger client to find info about a person whose email address is tmc@classroom.net.

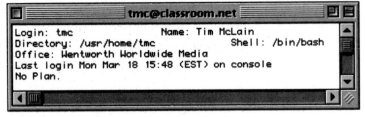

```
Login: tmc              Name: Tim McLain
Directory: /usr/home/tmc              Shell: /bin/bash
Office: Wentworth Worldwide Media
Last login Mon Mar 18 15:48 (EST) on console
No Plan.
```

Figure 10.4
By using Finger, we were able to find this person's full name and the name of the company hosting his email address.

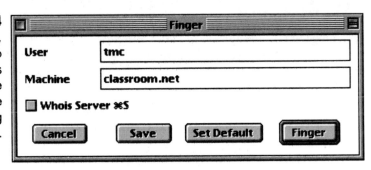

Finger

| User | tmc |
| Machine | classroom.net |

☐ Whois Server ⌘S

Cancel   Save   Set Default   Finger

Figure 10.5
This Finger query netted a little more information.

```
Login name: jwolfe       In real life: John G. Wolfe
Directory: /usr/users/jwolfe          Shell: /bin/ksh
Last login Thu Oct 12 14:21 on :0
No Plan.

Login name: john         In real life: John Banghart
Office: SuperNet, 3937635
Directory: /usr/users/john            Shell: /bin/csh
Last login Mon Mar 18 08:59 on ttyp1 from lily.redrose.net
No Plan.
```

ISP. It includes your real name, service provider name, and perhaps even an address and phone number.) Back in the days when the (much smaller) Internet was mainly the province of scientists and network engineers, many more users maintained plans. Today, though, with millions of people who have little network knowledge connected to the Internet, relatively few users have Finger information files.

To return to the example, by Fingering user tmc@classroom.net, we at least get the person's full name and name of the company hosting his email address. Of course, we have to hope that this information isn't fictional, but at least it's something to go on. (See Figure 10.4.)

Figure 10.5 provides an example of a Finger query that netted a little more information. Fingering john@success.net provides details on two people who use the success.net Internet computer, including a phone number for one of the users.

Besides using Finger client software or UNIX command lines to Finger, you can also access Finger via the World Wide Web.

URL: http://www.cs.indiana.edu:800/Finger/gateway

HOW TO USE WHOIS

Whois is another application for looking up somebody on the Internet. It's often used by network administrators to determine whether a username is valid. Instead of contacting the user's or host's machine for an individual's plan file, Whois does a lookup on InterNIC's database. The database contains administrative and technical contact information for entire networks, including email and postal addresses, telephone numbers of network users, data about networks and domains, and more. Graphical programs such as WinWhois make it easy to do Whois lookups.

A Whois query via InterNIC will only work if a site has a registered domain name. That's because the information for this database is gathered when organizations register their domain names. If a site has no domain name (instead of something.com, the address is 198.51.43.86), then it does not have to register with InterNIC, and therefore does not have to enter their information into the database.

Besides the InterNIC Whois database, several databases are independently maintained by Internet sites that provide information about their own staff members or students. If you'd like to do a Whois lookup, you can access a comprehensive directory of all the Whois servers located at business, government organizations, and universities around the world at the gopher site below.

If you know that an individual is sending mail from the University of Maryland, for example (perhaps the email address ends with umd.edu), you can target the university's Whois database to find more information.

Gopher to: sipb.mit.edu

Look in *Internet Whois servers*. Visit the gopher site for links to dozens of non-InterNIC Whois databases.

Figure 10.6

This is a typical response to a Whois query.

```
[vt220] InterNIC > whois networkings.com
Connecting to the rs Database . . . . . .
Connected to the rs Database
NetWork Interactive Services (NETWORKINGS-DOM)
    1613A Chadwick Circle
    Lancaster, PA 17603
    USA

Domain Name: NETWORKINGS.COM

Administrative Contact:
    Ryan, Dave  (DR601)  dryan@WENTWORTH.COM
    (717) 627-4757
Technical Contact, Zone Contact:
    Banghart, John [System Administrator]  (JB326)  admin@SUCCESS.NET
    (717) 738-7059

Record last updated on 03-Oct-95.
Record created on 03-Oct-95.

Domain servers in listed order:

HOST1.REDROSE.NET            204.249.184.2
```

If you don't have access to a graphical Internet account, you can also use telnet to access the InterNIC Whois database.

Telnet to: Whois.internic.net

Type WHOIS at the prompt to launch the remote lookup program. Then type WHOIS plus the domain name for which you'd like information. In a few seconds you'll get a response like the one in Figure 10.6.

WHERE TO FIND FINGER/WHOIS CLIENT SOFTWARE

You can choose from a variety of freeware and shareware Finger and Whois clients on the Internet. Most are pretty easy to use because they employ graphical interfaces and menu commands. Those with some UNIX experience may prefer to use standard UNIX commands to look up information about people and places on the Net. Note that Macintosh users can use the same Finger program used in the examples above to do Whois lookups by simply checking the Whois Server box.

◯∘ Finger and Whois for Windows 95
    URL: http://ns2.helenet.com/tx/computer/cadl/95ftp.html
◯∘ Finger and Whois for Windows 3.11
    URL: http://www.is.co.za/resources/ftpsite/tucows/softfin.html

- Mac Finger/Whois program from Classroom Connect ftpsite
  ftp to: ftp.classroom.net
  Select the *wentworth/Internet-Software/Mac* subdirectory
  and look for *Finger.sea*.
- DOS Finger client from Classroom Connect ftp site:
  ftp to: ftp.classroom.net
  Select the *wentworth/Internet-Software/IBM* subdirectory
  and look for *Finger.exe*.

TRACKING DOWN USENET POSTERS

The most effective way to find information about someone posting to a Usenet newsgroup is to run a Finger or Whois lookup
on their email address or host, as described above, or to use
DejaNews. With DejaNews, you can search a large collection of
newsgroup articles by email address or name. You may not get a
specific name, address, or phone number, but DejaNews may
generate a comprehensive report of all the person's posts over
the past few years. Scan through the posts for clues that would
help you or a law enforcement agency locate the individual.

Figure 10.7 shows an example of a DejaNews search on the
email address **tmc@classroom.net**. You can either click on an article
subject (middle) to read the post, or click on the author's email
address (far right) to get an "Author Profile" that shows all the

Deja News Results of Query:	Tim McLain

38 Hits:

Date	Scr	Subject	Newsgroup	Author
1. 03/09	022	Re: WWW publication/AUPs	**k12.ed.tech**	tmc@wentworth.com (T
2. 01/31	022	Re: Keypal Lists -- Here	**schl.sig.lmnet**	Tim McLain <tmc@CLAS
3. 01/14	022	WTB: Original Newton or	**misc.forsale.compute**	tmc@wentworth.com
4. 01/12	021	VME bus buyer's guide	**comp.arch.bus.vmebus**	tmclain@oz.et.byu.ed
5. 01/25	020	Re: Windows Screen Captu	**schl.sig.lmnet**	Tim McLain <tmc@WEN
6. 01/09	019	"Blizzard Cam" available	**k12.chat.teacher**	tmc@classroom.net (T
7. 03/14	018	BOOK> How do students us	**misc.education.multi**	tmc@wentworth.com
8. 03/14	018	.....How to YOU use the	**k12.chat.senior**	tmc@wentworth.com (T
9. 03/09	018	....BOOK> How do student	**uk.education.teacher**	tmc@wentworth.com (
10. 03/09	018	....BOOK> How do student	**k12.chat.teacher**	tmc@wentworth.com (T
11. 03/09	018	....BOOK> How do student	**k12.ed.health-pe**	tmc@wentworth.com (T
12. 03/09	018	....BOOK> How do student	**k12.lang.art**	tmc@wentworth.com (T
13. 02/13	018	...How to Cite Inter#2/2	**schl.sig.lmnet**	Tim McLain <tmc@CLAS
14. 02/01	018	...Search for K12 Web Si	**k12.ed.comp.literacy**	tmc@classroom.net (T
15. 02/01	018	...Search for K12 Web Si	**k12.chat.teacher**	tmc@classroom.net (T
16. 02/01	018	...Find K12 School Web s	**schl.sig.lmnet**	Tim McLain <tmc@CLAS
17. 02/01	018	Find K12 School Web site	**bit.listserv.edtech**	Tim McLain <tmc@clas
18. 01/04	018	UPDATED> Acceptable Use	**comp.internet.net-ha**	Gleason Sackman <s
19. 01/16	017	Re: Free Microsoft Semin	**slo.general**	tsawchuc@kestrel.pun

Figure 10.7
DejaNews allows
you to search a
massive collection
of newsgroup
articles by email
address or name.

Figure 10.8
It would be easy
to learn more
about
tmc@classroom.net
because his
signature file
includes detailed
contact infor-
mation. This is not
always the case,
as some people
choose to post
anonymously.

Morning all!

Just wanted to remind everyone about Classroom Connect's Keypal listing...
You can add your own calls for keypals to the list, as well as participate
with other classes the world over.

To get a copy of the list, which is updated several times each DAY by the
staff, send email to:

info@classroom.net

...and in the body of the message, type:

send keypals

Enjoy!

:-)

=========================
Tim McLain
Senior Internet Writer
Classroom Connect
Email: tmc@classroom.net
URL: http://www.classroom.net
=========================

newsgroups to which he or she has posted. When you click on a
newsgroup name from this Author Profile screen you're shown
only the posts that the person made to that particular
newsgroup.

By browsing through some of these posts you may be able
to find the person's full name, address, phone number, home
page address, employer, or anything else they might have
included in their various posts to Usenet newsgroups. (See
Figure 10.8.)

In this case, of course, tmc@classroom.net is none other than our
very own Tim McLain—our Internet guru and the head
writer for *Classroom Connect*. It would be pretty easy for
anyone to learn more about who tmc@classroom.net is, since the
signature file for all his posts includes contact information for
his company.

It may not be quite as simple when you search for other
persons, since some people don't include much contact information in their posts, or worse, they post anonymously. We
could have used a more realistic example, but we didn't want to
violate anyone's privacy by publishing such information in this
book.

USER PROFILES ON COMMERCIAL ONLINE SERVICES

If you're having problems with a person on a commercial online service, the first thing you should do is follow the instructions that the service has provided for alerting the service of a problem. America Online, Prodigy, and CompuServe staff members are usually very interested in hearing about activities on the service that violate their Terms of Service agreements. Many people have had their accounts discontinued for inappropriate behavior.

These services realize that, since a large portion of their subscriber base consists of families, it's in their best interest to stop online harassers, pedophiles, and other troublemakers right away. Check with your service's online help area for full information on how and where to post a complaint about an individual or activity.

Most of the commercial online services also offer member directories where you can look up all sorts of information about a user. In America Online, for example, every subscriber can fill out a member profile that includes their name, address, hobbies, and so forth. The problem with this is that the worst offenders are smart enough to know *not* to submit an online profile so they cannot be easily identified. Or else they log on and commit violations with temporary trial accounts or "AOHell" hacker software that lets them freely roam through the service. Your best bet for commercial services is to notify the service and give them as much information as you possibly can about any objectionable activities.

BE VIGILANT

Now that you've seen some of the tools available to you in case of an online incident, you should feel a little better that you at least have *something* to fight back with.

Of course, the best tool you can use is simply being vigilant about your children's or students' activities. By being involved in their online life, you can be ready to jump to their defense should they ever be unfortunate enough to encounter trouble on the Internet.

Resources LEARN MORE ABOUT IT!

Related Internet Sites

⊡ **Guide to Network Resource Tools**
URL: http://www.earn.net/gnrt/s

⊡ **ED3361—Internet Literacy**
URL: http://cnet.unb.ca/nbco/ed3361/index.html

⊡ **Anonymous Email**
URL: http://www.lookup.com/Homepages/64499/anon.html

⊡ **Anonymity and Privacy on the Internet**
URL: http://www.stack.urc.tue.nl/%7Egalactus/remailers/

⊡ **Pretty Good Privacy (PGP) Resource Page**
URL: http://netaccess.on.ca/ugali/crypt/

⊡ **American Psychological Association**
URL: http://www.apa.org

⊡ **APA Warning Signs of Trauma-related Stress**
URL: http://www.apa.org/ptsd.html

⊡ **Traumatic Memories**
URL: http://www.access.digex.net/~sidran/traumabr.html

⊡ **Trauma Affects All Age Groups**
URL: http://ion1.ionet.net/opubco/trauma.html

ACCEPTABLE USE POLICIES

The best way to learn about Acceptable Use Policies is to read actual AUPs schools are using. In this Appendix you'll find the full text of four AUPs and parental consent forms.

Use the Web addresses of these schools to find revisions or updates and to contact staffers to learn more about the policies. These AUPs are not edited for content in any way.

AUP 1: THE BELLINGHAM PUBLIC SCHOOLS

The AUP for Bellingham Public Schools includes language that is a good example of how to explain the Net's value in schools and how it fits in with a particular district's view of its educational mission. Their URL is:

http://www.bham.wednet.edu/

Their AUP is divided into three main sections:

1. The Board Policy on Student Access to Networked Information Resources.
2. Internet and Electronic Mail Permission Form.
3. Copyright Compliance Instruction (See Chapter 7).

For additional information, contact Jamieson McKenzie, Director of Technology. Email to: jmckenzie@msmail.bham.wednet.edu

BOARD POLICY: STUDENT ACCESS
TO NETWORKED INFORMATION RESOURCES
The Board recognizes that as telecommunications and other new technologies shift the ways that information may be accessed, communicated, and transferred by members of the society, those changes may also alter instruction and student learning. The Board generally supports access by students to rich information resources along with the development by staff of appropriate skills to analyze and evaluate such resources. In a free and democratic society, access to information is a fundamental right of citizenship.

Telecommunications, electronic information sources, and networked services significantly alter the information landscape for schools by opening classrooms to a broader array of resources. In the past, instructional and library media materials could usually be screened—prior to use—by committees of educators and community members intent on subjecting all such materials to reasonable selection criteria. Board Policy 2311 requires that all such materials be consistent with district adopted guides, supporting and enriching the curriculum while taking into account the varied instructional needs, learning styles, abilities and developmental levels of the students.

Telecommunications, because they may lead to any publicly available fileserver in the world, will open classrooms to electronic information resources which have not been screened by educators for use by students of various ages.

Electronic information research skills are now fundamental to preparation of citizens and future employees during an Age of Information. The Board expects that staff will blend thoughtful use of such information throughout the curriculum and that the staff will provide guidance and instruction to students in the appropriate use of such resources. Staff will consult the guidelines for instructional materials contained in Board Policy 2311 and will honor the goals for selection of instructional materials contained therein.

Students are responsible for good behavior on school computer networks just as they are in a classroom or a school hallway. Communications on the network are often public in nature. General school rules for behavior and communications apply (see Board Policy 3200). The network is provided for students to conduct research and communicate with others. Access to network services will be provided to students who agree to act in a considerate and responsible manner.

Independent student use of telecommunications and electronic information resources will be permitted upon submission of permission forms and agreement forms by parents of minor students (under 18 years of age) and by students themselves. Regional networks such as WEDNET require agreement by users to acceptable use policies outlining standards for behavior and communication.

Access to telecommunications will enable students to explore thousands of libraries, databases, and bulletin boards while exchanging messages with people throughout the world. The Board believes that the benefits to students from access in the form of information resources and opportunities for collaboration, exceed the disadvantages. But ultimately, parents and guardians of minors are responsible for setting and conveying the standards that their children should follow when using media and information sources. To that end, the Bellingham Public Schools support and respect each family's right to decide whether or not to apply for independent access.

The Board authorizes the Superintendent to prepare appropriate procedures for implementing this policy and for reviewing and evaluating its effect on instruction and student achievement.

INTERNET AND ELECTRONIC MAIL PERMISSION FORM

We are pleased to offer students of the Bellingham Public Schools access to the district computer network for electronic mail and the Internet. To gain access to email and the Internet, all students under the age of 18 must obtain parental permission and must sign and return this form to the Library Media Specialist. Students 18 and over may sign their own forms.

Access to email and the Internet will enable students to explore thousands of libraries, databases, and bulletin boards while exchanging messages with Internet users throughout the world. Families should be warned that some material accessible via the Internet may contain items that are illegal, defamatory, inaccurate, or potentially offensive to some people. While our intent is to make Internet access available to further educational goals and objectives, students may find ways to access other materials as well. We believe that the benefits to students from access to the Internet, in the form of information resources and opportunities for collaboration, exceed any disadvantages. But ultimately, parents and guardians of minors are responsible for setting and conveying the standards that their children should follow when using media and information sources. To that end, the Bellingham Public Schools support and respect each family's right to decide whether or not to apply for access.

DISTRICT INTERNET AND EMAIL RULES

Students are responsible for good behavior on school computer networks just as they are in a classroom or a school hallway. Communications on the network are often public in nature. General school rules for behavior and communications apply.

The network is provided for students so that they may conduct research and communicate with others. Access to network services is given to students who agree to act in a considerate and responsible manner. Parental permission is required. Access is a privilege—not a right. Access entails responsibility.

Individual users of the district computer networks are responsible for their behavior and communications over those networks. It is presumed that users will comply with district standards and will honor the agreements that they have signed. Beyond the clarification of such standards, the district is not responsible for restricting, monitoring, or controlling the communications of any individuals utilizing the network.

Network storage areas may be treated like school lockers. Network administrators may review files and communications to maintain system integrity and insure that users are using the system responsibly.

Users should not expect that files stored on district servers will always be private. Within reason, freedom of speech and access to information will be honored. During school, teachers of younger students will guide them toward appropriate materials. Outside of school, families bear the same responsibility for such guidance as they exercise with information sources such as television, telephones, movies, radio, and other potentially offensive media.

As outlined in Board Policy and Procedures on Student Rights and Responsibilities (3200), copies of which are available in school offices, the following actions are not permitted:

- Sending or displaying offensive messages or pictures
- Using obscene language
- Harassing, insulting, or attacking others
- Damaging computers, computer systems, or computer networks
- Violating copyright laws
- Using another's password
- Trespassing in another's folders, work, or files
- Intentionally wasting limited resources
- Employing the network for commercial purposes

Violations may result in a loss of access as well as other disciplinary or legal action.

USER AGREEMENT AND PARENT PERMISSION FORM—1995
As a user of the Bellingham Public Schools computer network, I hereby agree to comply with the above stated rules—communicating over the network in a reliable fashion while honoring all relevant laws and restrictions.

_____

Student Signature

As the parent or legal guardian of the minor student signing above, I grant permission for my son or daughter to access networked computer services such as electronic mail and the Internet. I understand that individuals and families may be held liable for violations. I understand that some materials on the Internet may be objectionable, but I accept responsibility for guidance of Internet use—setting and conveying standards for my daughter or son to follow when selecting, sharing, or exploring information and media.

Parent Signature _____

Date _____

Name of Student _____

School _____

Grade _____

Social Security Number _____

Birth Date _____

Street Address _____

Home Telephone _____

AUP 2: BOULDER VALLEY SCHOOL DISTRICT

Boulder Valley has been in the forefront of schools implement-ing Internet technology. It includes a teacher/staff application for an Internet account. Its URL is:

http://bvsd.k12.co.us/docs/agreement.html

APPLICATION FOR ACCOUNT AND TERMS
AND CONDITIONS FOR USE

Please read the following carefully before signing the attached contract. This is a legally binding document.

Internet access is now available to students and teachers in the Boulder Valley School District. The access is being offered as part of a collaborative project involving the Boulder Valley School District (BVSD), The University of Colorado at Boulder (UCB), Colorado SuperNet (CSN), WestNet and the National Science Foundation.

We are very pleased to bring this access to Boulder Valley and believe the BVSDNet offers vast, diverse, and unique resources to both students and teachers. Our goal in providing this service to teachers and students is to promote educational excellence in the Boulder Valley Schools by facilitating resource sharing, innovation, and communication.

The BVSDNet is an electronic network which accesses the Internet. The Internet is an electronic highway connecting thousands of computers all over the world and millions of indi-vidual subscribers. Students and teachers have access to elec-tronic mail communication with people all over the world; information and news from NASA as well as the opportunity to correspond with the scientists at NASA and other research insti-tutions; public domain and shareware software of all types; discussion groups on a plethora of topics ranging from Chinese culture to the environment to music to politics; access to many University Library Catalogs, the Library of Congress, CARL and ERIC.

With access to computers and people all over the world also comes the availability of material that may not be considered to be of educational value in the context of the school setting.

BVSD, UCB, and CSN have taken available precautions, which are limited, to restrict access to controversial materials. However, on a global network it is impossible to control all materials and an industrious user may discover controversial information. We (BVSD, UCB, and CSN) firmly believe that the valuable information and interaction available on this worldwide network far outweighs the possibility that users may procure material that is not consistent with the educational goals of this Project.

Internet access is coordinated through a complex association of government agencies and regional and state networks. In addition, the smooth operation of the network relies upon the proper conduct of the end users who must adhere to strict guidelines. These guidelines are provided here so that you are aware of the responsibilities you are about to acquire. In general this requires efficient, ethical and legal utilization of the network resources. If a BVSD user violates any of these provisions, his or her account with BVSDNet will be terminated and future access could possibly be denied.

Your signature(s) on the attached contract is (are) legally binding and indicates the party (parties) who signed has (have) read the terms and conditions carefully and understand(s) their significance.

BVSDNet—Terms and Conditions

1. *Acceptable Use*—The purpose of our use of the Internet, is to support research and education by providing access to unique resources and the opportunity for collaborative work. The use of your account must be in support of education and research and consistent with the educational objectives of the Boulder Valley School District. Use of other organization's networks or computing resources must comply with the rules appropriate for that network. Transmission of any material in violation of any U.S. or state regulation is prohibited. This includes, but is not limited to: copyrighted material, threatening or obscene material, or material protected by trade secret. Use for commercial activities by for-profit institutions is generally not acceptable. Use for product advertisement or political lobbying is also prohibited. Illegal activities are strictly prohibited.

2. *Privileges*—The use of BVSDNet is a privilege, not a right, and inappropriate use will result in a cancellation of those privileges. (Each student who receives an account will be part of a discussion with a BVSD faculty member pertaining to the proper use of the network.) Based upon the acceptable use guidelines outlined in this document, the system administrators will deem what is inappropriate use and their decision is final. Also, the system administrators may close an account at any time as required. The administration, faculty, and staff of BVSD may request the system administrator to deny, revoke, or suspend specific user accounts.

3. *Netiquette*—You are expected to abide by the generally accepted rules of network etiquette. These include (but are not limited to) the following:

   - Be polite. Do not write or send abusive messages to others. Use appropriate language. Do not swear, use vulgarities or any other inappropriate language.
   - Do not reveal your personal address or phone numbers of students or colleagues.
   - Note that electronic mail (email) is not guaranteed to be private. People who operate the system do have access to all mail. Messages relating to or in support of illegal activities may be reported to the authorities.
   - Do not use the network in such a way that you would disrupt the use of the network by other users (e.g. downloading huge files during prime time; sending mass email messages; annoying other users using the talk or write functions).
   - All communications and information accessible via the network should be assumed to be private property.

4. *Reliability*—BVSD, CSN, and UCB make no warranties of any kind, whether expressed or implied, for the service it is providing. BVSD, CSN, and UCB will not be responsible for any damages you suffer. This includes loss of data resulting from delays, nondeliveries, misdeliveries, or service interruptions caused by its own negligence or your errors or omissions. Use of any information obtained via BVSD, CSN, or UCB is at your own risk. BVSD, CSN, and UCB deny any responsibility for the accuracy or quality of information obtained through its services.

5. *Security*—Security on any computer system is a high priority, especially when the system involves many users. If you feel you can identify a security problem on BVSDNet, you must notify a system administrator or email help@bvsd.k12.co.us. Do not demonstrate the problem to other users. Do not use another individual's account without written permission from that individual. Do not give your password to any other individual. Attempts to log in to the system as any other user will result in cancellation of user privileges. Attempts to login to BVSDNet as a system administrator will result in cancellation of user privileges. Any user identified as a security risk or having a history of problems with other computer systems may be denied access to BVSDNet.

6. *Vandalism*—Vandalism will result in cancellation of privileges. Vandalism is defined as any malicious attempt to harm or destroy data of another user, BVSDNet, or any of the above listed agencies or other networks that are connected to CSN, or the NSFNet Internet backbone. This includes, but is not limited to, the uploading or creation of computer viruses.

7. *Updating Your User Information*—BVSDNet may occasionally require new registration and account information from you to continue the service. You must notify BVSDNet of any changes in your account information (address, etc.). Currently, there are no user fees for this service.

8. *Exception of Terms and Conditions*—All terms and conditions as stated in this document are applicable to the Boulder Valley School District, the University of Colorado, in addition to Colorado SuperNet, WestNet, and NSFNet. These terms and conditions reflect the entire agreement of the parties and supersede all prior oral or written agreements and understandings of the parties. These terms and conditions shall be governed and interpreted in accordance with the laws of the State of Colorado, United States of America.

Any Boulder Valley School District student or staff may apply for an Internet Account. To do so you must complete the attached contract and application. Students should return the contract to the person from whom they received the contract. Staff should return the contract to Libby Black in the Curriculum Office at the Ed Center. You may retain this copy of the Terms and Conditions for your files.

STUDENT

Last Name: _____

First Name: _____

Expected Year Of Graduation from 12th grade: _____

Class Period: _____

STUDENT CONTRACT AGREEMENT AND APPLICATION FOR
BOULDER VALLEY SCHOOL DISTRICT INTERNET ACCOUNT
Directions: After reading the BVSDNet Application for Account
and Terms and Conditions (version 2.0) please read and fill out
the appropriate portions of the following contract completely
and legibly. The signature of a parent or guardian is also
required. Please return the contract to your teacher. Any questions should be addressed to your teacher as well.

CONTRACT PORTION OF DOCUMENT
I have read the BVSDNet Terms and Conditions. I understand
and will abide by the stated Terms and Conditions for BVSDNet.
I further understand that violation of the regulations is unethical
and may constitute a criminal offense. Should I commit any violation my access privileges may be revoked, school disciplinary
action may be taken and/or appropriate legal action.

User Name (please print): _____

User Signature: _____

Date: _____

Parent or Guardian _____

(If the applicant is under the age of 18 a parent or guardian most
also read and sign this agreement.) As the parent or Guardian of
this student I have read the Terms and Conditions for BVSDNet
(version 2.0). I understand that this access is designed for educational purposes and BVSD, UCB, and CSN have taken available
precautions to eliminate controversial material.

However, I also recognize it is impossible for BVSD, UCB, or CSN to restrict access to all controversial materials and I will not hold them responsible for materials acquired on the network. Further, I accept full responsibility for supervision if and when my child's use is not in a school setting. I hereby give my permission to issue an account for my child and certify that the information contained on this form is correct.

Parent or Guardian (please print): _____

Signature: _____

Date: _____

Daytime Phone Number: _____

Evening Phone Number: _____

SPONSORING TEACHER

I have read the Terms and Conditions of BVSDNet (version 2.0) and agree to promote this agreement with the student. Because the student may use the network for individual work or in the context of another class, I cannot be held responsible for the student's use of the network. As the sponsoring teacher I do agree to instruct the student on acceptable use of the network and proper network etiquette.

Teacher's Name (please print): _____

Teacher's Signature: _____

Date: _____

APPLICATION PORTION OF DOCUMENT

Student's Full Name (please print): _____

Student ID Number (accounts cannot be issued without this): _____

I expect to graduate from 12th grade in _____ (year).

Your Home Address: _____

_____

_____

Home Phone: _____

Current School: _____

When your account is established your teacher will notify you of your logon name and user password. Thank you for your interest and support of this exciting new resource in the Boulder Valley Schools.

TEACHER/STAFF APPLICATION

Last Name: _____

First Name: _____

Circle One: teacher, media specialist, administrator, support
staff, community member

STAFF CONTRACT AGREEMENT AND APPLICATION FOR BOULDER VALLEY SCHOOL DISTRICT INTERNET ACCOUNT

Directions: After reading the BVSDNet Application for Account and Terms and Conditions (version 2.0) please read and fill out the appropriate portions of the following contract completely and legibly. Please return the contract to Libby Black in the Curriculum Office at the Ed Center.

Full Name (please print): _____

Social Security Number (accounts cannot be issued without this): _____

Home Address: _____

_____

_____

Home Phone: _____

Work Phone: _____

I am a. . . . (check one)

_____ BVSD teacher, teaching _____ (subject/grade)

at _____ (school)

_____ BVSD staff working at _____ (location)

in the capacity of _____

_____ Boulder Valley School District community member.

I have read the BVSDNet Terms and Conditions. I understand and will abide by the stated Terms and Conditions for BVSDNet. I further understand that violation of the regulations is unethical and may constitute a criminal offense. Should I commit any violation my access privileges may be revoked and/or appropriate legal action taken. I understand that if I switch schools or leave the Boulder Valley School District I must notify the Internet Director.

User Name (please print): _____

User Signature: _____

Date: _____

When your account is established you will be notified of your password and logon. Thank you for your interest and support of this exciting new resource in the Boulder Valley Schools.

AUP 3: SHORECREST AUP FOR EDUCATIONAL TECHNOLOGY

This policy is an example of a brief, to-the-point AUP.

Shorecrest (http://www.shorecrest.org/Txt/AccUsePolicy.html) has made and will continue to make a significant investment of time and financial resources to bring technology into the classroom. Along with the increased educational resources that telecomputing brings to teachers and students comes an increased need to use them wisely and responsibly. Please become familiar with the following Shorecrest Acceptable Use Policy for Educational Technology. When you have read this policy, please obtain both parent and student signatures and return the signed copy to your respective school office. Students who have not returned the policy will not be given access to Shorecrest's computers and computer network.

SHORECREST ACCEPTABLE USE POLICY FOR EDUCATIONAL TECHNOLOGY

Students who wish to use Shorecrest's computers and computer network must comply with the following policies. Violation of these policies will result in the loss of access and may result in further disciplinary action.

- Do not disclose personal information over the Internet or other open systems.

- Do not reveal your real name, telephone number, address, password, credit information, or other information that could be used against you. Follow the specific guidelines you will identify.

- Do not attempt to access material that is sexually explicit or obscene. Use the Internet and other resources only for purposes related to schoolwork.

- Avoid irrelevant material and comply with teachers' instructions about specific areas.

- Use only your own computer identity; do not log on as anyone else or use anyone else's account.

- Respect software copyright restrictions. Do not duplicate commercial software.

- Leave software in place on computers unless otherwise instructed; do not delete, alter, or reposition files. Do not open other students' files.

- Do not attempt to defeat security software.

- Do not place any software on a Shorecrest computer or network without permission of a teacher. Get permission before downloading software or files from the Shorecrest network.

- Take proper precautions not to bring viruses or other damaging software into any Shorecrest computer or network. Before using a floppy disk that has been off campus, check it for viruses.

- Keep passwords secret; never disclose them to anyone. Follow guidelines on password security.

- Protect our computer hardware. Do not eat or drink near computers. Follow the shut-down procedure before switching off. Do not attach or detach any peripherals unless all components are powered down and unplugged. Do not tolerate any damage or theft by anyone.

- Respect others. Communicate through computers as you would deal with people in person.

I have read, understood, and agree to abide by the above policy.

Student Signature: _____

Date: _____

Parent Signature: _____

Date: _____

....

AUP 4: NORFOLK PUBLIC SCHOOLS

This is another example of a fairly brief AUP. Norfolk Public Schools URL is:

http://www.norfolk.k12.ma.us/

It is the policy of the Norfolk School Committee that all users of the Internet in the Norfolk Public Schools read, sign and agree to the terms of the following Acceptable use policy. Please read this document carefully before signing.

Internet access is now available to students, teachers and staff of the Norfolk Public Schools through NorNet—Norfolk's Educational Information. This exciting technology allows for communication and access to information on a global scale including but not limited to:

- Electronic mail communication with people all over the world
- Information and news from NASA as well as the opportunity to correspond with the scientists at NASA and other research institutions
- Public domain software and shareware of all types
- Discussion groups on a variety of topics ranging from Chinese culture to the environment to music to world history
- Access to university library catalogs, the Library of Congress and ERIC
- World Wide Web sites that offer thousands of educational resources

With access to computers and people all over the world also comes the availability of material that may not be considered to be of educational value in the context of the school setting. The Norfolk

Schools have taken precautions to restrict access to controversial materials. However, on a global network it is impossible to control all materials and an industrious user may discover controversial information. The Norfolk Schools believe that the valuable information and interaction available on this worldwide network far outweighs the possibility that users may procure material that is not consistent with the educational goals of the District.

Internet access is coordinated through a complex association of government agencies and regional and state networks. In addition, the smooth operation of the network relies upon proper conduct of the end users who must adhere to strict guidelines. In general, this requires efficient, ethical, and legal utilization of the network resources. If a Norfolk School user violates any of these provisions, his or her account will be terminated and future access could possibly denied. The signature(s) at the end of this document is (are) legally binding and indicates the party (parties) who signed has (have) read the terms and conditions carefully and understand(s) their significance.

INTERNET—TERMS AND CONDITIONS

1. Acceptable Uses: The use of your account must be in support of education and research and in accordance with the educational objectives of the Norfolk Public Schools. Unacceptable use includes but is not limited to the following:
   - Users should not lend their Internet account and/or password to other users, or use another's account.
   - Use for commercial purposes or political lobbying is prohibited.
   - The malicious attempt to harm or destroy data of another user or the Internet, including the uploading or creation of computer viruses, is forbidden.
   - Transmission of any material in violation of any U.S. or state regulation is prohibited. This includes, but is not limited to: copyrighted material; threatening, racist, sexist, pornographic, and obscene material; or information protected by trade secret.
   - Abusive or otherwise objectionable language is forbidden.
2. Netiquette: Users are expected to abide by the generally accepted rules of network etiquette. These include but are not limited to the following:

- Be polite. Do not get abusive in your messages to others. Use appropriate language.
- Do not reveal your personal address or phone numbers of students or colleagues.
- Assume that email is NOT secure or confidential. Never send anything that you would hesitate to have viewed by others.
- Use upper and lower case letters (all caps is considered the equivalent of shouting), and be mindful of spelling.
- Keep paragraphs and messages short and to the point.
- Check email regularly and delete unwanted messages as quickly as possible.
- Respect other people's privacy regarding mail or files.
- Avoid use of sarcasm in electronic communications.

3. Vandalism: Vandalism will result in cancellation of access privileges. Vandalism is defined as any malicious attempt to harm or destroy data of another user, the Internet, or any of the above listed agencies or other networks that are connected to the Internet backbone. This includes the uploading or creation of computer viruses. The use of the Internet is a privilege, not a right, and inappropriate use will result in a cancellation of those privileges. The system administrators will deem what is inappropriate and their decision is final. The administration, faculty, and staff of the Norfolk Schools may request of the system administrators to deny, revoke, or suspend specific user accounts.

INTERNET USE AGREEMENT

I understand and will abide by the above Internet Acceptable-Use Policy. I further understand that if I commit any violation of the regulations above, my access privileges may be revoked, school disciplinary and/or appropriate legal action may be taken.

User Signature: _____

PARENT OR GUARDIAN

As the parent or guardian of this student, I have read the Internet Acceptable Use Policy. I understand that this access is designed for educational purposes. I recognize it is impossible

for Norfolk Schools to restrict access to all controversial materials and I will not hold them responsible for materials acquired
on the network. I hereby give permission to issue an account for
my child.

Parent or Guardian's Name (please print): _____

Signature: _____

Date: _____

SPONSORING TEACHER
I have read the Internet Acceptable Use Policy and agree to
promote this agreement with the student. As the sponsoring
teacher I agree to instruct the student on acceptable use of the
network and proper network etiquette.

Teacher's Name (please print): _____

Signature: _____

Date: _____

. . . .

AUP 5: COMMUNITY HIGH SCHOOL INTERNET POLICY STATEMENT

This AUP applies not to an entire district, but to a specific
school. Their URL is:

http://chs-web.umdl.umich.edu/

It includes an Internet Code of Conduct and specific guidelines
for World Wide Web publishing.

MISSION
The mission of the Community High School Internet initiative
is to improve learning and teaching through interpersonal communication, student access to information, research, teacher
training, collaboration, and dissemination of successful educational practices, methods, and materials.

Rights and Responsibilities

Community High School will be connected to the Internet through the National Science Foundation (NSF) and the University of Michigan Digital Library Initiative (UMDL). This connection will provide access to local, national, and international sources of information and collaboration vital to intellectual inquiry in a democracy. In return for this access, every Digital Library user has the responsibility to respect and protect the rights of every other user in our community and on the Internet. In short, account holders are expected to act in a responsible, ethical, and legal manner, in accordance with the Community High School Internet Code of Conduct, the missions and purposes of the other networks they use on the Internet, and the laws of the states and the United States.

Community High School Internet Code of Conduct

The Internet Code of Conduct applies to all users of the CHS network. It reads: "I will strive to act in all situations with honesty, integrity, and respect for the rights of others and to help others to behave in a similar fashion. I will make a conscious effort to be of service to others and to the community. I agree to follow the access, usage, and content rules as put forth in the Community High School Internet Policy Statement."

Access to Accounts

A UMDL sponsored Internet account is a privilege offered each academic year to the following: all Community High School Foundations of Science students and their parent(s) or guardian(s); all educators who are working with Foundations students, including classroom teachers, support personnel, administrators, tutors, music staff, specialists, and mentors; educators and students from other educational institutions who are working in partnership with Community High School for specific purposes over a limited period of time.

Usage Guidelines

The Internet account holder is held responsible for his/her actions and activity within his/her account. Unacceptable uses of the network will result in the suspension or revoking of these privileges. Some examples of such unacceptable use are:

1. Using the network for any illegal activity, including violation of copyright or other contracts;
2. Using the network for financial or commercial gain;
3. Degrading or disrupting equipment, software, or system performance;
4. Vandalizing the data of another user;
5. Wastefully using finite resources;
6. Gaining unauthorized access to resources or entities;
7. Invading the privacy of individuals;
8. Using an account owned by another user;
9. Posting personal communications without the original author's consent;
10. Posting anonymous messages;
11. Downloading, storing, or printing files or messages that are profane, obscene, or that use language that offends or tends to degrade others;
12. Violating the Content Guidelines as outlined below.

CONTENT GUIDELINES

Students will be allowed to produce materials for electronic publication on the Internet. Network administrators will monitor these materials to ensure compliance with content standards. The content of student materials is constrained by the following restrictions:

1. No personal information about a student will be allowed. This includes home telephone numbers and addresses as well as information regarding the specific location of any student at any given time.
2. All student works must be signed with the student's full name.
3. Individuals in pictures, movies, or sound recordings may be identified only by initials (e.g. JQP for John Q. Public). Absolutely no first or last names may appear in reference to individuals in any image, movie, or sound recording.
4. No text, image, movie, or sound that contains pornography, profanity, obscenity, or language that offends or tends to degrade others will be allowed.

COMMUNITY HIGH SCHOOL INTERNET CONSENT AND WAIVER FORM

The consent forms are standard University of Michigan CAEN network access documents which have been slightly modified for use with the UMDL project.

By signing the UMDL Conditions of Use and Account Request forms, the requester and his/her parent(s) or guardian(s) agree to abide by the restrictions outlined in this policy. The student and his/her parent(s) or guardian(s) should discuss these rights and responsibilities. Ultimately, parent(s) and guardian(s) of minors are responsible for setting and conveying the standards that their child or ward should follow. To that end, Community High School supports and respects each family's right to decide whether or not to apply for Internet access.

The UMDL is an experimental system being developed to support Community High School's educational responsibilities and mission. The specific conditions and services being offered may change from time to time. Community High School makes no warranties with respect to Internet service or content.

Further, the requester and his/her parent(s) or guardian(s) should be aware that Community High School does not have control of the information on the Internet, nor can it provide barriers to account holders accessing the full range of information available. Other sites accessible via the Internet may contain material that is illegal, defamatory, inaccurate, or potentially offensive to some people. Similarly, while Community High School supports the privacy of electronic mail, account users must assume that this cannot be guaranteed.

Community High School believes that the benefits to educators and students from access to the Internet, in the form of information resources and opportunities for collaboration, far exceed any disadvantages of access. We hope you and your student will join us on the Internet.

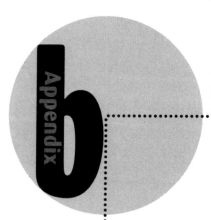

INFORMATION LITERACY

Appendix

b

In its Acceptable Use Policy, The Bellingham School District included an entire section on copyright compliance and fair use.

Drawing heavily upon the Copyright Act of 1976, the policy includes detailed copyright compliance information for teachers and administrators.

This policy may be copied.
BELLINGHAM SCHOOL DISTRICT 501
2314
BOARD POLICY

COPYRIGHT COMPLIANCE INSTRUCTION

The board recognizes that federal law makes it illegal to duplicate copyrighted materials without authorization of the holder
of the copyright, except for certain exempt purposes. Severe
penalties may be imposed for unauthorized copying or using of
audiovisual or printed materials and computer software, unless
the copying or using conforms to the "fair use" doctrine.

Under the "fair use" doctrine, unauthorized reproduction of
copyrighted materials is permissible for such purposes as criticism, comment, news reporting, teaching, scholarship, or
research. If duplicating or changing a product is to fall within
the bounds of fair use, these four standards must be met for any
of the foregoing purposes:

A. *The Purpose and Character of The Use.* The use must be for
   such purposes as teaching or scholarship and must be nonprofit.
B. *The Nature of the Copyrighted Work.* Staff may make single
   copies of the following for use in research, instruction, or
   preparation for teaching: book chapters; articles from periodicals or newspapers; short stories, essays, or poems; and
   charts, graphs, diagrams, drawings, cartoons, or pictures
   from books, periodicals, or newspapers in accordance with
   these guidelines.
C. *The Amount and Substantiality of the Portion Used.* In most
   circumstances, copying the whole of a work cannot be considered fair use; copying a small portion may be if these
   guidelines are followed.
D. *The Effect of the Use upon the Potential Market for or Value
   of the Copyrighted Work.* If resulting economic loss to the
   copyright holder can be shown, even making a single copy of
   certain materials may be an infringement, and making multiple copies presents the danger of greater penalties.

While the district encourages its staff to enrich the learning
programs by making proper use of supplementary materials, it is

the responsibility of district staff to abide by the district's copying procedures and obey the requirements of the law. In no circumstances shall it be necessary for district staff to violate copyright requirements in order to perform their duties properly. The district cannot be responsible for any violations of the copyright law by its staff.

Any staff member who is uncertain as to whether reproducing or using copyrighted material complies with the district's procedures or is permissible under the law should contact the superintendent or the person designated as the copyright compliance officer. The latter will also assist staff in obtaining proper authorization to copy or use protected material when such authorization is required.

Legal References: P.L. 94–553 Federal Copyright Law of 1976 (U.S. Code, Title 17) Adopted: 1-12-95

BELLINGHAM SCHOOL DISTRICT 501
2314p
ADMINISTRATIVE PROCEDURE

COPYRIGHT COMPLIANCE INSTRUCTION

Staff may make copies of copyrighted school district materials that fall within the following guidelines. Where there is reason to believe the material to be copied does not fall within these guidelines, prior permission shall be obtained from the principal. Staff members who fail to follow this procedure may be held personally liable for copyright infringement.

AUTHORIZED REPRODUCTION AND USE OF COPYRIGHTED MATERIAL IN BOOKS AND PERIODICALS

In preparing for instruction, a teacher may make or have made a single copy of:

A. A chapter from a book;
B. An article from a newspaper or periodical;
C. A short story, short essay, or short poem; or
D. A chart, graph, diagram, drawing, cartoon, or picture from a book, periodical, or newspaper.

A teacher may make multiple copies, not exceeding more than one per pupil, for classroom use or discussion if the copying meets the tests of "brevity, spontaneity, and cumulative effect" set by the following guidelines. Each copy must include the notice of copyright present in the original work.

A. Brevity.
   1. A complete poem, if less than 250 words and if printed on not more than two pages, may be copied; excerpts from longer poems cannot exceed 250 words;
   2. Complete articles, stories, or essays of less than 2500 words may be copied. Excerpts from prose works of not more than 1000 words or 10% of the work—whichever is smaller—may be copied, but in any event, a minimum of 500 words may be copied.
   3. Each numerical limit set forth above may be expanded to permit the completion of an unfinished line of a poem or an unfinished prose paragraph;
   4. One chart, graph, diagram, drawing, cartoon, or picture per book or periodical issue may be copied.
   5. "Special" works cannot be reproduced in full under any circumstances; however, an excerpt of not more than two published pages containing not more than 10% of the words in the text of such special work may be reproduced. What constitutes a "special" work is not clearly defined; however, special works include children's books combining poetry, prose, or poetic prose with illustrations and which are less than 2500 words in their entirety. For a further discussion on what constitutes a "special" work, see Agreement on Guidelines for classroom coping in Not-for-Print educational institutions with respect to books and periodicals.

B. Spontaneity. Copying should be at the "instance and inspiration" of the individual teacher; and the inspiration and decision to use the work and the moment of its use for maximum teaching effectiveness are so close in time that it would be unreasonable to expect a timely reply to a request for permission.

C. Cumulative Effect. Teachers are limited to using copied material for only one course in the school in which copies are made. No more than one short poem, article, story, essay, or two excerpts from the same author may be copied, and no more than three works or excerpts can be copied from a collective work or periodical volume during one class term. Teachers are limited to nine instances of multiple copying for one course during one class term. The numerical limitations set forth above do not apply to current news periodicals, newspapers, and current news sections of other periodicals.

Performances by teachers or students of copyrighted dramatic works without authorization from the copyright owner are permitted as part of a teaching activity in a classroom or instructional setting. All other performances require permission from the copyright owner.

Not withstanding any of the foregoing, the copyright law prohibits using copies to create, replace, or substitute for anthologies, compilations, or collective works. There shall be no copying of or from works intended to be "consumable" in the course of study or of teaching. "Consumable" works include: workbooks, exercises, standardized tests, test booklets, and answer sheets. Teachers cannot substitute copies for the purchase of books, publishers' reprints, or periodicals, nor can they repeatedly copy the same item from term-to-term. Copying cannot be directed by a "higher authority," and students cannot be charged more than actual cost of photocopying. Teachers may use copyrighted material in overhead or opaque projectors for instructional purposes.

AUTHORIZED REPRODUCTION AND USE OF COPYRIGHTED MATERIALS IN THE LIBRARY

A library may make a single copy (containing the notice of copyright present on the original work) of:

A. An unpublished work which is in its collection solely for purposes of preservation and security or for deposit for research use in another qualified library or archives.
B. A published work in order to replace it because it is damaged, deteriorated, lost, or stolen, provided that an unused replacement cannot be obtained at a fair price.

A library may provide a single copy of copyrighted material to a student or staff member at no more than the actual cost of photocopying. The copy must be limited to one article of a periodical issue or a small part of other material, unless the library finds that the copyrighted work cannot be obtained elsewhere at a fair price. In the latter circumstance, the entire work may be copied. In any case, the copy shall contain the notice of copyright present in the original work and the student or staff member shall be notified that the copy is to be used only for private study, scholarship, or research. Any other use may subject the person to liability for copyright infringement and the library shall not make a copy if it has notice of any other use. The foregoing reproduction right shall not apply to musical works, motion pictures, or other audiovisual works (other than an audiovisual work dealing with news), or pictorial, graphic, or sculptural works (other than pictorial or graphic works published as illustrations, diagrams, or similar adjuncts to works of which copies are reproduced hereunder).

At the request of a teacher, copies may be made for reserve use. The same limits apply as for single or multiple copies designated in "Authorized Reproduction and Use of Copyrighted Material in Print."

AUTHORIZED REPRODUCTION AND USE OF COPYRIGHTED MUSIC

For academic purposes, other than performance, teachers may make a single copy of an entire performable unit (section), movement, aria, etc., from a printed musical work that is (1) confirmed by the copyright proprietor to be out of print or (2) unavailable except in a larger work, for purposes of preparing for instruction.

A teacher may make multiple copies not exceeding one copy per pupil for classroom use of an excerpt of not more than 10% of a printed musical work if it is to be used for academic purposes other than performance, provided that the excerpt does not comprise a part of the whole musical work which would constitute a performable unit such as a selection, movement, or aria.

In an emergency, a teacher may make and use replacement copies of printed music for an imminent musical performance when the purchased copies have been lost, destroyed or are otherwise not available, provided that purchased copies shall be substituted in due course.

A teacher may make and retain a single recording of student performances of copyrighted material when it is made for purposes of evaluation or rehearsal.

A teacher may make and retain a single copy of excerpts from recordings of copyrighted musical works owned by the school or the individual teacher for use as aural exercises or examination questions.

A teacher may edit or simplify purchased copies of music provided that the fundamental character of the music is not distorted. Lyrics shall not be altered or added if none exist.

Copying cannot be used to create, replace, or substitute for anthologies, compilations, or collective works; copying of consumable works is prohibited.

Copying for the purpose of performance is prohibited, except in the case of an emergency as set forth above, and copying for the purpose of substituting for the purchase of music is prohibited, except as set forth in the first and second paragraphs above. All copies must include the copyright notice appearing on the printed copy.

Performance by teachers or students of copyrighted musical works is permitted without the authorization of the copyright owner as part of a teaching activity in a classroom or instructional setting. The purpose shall be instructional rather than for entertainment.

If the requirements of the foregoing paragraph are not satisfied, performances of nondramatic musical works which are copyrighted are permitted without the authorization of the copyright owner, provided that:

A. The performance is not for a commercial purpose;
B. None of the performers, promoters, or organizers are compensated; and
C. (1) There is no direct or indirect admission charge; or
   (2) Admission fees are used for educational or charitable purposes only; provided that the copyright owner has not objected to the performance.

All other musical performances require permission from the copyright owner.

OFF-AIR RECORDING OF COPYRIGHTED PROGRAMS
Television programs transmitted by television stations for reception by the general public without charge (hereinafter referred to as "broadcast programs") may be recorded off-air

simultaneously with broadcast transmission (including simultaneous cable retransmission) and retained by a school for a period not to exceed the first forty-five (45) consecutive calendar days after date of recording. Upon conclusion of this retention period, all off-air recordings must be erased or destroyed immediately.

Off-air recordings may be used once by individual teachers in the course of relevant instructional activities, and then repeated once only when instructional reinforcement is necessary in classrooms and other similar places devoted to instruction, during the first ten (10) consecutive school days in the forty-five (45) calendar day retention period. "School days" are school session days—not counting weekends, holidays, vacations, examination periods, or other scheduled interruptions.

Off-air recordings may be made only at the request of and used by individual teachers, and may not be regularly recorded in anticipation of requests. No broadcast program may be recorded off-air more than once at the request of the same teacher, regardless of the number of times the program may be broadcast.

A limited number of copies may be reproduced from each off-air recording to meet the legitimate needs of teachers under these guidelines. Each additional copy shall be subject to all provisions governing the original recording.

After the first ten (10) consecutive school days, off-air recordings may be used up to the end of the forty-five (45) calendar day retention period only for teacher evaluation purposes, i.e., to determine whether or not to include the broadcast program in the teaching curriculum. Permission must be secured from the publisher before the recording can be used for instructional purposes or any other nonevaluation purpose after the ten (10) day period.

Off-air recordings need not be used in their entirety, but the recorded programs may not be altered from their original content. Off-air recordings may not be physically or electronically combined or merged to constitute teaching anthologies or compilations.

All copies of off-air recordings must include the copyright notice on the broadcast program as recorded.

Authorized Reproduction and Use of Video Rentals or Videos Purchased for Home

Videos may only be rented for classroom use from agencies or companies which allow for such use. Many retail video rental stores have strict license agreements prohibiting use with large, non-home audiences. These restrictions may also apply to the use of videos purchased for home use. Staff is expected to review and honor these agreements.

Authorized Reproduction and Use of Copyrighted Computer Software and CD-ROM Products

Schools have a valid need for high quality software at reasonable prices. To assure a fair return to the authors of software programs, the school district shall comply with the copyright laws and any usage agreements that are applicable to the acquisition of software programs. To this end, the following guidelines shall be in effect:

A. All copyright laws and license agreements between the vendor and the district shall be observed;

B. Staff members shall take reasonable precautions to prevent copying or the use of unauthorized copies on school equipment, to avoid the installation of privately purchased software on school equipment and to avoid the use of single copy software or CD-ROM products across a network with multiple users unless such use is permitted by the applicable license agreement;

C. A backup copy shall be purchased for use as a replacement when a program is lost or damaged. If the vendor is not able to supply such, the district shall make a backup program in accordance with the terms of the applicable license agreement or 17 U.S.C. and 117 and attest that the program will be used for replacement purposes only;

D. The principal is authorized to sign a software license agreement on behalf of the school. A copy of said agreement shall be retained by the principal.

Copying Limitations

Circumstances will arise when staff are uncertain whether or not copying is prohibited. In those circumstances, the superintendent or designated copyright compliance officer should be contacted. The following prohibitions have been expressly stated in guidelines agreed to by representatives of educators and authors/publishers:

A. Reproduction of copyrighted material shall not be used to create or substitute for anthologies, compilations, or collective works.
B. Unless expressly permitted by agreement with the publisher and authorized by district action, there shall be no copying from copyrighted consumable materials such as workbooks, exercises, test booklets, answer sheets, and the like.
C. Staff shall not:
    1. Use copies to substitute for the purchase of books, periodicals, music recordings, computer software, or other copyrighted material except as permitted by district procedure;
    2. Copy or use the same item from term to term without the copyright owner's permission;
    3. Copy or use more than nine instances of multiple copying of protected material for one course in any one term;
    4. Copy or use more than one short work or two excerpts from works of the same author in any one term; or
    5. Copy or use protected material without including the notice of copyright present in the original work; the following is a satisfactory notice:
    Notice: This Material May Be Protected by Copyright Law.

··········
NOTE

This document and other sections about copyright law in this book are included for informational purposes only and are not intended as legal advice. For specific legal advice or information, contact your lawyer or your school's legal counsel. Wentworth Worldwide Media and *Classroom Connect* will not be responsible for any actions you take based on information provided in this book. You may wish to refer to the guide, *Creating Acceptable Use Policies for K–12 Schools*, by Classroom Connnect: 800-638-1639.

ELECTRONIC FRONTIER FOUNDATION

Founded in 1990 to "ensure that the principles embodied in the Constitution and Bill of Rights are protected as new communications technologies emerge," the Electronic Frontier Foundation (EFF) engages in a variety of activities in the interest of protecting Internet citizens, preserving free speech, and making the Internet safer for all.

The following information comes from the Electronic Frontier Foundation's home page and provides more information about the group. The EFF:

- Sponsors cases. . . in which users' online civil liberties have been violated. Additionally, EFF submits amicus briefs and finds pro bono counsel when possible for important legal cases. We continue to monitor the online community for legal actions that merit EFF support.
- Works to ensure that communications carriers do not deny service to network users solely on the basis of the content of their messages and that carriers do not bear undue liability for harm stemming from the content of messages where that harm is actually caused by users.
- Produces legal white papers that inform BBS operators, telephone companies, and public utility commissions about the civil liberties implications of their actions. We monitor legislation and agency actions affecting the online community. We also work with EFF members and groups of members on state and local levels to effect change in local legislation.
- Provides a free telephone hotline for members of the online community who have questions regarding their legal rights.
- Speaks to law enforcement organizations, state attorney bar associations, conferences and summits, and university classes on the work that we do and how these groups can get involved.

REPRESENTING THE INTERESTS OF "NETIZENS"

EFF works to make sure that common carriage principles are upheld in the information age. Common carriage principles require that network providers carry all speech, regardless of its controversial content. EFF supports a new common carriage system in which system operators are shielded from liability for the actions of users, but without the regulatory burden presently associated with common carriage.

EFF also works to convince Congress that all measures that support broader public access to information should be enacted into law. EFF supports an Electronic Freedom of Information

Act and other legislation to make government information more accessible to citizens.

EFF supports both legal and technical means to enhance privacy in communications. We, therefore, advocate measures that ensure the public's right to use the most effective encryption technologies available, and have testified before Congress as well as conducted online campaigns against the NSA's "Clipper Chip" initiative.

EFF supports an Open Platform model of the global information infrastructure, providing nondiscriminatory access, based on open, private sector standards, and free from burdensome regulation.

Finally, EFF works to craft policies that enable public and private information providers to distribute and sell their information products over the Internet. We encourage the government to provide support for schools, universities, and research labs that buy Internet services on the open market. We work on policies that encourage the government to stimulate the development of experimental, precompetitive, network technologies and to fund the development of applications that are of use to "low-end" users, who are traditionally underserved by advanced digital media.

PROTECTING CHILDREN WITH SURFWATCH

SurfWatch is an Internet access management utility to control children's access to the Internet. It gives parents and teachers control over children's access to the Internet.

It's included free on the CD-ROM at the back of this book! This Appendix provides a brief overview and instructions for installing the software.

USING SURFWATCH

SurfWatch is an Internet access management utility used by parents and teachers to control children's access to the Internet. It's a breakthrough software product that helps you deal with inappropriate, sexually explicit and potentially upsetting material on the Internet. When SurfWatch software is installed on a computer, children have less chance of accidentally or deliberately being exposed to unwanted material. A password-protected on/off switch lets parents and teachers allow or prevent access to various categories of material.

When installed, SurfWatch runs in the background and monitors the flow of information into your computer from the Internet. There are several ways SurfWatch informs the computer user that a site has been blocked. Usually, he or she will see a "Blocked by SurfWatch" message.

SurfWatch comes ready to block thousands of Internet sites containing objectionable material, including Web, ftp, Gopher, newsgroups, and chat areas. However, new sites appear daily on the Internet. For this reason, SurfWatch offers a *Maintenance Plan* that periodically updates its list of inappropriate sites.

Once installed, SurfWatch is automatically operational, and you never have to touch it again unless you want to turn it off or remove it.

INSTALLATION INSTRUCTIONS FOR MAC

Some antivirus software may interfere with the installation of SurfWatch. You may want to restart your Mac with extensions off before installing SurfWatch.

1. Double click on the Install SurfWatch icon and follow the instructions on the screen.
2. After your machine restarts, SurfWatch will be functional on your machine and turned on to begin blocking access to inappropriate Internet sites.
3. The first time you Restart after installation, SurfWatch will automatically update your computer with the most current site database.

INSTALLATION INSTRUCTIONS
FOR WINDOWS

1. Choose File/Run from the Program Manager menu. Type **a:setup** or **b:setup** in the dialog box that appears. Press Enter or click OK to start the setup program.
2. Follow the instructions on your screen. You must create your own password.
3. When setup is complete, SurfWatch will be installed and running on your machine.

Directory of Child-Safe Internet Sites

It's easy to get confused by the barrage of information and the sheer number of sites on the Internet. You may wonder:

"What sites can I feel safe about sending my child to?"

Well, we've compiled the following list of URLs that will delight your kids an give you peace of mind.

CHILDREN UP TO 7

▣ The Wizard of Oz Story Page
http://seamonkey.ed.asu.edu/oz/wizard1.html
The beloved story, as told and illustrated online by the kindergarten and first-grade students at Carminati Elementary School in Arizona. Enchanting!

▣ The Bowen Family Home Page
http://www.comlab.ox.ac.uk/oucl/users/jonathan.bowen/children.html
An adorable collection of stories, poems, pictures, and sounds from 7- and 10-year-old sisters in England. Great links and creativity.

▣ The Adventures of Quitsie Dog
http://www.scruz.net/~wave/quitsie.html
The delightful adventures of Quitsie, including her travels and friends. Large type and great illustrations.

▣ Virtual Whale Watch
http://www.neaq.org/KIDS/vt.ww.intro.html
Take a trip aboard the Voyager II whale boat to see humpback whales outside Boston Harbor.

▣ Carlos' Coloring Book
http://www.ravenna.com/coloring/
Choose one of several pictures, choose colors one at a time with your mouse, then print it!

▣ Theodore Tugboat Home Page
http://www.cochran.com/.html
Read the interactive story about Theodore, the tugboat, and follow his latest adventure.

▣ Muppet Songs Page
http://www.cs.unc.edu/~arthur/muppet-songs.html
Lyrics to all of your favorite Muppet songs, from the television show and their movies, to sing over and over again.

▣ Cyber-Seuss
http://www.gnn.com/gnn/wic/wics/ed.81.html
All the texts of all of the good doctor's humorous books, including his beginning readers series. The site is lacking in graphics, but the stories and rhymes are great fun.

▣ The Littlest Knight
http://www.pacificnet/~cmoore/lk/index.htm
A beautifully illustrated original story about a petite knight who falls in love with a princess. Large type makes for easy reading.

▣ Nikolai's Web Site
http://www.h-plus-a.com/nikolai/nnn.htm
Build your own little paper town, make paper dolls and lots of other fun things at this activity-filled site. Large type, colorful illustrations.

▣ Personalized Book—Space Travel
http://www.ot.com:80/cgi/kidsbook/
Type in your child's name and the names of two friends, and watch as they are written into a story of space travel. Fun illustrations, large type.

▣ Alphabet
http://www.klsc.com/children/
Learning the alphabet and numbers are fun here at this creative interactive site.

▣ Kid Crafts

http://ucunix.san.uc.edu/~edavis/kids-list/crafts.html

A zillion practical, easy, and fun ideas for crafts at home with your children, including macaroni necklaces and painting with cut-up sponges. Try out the silly putty recipes too!

▣ The Sugar Bush

http://intranet.ca/~dlemire/sb_kids.html

Cute stories, activities with leaves, and a how-to lesson on making a simple bird feeder highlight this pleasant page. Large type.

▣ Crayola—How Are Crayons Made?

http://www.crayola.com:80/crayons/home.html

Take a virtual tour of the Crayola factory, and learn how they are made from start to finish.

▣ Peace In Pictures Project—Children's Drawings of Peace

http:///www.macom.co.il/peace/index.html

Draw or paint a picture of what peace looks like to you, then send it to Jerusalem, Israel, where it will be on this Website.

▣ Royal Tyrrell Museum Tour: Dinosaur Hall

http://www.tyrrell.com/tour/dinohall.html

From Albertosaurus to Tyrannosaurus Rex, they are all here with facts, pictures, and more facts for your favorite dinosaur fan.

▢ Games Kids Play
http://www.corpcomm.net/~gnieboer/gamehome.htm
Remember a game you played as a kid, but you can't
exactly remember the rules? Well, check for them here in
a sort of rules database—-and share your childhood games
with your kids.

▢ Kid Safety
http://www.uoknor.edu/oupd/kidsafe/start.htm
A site to help teach your child what to do in the event of
an accident or emergency.

▢ Underwater World Home Page
http://pathfinder.com/@@AqyOBmGLBgAAQJua/pathfinder/kidstuff/underwater/
Come visit the Monterey Bay Aquarium and try all the fun
activities—dive with a diver and study the sizes of fish
mouths. Don't forget to explore the site's "Freaky Fishes"
challenge!

▢ Cool Dog Teddy
http://www2.best.com/~stevesch/morningwalk.html
Enjoy the cute stories and the child-provided illustrations
of this fun-to-read series.

▢ Yukon Quest 96
http:www2.northstar.k12.ak. us/schools/upk/quest/quest.html
A detailed report on the 1995 Yukon Quest International
Sled Dog, from Alaska to Canada. The page is set up by
third-graders in Alaska. Contains pictures and other links.

▢ Judy and David's Online Songbook
http://www.io.org/~jandd/songbook/songbookcover.html
Click a letter to look for the words of your favorite children's songs, from "Alice the Camel" to "Zum Gali Gali."

▣ My Hero
http://myhero.com/
Here, regular people are lauded for going above and beyond the call of duty.

▣ Mapquest
http://www.mapquest.com
Type in an address—just about any in the nation—and let the Mapquest database find the address and pull out a map to show you.

CHILDREN 8 TO 12 YEARS OLD

▣ The Dinosauria
http://ucmp1.berkeley.edu/exhibittext/dinosaur.html
The ultra-searchable site of the Museum of Paleontology at the University of California, with great links to geologic periods and many more topics. For the dinosaur lover in your home.

▣ 1000 Cranes Project
http://www.csi.ad.jp/suzuhari-es/1000cranes/index.html
The touching story of "Sadako and the 1000 Cranes," about a little girl in Hiroshima, Japan, after the atomic bomb ended World War II. With links to the A-bomb Web Museum and more.

▣ NASA Homepage
http://www.nasa.gov/
A space lovers dream site. Great links not to be missed, such as "Today@NASA" and "NASA Newsroom." Great photos from the Hubble Space Telescope. A site for hours of exploration.

▣ The World Series
http://www.delphi.com/sports/baseball/series/index.htm
A delightful online tour of baseball's Fall Classic, with complete results through 1993 and film and video clips galore.

▣ The Solar System
http://www.hq.nasa.gov/office/solar_system/
Discover the planets, their moons, and the myriad other mysteries of the solar system in this well-linked site.

▣ Horse Country
http://www.pathology.washington.edu/Horse/
A young horse enthusiast's dream site, with stories, trainer's tips, care information, and a large photo collection.

▣ The White House for Kids
http://www.whitehouse.gov/WH/kids/html/home.html
A guided tour of the White House, it's history, and the Clinton family by none other than Socks, the First Cat. You can even send email to the President, to Vice President Gore, or to Socks!

▣ The Wolf Home Page
http://www.usa.net/WolfHome/
Learn about wolves, their natural habitats, and efforts to restore their populations in the Midwest. This is the site of the Wolf Park natural area in Indiana.

▣ Ports & Pilots Flag Game
http://www.nav.com/ports/game.htm
Spell your name using signal flags as you learn all about how signal flags and semaphores are used by sailors to communicate with other ships.

▣ MayaQuest 96

http://www.mecc.com/MAYA/More.html

Follow a group of five explorers who head to Central
America to learn more about ancient Mayan civilization.
Check the "Archives" to see all the interesting discoveries
they made in their 1995 trip.

▣ OK Pen-Pals

http://web2.starwave.com/outside/online/kids/penpals/pal.html

Choose a pen-pal from lists of kids just like yourself and
send them email right from the Web!

▣ Kid's Crambo

http://www.primenet.com/~hodges/kids_crambo.html

Fun word games, including making up your own rhymes
and silly definitions.

▣ National Air & Space Museum

http://www.nasm.edu/NASMDOCS/NASMAP.html

Click any gallery in the museum map and be immersed in
the history of manned and unmanned spaceflight. Great
links and beautiful photos in an extensive historical
collection.

▣ The Yuckiest Site on the Internet

http://www.nj.com/yucky/index.html

Learn all about cockroaches in this interactive site at the
Liberty Science Center. Don't miss "A Day in the Life of
Rodney Roach!"

▣ Paper Airplanes of the Month

http://pchelp.inc.net/paper_ac.htm

Fold and fly a great assortment of unusual paper airplanes.

▣ The Field Museum Natural History Exhibits
http://www.bvis.uic.edu/museum/exhibits/Exhibits.html
Tour the fossils, dinosaur exhibits, and many other online features of this wonderful museum.

▣ Invention Dimension
http://web.mit.edu/afs/athena.mit.edu/org/i/invent/
Visit MIT's featured inventor site to learn all about American inventors and their amazing discoveries. Past featured inventors are also searchable, as well as many links.

▣ Nye Labs Online
http://nyelabs.kcts.org/
Homepage of Bill Nye, PBS Television's "Science Guy," featuring online experiments, info, and much more. Be sure to visit the "Demo of the Day."

▣ Ask An Expert
http://njnie.dl.stevens-tech.edu/curriculum/aska.html
Have questions you can't answer about science, math, or technology? Then send your question to one of these experts for help. Ask a meteorologist, geologist, astronomer, and more!

▣ Charlotte—The Vermont Whale
http://mole.uvm.edu/whale/Introduction.html
Learn how and why the fossilized bones of an 11,000-year-old whale were found buried in rural Vermont, 150 miles inland from the ocean.

The Michael Jordan Page
http://gagme.wwa.com/~boba/mj.html
Everything you ever wanted to know about the Chicago
Bulls star, including stats, profiles, and much more.

CyberKids Online Magazine
http://www.mtlake.com/cyberkids/
Read stories written by kids, do projects, play games, and
enjoy lots of other online activities. You can even send in
your own stories and artwork.

Welcome to Connect Four
http://csugrad.cs.vt.edu/htbin/Connect4.perl
Play a game or two (or ten—it's addictive!) of the game
Connect Four against a computer and seek utter
domination.

The Flag of the United States
http://asimov.elk-grove.k12.il.us/usflag/toc.html
The ultimate source for all of your questions on the
American flag, its history, customs, care, and more. Great
links to American historical sites, including the
Declaration of Independence.

The Piano Education Page—Just for Kids
http://www.unm.edu/~loritaf/pnokids.html
Read all about the featured composer and get tips on having more fun with your piano lessons. Beautiful classical
music compositions can be downloaded here also.

CHILDREN 13 TO 18 YEARS OLD

▣ Bullpen Ace
http://www.dtd.com/ace/

You are the "closer" in the bottom of the ninth inning of a baseball game. They score—you lose. Win the game by correctly answering three baseball trivia questions—for three strikes! He's out!

▣ Franklin Institute, The Heart: A Virtual Exploration
http://sln.fi.edu/biosci/heart.html

An interactive and searchable site about the detailed inner workings of the human heart, complete with animations, sounds, on-line activities, and more. Be sure to check the links to the museum!

▣ NASA Historical Archive
http://www.ksc.nasa.gov/history/history.html

A virtual history book of U.S. spaceflight, from unmanned satellites to mission-by-mission descriptions of the Space Shuttles. Incredible historical links to related sites.

▣ National Park Service
http://www.nps.gov/

A great place to explore the national parks across the U.S., with pictures, maps, and history. Plan your summer vacation or research a school project! Links to the states. Click the name of the park!

▣ NASCAR Online
http://www.nascar.com

The source of information for stock car racing fans, with the latest race information and results, video clips, driver and team profiles, and more.

▣ Jane Austen Home Page

http://uts.cc.utexas.edu/~churchh/janeinfo.html

A great source for info on the popular English writer who lived from 1775 to 1817. Her novels and other writings are all here, as well as lots of other interesting information about her and her times.

▣ Kristi Yamaguchi Home Page

http://www.polaris.net/user-www/shanhew/

Photos of the Olympic medal winner, her biography and more, plus great links for skating fans to sites of other skating stars. Full events schedule and much more.

▣ Civil War Letters

http://www.ucsc.edu/civil-war-letters/home.html

A fascinating true account of the Civil War through the eyes of a soldier as he writes letters to his sweetheart back home. Private Newton Robert Scott shares his experiences with us.

▣ National Museum of American Art

http://www.nmaa.si.edu:80/masterdir/pagesub/tourthegallery.html

Almost 1000 works of art, plus voice clips and more highlight this interactive and searchable art gallery in Washington, D.C.

▣ International Museum of the Horse

http://www.horseworld.com/imh/imhmain.html

History of horses and racing through the centuries, with links to the National Cowboy Hall of Fame, shows, and more.

▣ Animals Around the World

http://www.chicojr.chico.k12.ca.us/staff/gray/animals.html

A site maintained as a research project for seventh-grade students, this is an incredible resource for info on just about every species of animal. Extensive links to every animal species and more.

▣ The Electric Postcard

http://postcards.www.media.mit.edu/Postcards/

Send an electronic postcard of a painting, photograph, or even a mural to a friend via email! It's cool and it's free!

▣ The Klingon Language Institute

http://www.kli.org/KLIhome.html

A web site designed to foster the Klingon language, based on the television series *Star Trek*.

▣ Los Angeles River Virtual Tour

http://www.lalc.k12.ca.us/laep/smart/river/tour/index.html

Take a fascinating tour of how an urban area gets its drinking water, with great text and photos and superb links to the plants, wildlife, and people along the river.

▣ Cool Word of the Day Page

http://www.dsu.edu/projects/word_of_day/word.html

Expand your vocabulary or test your knowledge with this fun page, sponsored by Dakota State University.

▣ Treasures of the Czars

http://www.times.st-pete.fl.us/Treasures/Default.html

Visit this interesting exhibit of the Czars of Russia at the Florida International Museum. Be sure to also visit the museum's link to its "Splendors of Ancient Egypt" exhibit.

▣ CNN Interactive
http://www.cnn.com/
All the news of the day, online and up-to-date, from CNN News around the globe.

▣ The Human Languages Page
http://www.willamette.edu~tjones/languages/Language-Page.html
Studying a foreign language? Interested in other languages? Here's a great resource for more than 550 languages from A to Z, with dictionaries and sound files for pronunciations.

▣ World of Escher
http://www.texas.net/escher/
The art and life of M.C. Escher, the Dutch graphic artist whose work continues to fascinate viewers.

▣ Encyclopedia Mystica
http://www.pantheon.org/myth
From Greek mythology to folklore and legends and more, here is a great source of information.

▣ Juggling Information Service
http://www.juggling.org
All about the art of juggling, beginning with the classic three-ball juggle and progressing to more difficult tricks. Start at "Juggling Help" to learn the ropes, and don't miss the "Hall of Fame."

▣ John Skilton's Baseball Links
http://www.pc-professor.com/baseball/
If it's about baseball—from youth ball to the pros—it's here. Be sure to visit the "Cal Ripken—One For the Ages" link! Incredible resource for fans.

▣ WebMuseum: Bienvenue!

http://sunsite.unc.edu/wm/

Visit incredible art museums in Paris, see paintings come alive on your screen. Don't forget to take the detailed "Visit Paris" tours.

▣ The Library of Congress

http://www.loc.gov

Everything you ever wanted to know about U.S. government, from the president to the Congress to the CIA, the Department of Agriculture, and more. See the "Explore the Internet" link, too.

▣ Battleship

http://csugrad.cs.vt.edu/htbin/battleship

The classic game of naval strategy—but this time it is you against a computer. Good luck, Captain Queeg.

Glossary

Acceptable Use Policy (AUP)
A binding document signed by all users that explains the rules of Internet use at an institution.

Anonymous FTP
A publicly available Internet file site. Users must sign on as "anonymous" and enter their email addresses to connect to an anonymous ftp site.

Archie
A program that locates files that are freely available on anonymous ftp sites across the Internet. To use Archie, telnet to one of these sites and login as archie.

archie.internic.net
archie.ans.net
archie.rutgers.edu
archie.sura.net
archie.unl.edu
archie.au
archie.doc.ic.ac.uk

Type help for full instructions.

Bitnet
An autonomous network of academic and research sites.

Browser
Software that allows users to access and navigate the World Wide Web. Some Web browsers, such as Mosaic and Netscape, are graphical. Lynx is a text-based browser used on UNIX computers.

Bulletin Board Service (BBS)
A forum for users to browse and exchange information. Computer BBSs are accessible by telephone via personal computer and a modem. Many BBSs are small operations run by a single person that allow only several users to logon at the same time. Some are much larger and allow hundreds of users to logon. America Online, Prodigy, and CompuServe are commercial BBSs.

Commercial online service

A company that, for a fee, allows computer users to dial in via modem to access its information and services, which can include Internet access. Examples include America Online, CompuServe, and Prodigy.

Database

A computer holding large amounts of information that can be searched by a user. A storehouse of information on the Net.

Dial-up Internet connection

Lets a user dial into an Internet service provider using a modem and telephone line to access the Internet. The user is presented with a text-based set of menus that are used to navigate the Internet. (See **SLIP or PPP connections**)

Directory

A list of files or other directories on a computer at an Internet site.

Download/upload

To download is to transfer a file from another computer to the user's computer. To upload is to send a file to another computer.

Email

Allows users to send and receive messages to each other over the Internet.

Emoticons

Smileys and other character art used to express feelings (to compensate for the lack of body language) in email communication.

File Transfer Protocol (ftp)

Allows files to be transferred between Internet-connected computers.

Filter

Hardware or software that is designed to restrict a person's access to certain areas on the Internet.

Finger

Software that allows the user to enter the address of an Internet site in order to find information about that system's users or a particular user. Some finger addresses return other topic-specific information.

Flame

To send a harsh, critical email message to another Internet user, usually someone who has violated the rules of Netiquette.

Free-Net
Any one of more than two dozen freely accessible Internet sites, primarily offering community and educational information.

Frequently Asked Questions (FAQ)
FAQ files answer frequently asked questions on hundreds of Internet-related topics. They're freely available at many different locations on the Net. The ftp site given below holds every FAQ on the Net.

ftp to: rtfm.mit.edu

Go to the *pub/usenet/news.answers* subdirectory

Gopher
A menu-based system used for browsing Internet information.

Graphical interface
Software designed to allow the user to execute commands by pointing and clicking on icons or text.

Hacker
A computer user who illegally visits networked computers to look around or cause harm.

Home page
The main page on a World Wide Web site, usually the first page a user sees when visiting, unless brought by a hyperlink (see below).

HTML (Hypertext Markup Language)
The programming "language" of the World Wide Web, HTML software can turn a document into a hyperlinked World Wide Web page.

Hypertext/hyperlink
A highlighted word or graphic in a document that, when clicked upon, takes the user to a related piece of information at that or any other location on the Internet.

Infobot (or mailbot)
An email address that can automatically seek out, find, and return information on the Internet, as instructed by the user.

Internaut
Anyone who uses the Internet.

Internet

The global "network of networks" that connects more than four million computers, called hosts. The Internet is the virtual "space" in which users send and receive email, logon to remote computers (telnet), browse databases of information (gopher, World Wide Web, WAIS), and send and receive programs (ftp) contained on these computers.

Internet account

Purchased through an Internet Service Provider, the account assigns a password and email address to an individual or group.

Internet Relay Chat (IRC)

Interactive, real-time discussions between Internauts using text messages. Users logon to designated Net computers and join discussions already in progress. More information about IRC can be obtained via ftp.

ftp to: cs.bu.edu

Go to the *irc/support* subdirectory

Internet server

A computer that stores data that can be accessed via the Internet.

Internet Service Provider (ISP)

Any organization that provides access to the Internet. Many ISPs also offer technical assistance to schools looking to become Internet information providers by placing their school's information online. They also help schools get connected to the Net. A list of ISPs can be retrieved via ftp.

ftp to: ftp.classroom.net

Look in the *wentworth* subdirectory

Internet site

A computer connected to the Internet containing information that can be accessed using an Internet navigation tool such as ftp, telnet, gopher, or a Web browser.

IP address

The unique numerical address assigned to every computer on the Internet, such as 123.456.78.9.

Jughead

An Internet search tool that will scan one or a few gopher sites for material related to a keyword.

Keyword
A word or words that can be searched for in documents or menus.

Knowbot
Software that searches Internet "white pages" (lists of users at large institutions) to find a person's name and address.

Logon
To sign on to a computer system.

Mailing lists (or Listserv)
These are more than 4,000 topic-oriented, email-based message bases that can be read and posted to.

Users subscribe to the lists they want to read and receive messages via email. Mailing lists are operated using list-serv software. Thus, many Internauts call mailing lists "listservers."

There are two types of lists: moderated and unmod-erated. Moderated lists are screened by a human before being posted to subscribers. Messages to unmoderated lists are automatically for-warded to subscribers.

Menu
A list of information that leads to documents or other menus.

Modem
An electronic device that attaches to a computer and links that computer to the online world via a phone line.

Modems are available for any computer, can be installed inside the computer or placed next to it on the desk-top, and come in several speeds, known as the baud rate.

The higher the baud rate, the faster the modem. Until recently, the most popular modem was 14,400 (14.4) baud but 28,800 (28.8) baud modems are now the standard.

Most Internet service providers allow you to dial into their systems at 14,400, or even 28,800 baud.

Mosaic

Internet navigation software that allows Internauts to access information through a graphical, point-and-click interface rather than text-only screens or menus.

Mosaic is known as a Web browser because it accesses World Wide Web information formatted into special home pages using hypertext. Other graphical Web browsers include Netscape, WinWeb, Microsoft Internet Explorer, and Cello.

National Information Infrastructure (NII)

The official U.S. government name for the Internet and other computer networks. It's more commonly known as the Information Superhighway.

Netiquette

The rules of conduct for Internet users. Violating Netiquette could result in flaming or removal from a mailing list.

Some service providers will even cancel a user's Internet account, denying him or her access to the Net, if the violation is severe enough.

Net surfer

Someone who browses the Internet.

Network

A group of computers that are connected in some fashion. Most school networks are known as LANs, or local area networks, because they are networks linking computers in one small area. The Internet could be referred to as a WAN, or a wide area network, because it connects computers in more than one local area.

Online/Offline

When you are logged on to a computer through your modem, you are said to be online. When you're using your computer but are not connected to a computer through your modem, you're said to be working offline.

Posts

Email messages sent to a mailing list or a Usenet newsgroup to be read by subscribers or others on the Internet.

Request for Comments (RFC)

Online documents that have to do with technical standards for the Internet.

Serial Line Internet Protocol (SLIP) or Point to Point Protocol (PPP, a Dial-up IP)

Types of Internet connections. Both allow a computer to connect to the Internet using a modem and telephone line. Users then navigate the Internet using software on their own computer.

This is in contrast to using a dial-up Internet connection, where users are forced to navigate the Net using text-based sets of menus.

Signature file

Return address information such as name, phone number, and email address that users put at the bottom of email messages.

Telnet

Allows users to access computers and their data at thousands of places around the world, most often at libraries, universities, and government agencies.

Text-based Internet account

The user must use UNIX commands to navigate the Internet.

UNIX

A computer operating system commonly used on the Internet.

URL (Universal Resource Locator)

The address and method used to locate a specific resource on the Internet. A URL beginning with *http://* indicates that the site is a World Wide Web resource and that a Web browser will access it.

Usenet newsgroups

Message bases that can be read and posted to. There are more than 13,000 on the Internet. Also called newsgroups.

Veronica

Veronica is a computer program that helps Internauts find what they're looking for on gopher servers around the world.

Instead of looking through menus, Veronica allows users to enter keywords to locate the gopher site that holds the information they want.

Gopher to: veronica.scs.unr.edu

Virtual

A computer-generated environment.

WAIS (Wide Area Information Servers)

These servers allow users to conduct full-text keyword searches in documents, databases, and libraries that are connected to the Internet.

World Wide Web (WWW or Web)

A revolutionary Internet browsing system that allows point-and-click navigation of the Internet. The WWW is a spider web–like interconnection of millions of pieces of information located on computers around the world.

Web documents use hypertext, which incorporates text and graphical "links" to other documents and files on Internet-connected computers.

ndex

Internet Access Management Utility

CyberPatrol lets parents and teachers control children's access to the Internet, providing:
Automatic blocking of access to specified Internet sites
CyberNOT block list—researched Internet sites that parents may find questionable
First and only Internet filter that works with all browsers, including 32-bit browsers
Built-in support for the SafeSurf system
Restriction access to certain times of day
Limit total time spent on-line
Control local applications use

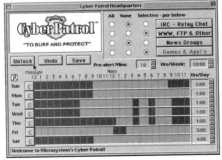

CyberPatrol's main administration screen lets parents, teachers, and others control children's use of a computer by hours of the day and by specific Internet locations.

CyberPatrol is an Internet access management utility that parents and teachers can use to control children's access to the Internet.

It allows those responsible for children to restrict access to certain times of day, limit the total time spent online in a day and block access to Internet sites deemed inappropriate. CyberPatrol also can be used to control access to the major online services and to local applications—such as games and personal financial managers.

CyberPatrol comes loaded with Microsystems Software's "CyberNOT Block List," a listing of researched Internet sites containing material that parents may find questionable. The list is divided into categories, and access can be managed down to the file directory or page level. Therefore, appropriate material at an Internet address need not be blocked simply because there is restricted material elsewhere at that address. Parents may select all or any of the categories to be blocked by content, time of day, or specific Internet site.

Parental Control

CyberPatrol allows parents to manage computer use in their own household. Cumulative duration of Internet (or applications) use can be captured and reported. In addition to providing a useful overview of computer usage, these reports can also be used to verify online provider and telephone bills.

CyberPatrol is available for Windows and Macintosh systems. CyberPatrol 3.0 for Windows provides control of children's access through Internet Applications and

web browsers, including America Online, America Online's MegaWeb Internet access service, CompuServe/Spry Mosaic, Netcruiser, Netscape, and Mosaic 2.0. CyberPatrol 3.0 also blocks sites accessed via a proxy server.

CyberPatrol 1.0 for Macintosh can block direct Internet access. This core functionality is required by the education market. Currently, the Macintosh product will intercept calls to the Macintosh TCP driver, and will block access from the popular Mac browsers and Internet applications such as Netscape, Mosaic and NewsWatcher.

CyberPatrol loads during start-up and runs in the background, controlling access to all associated applications. CyberPatrol is accessed via password, and offers two levels of parental password control. Several safeguards include controls which prevent children from disabling CyberPatrol or simply renaming blocked applications.

CyberNOT Block List

The sites on the CyberNOT Block List are reviewed by a team of professionals at Microsystems software, including parents and teachers. They use a set of criteria that categorizes Internet sites and resources according to the level of possibly objectionable content. The categories include: Violence/Profanity; Partial Nudity; Nudity; Sexual Acts/Text; Gross Depictions/Text; Racist/Ethnic; Satanic/Cult; Militant/Extremist; Drugs/Drug Culture; Alcohol, Beer, and Wine; Gambling; and Questionable/Illegal.

Parents can select the content categories they wish to block and allow access to any site on the CyberNOT List they deem appropriate. They can also deny access to sites not included on the CyberNOT List and control or block access to major online services as well as applications (games, for example).

The CyberNOT List is updated weekly and can be downloaded from the Internet using CyberPatrol.

How to Purchase

The $49 list price for CyberPatrol includes a six-month subscription to the CyberNOT Block List. **But by special arrangement with _Classroom Connect_, you can purchase CyberPatrol for only $29.95,** which includes a 12-month subscription to the CyberNOT Block List.

You can download a FREE 14-day working demo from _Classroom Connect:_ **www.classroom.net/cyberpatrol.** Call Classroom Connect at (800) 638-1639. Quantity discounts available.

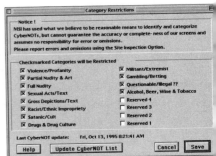

TM

◆ A complete online research library.

◆ Deep and broad consumer reference product.

◆ The best way for students and families to do research.

◆ Content is as safe as local public library.

◆ Accessible via the Internet.

◆ Updated daily via satellite.

The way you do research.™
http://www.k12.elibrary.com/classroom

Using The Electric Library, a student can pose a question in plain English and launch a comprehensive and simultaneous search through more than 150 full-text newspapers, over 900 full-text magazines, two international newswires, two thousand classic books, hundreds of maps, thousands of photographs as well as major works of literature and art.

In a matter of seconds, query results are returned to a user ranked in relevancy order, displaying reference data, file size, and grade reading level. With this easy-to-use product a researcher need only click on the document or image of interest and it is automatically downloaded. The materials can also be copied and saved into a word processing document with bibliographic information automatically transferred.

Included in The Electric Library database are materials from world renowned publishers such as Reuters, Simon and Schuster, Gannett, World Almanac, Times Mirror, and Compton's New Media. The Electric Library also incorporates a host of local, ethnic, and special interest publications.

All retrieved information can be downloaded and saved or transferred to a word processor in real time, and used for educational purposes. This includes both the text and images from The Electric Library's databases.

PARTIAL LIST OF ELECTRIC LIBRARY CONTENT

Magazines/Journals	Books/Reference Works	Newspapers/Newswires
Art Journal	3,000 Great Works of Literature	Baseball Weekly
The Economist	Monarch Notes	Jerusalem Post
Editor & Publisher	The Complete Works of	La Prensa
Inc.	Shakespeare	Los Angeles Times
Lancet	The World's Best Poetry	Magill's Survey of Cinema
Maclean's	Compton's Encyclopedia	Newsbytes News Service
Mother Jones	King James Bible	News India
National Review	Thematic Dictionary	New York Newsday
New Republic	Webster's Dictionary	Reuters
World Press Review	World Fact Book	USA Today

FREE
30-DAY TRIAL!
Offer made in special arrangement with Classroom Connect

PRICING
Individual User: 9^{95} per month
School Site License: $2,000 per year

(800) 638-1639

Monstrous Media Kit

(formerly Kid's Studio)

The award-winning multimedia creativity tool for kids ages seven to seventeen.

Produce, direct and star in your own multimedia productions. CyberPuppy's Monstrous Media Kit is an all-in-one multimedia application that offers children sophisticated tools for creating their own presentations. Kids can compose brilliant pages combining photo-realistic images with paint, text, and sound, and show off their work as full-screen slide shows, movies or printed stories. Features a "Treasure Chest" of images, Cookie-Cutter Technology, QuickTime™ or Video for Windows, and Kodak PhotoCDs.

Special pricing for the CD-ROM version:
- Home or School Edition — for one user $22
- Lab Pack with 5 CDs — for up to five users $65
- Classroom Pack with 5 CDs — for up to 30 users $185
- Network Pack with 5 CDs — for up to 50 users $325
- Site License with 5 CDs — unlimited use in one school building $400

For more information, contact:
CyberPuppy Software
2248 Park Boulevard
 Palo ALto, CA 94306
Telephone: (415) 326-2449
Fax: (415) 326-6301
URL: http://www.cyberpuppy.com

Minimum Requirements, Macintosh: Mac LC or higher; CD-ROM drive; System 7; 5 MB RAM, 5MB free hard disk space; 12-inch monitor with 256 colors/grays.

Minimum Requirements, Windows: 486SX; CD-ROM drive; Windows 3.1; 8MB RAM, 5 MB free hard disk space; VGA+ (640 x 480 at 256 colors)

Educator's INTERNET CD Club

Classroom-ready Internet™

New! Internet on CD-ROM

Join the Educator's Internet CD Club today — and receive a year's worth of Internet resources on CD-ROM. No Internet access required!

iCD — for every subject area and grade level

As an iCD Club member, you'll receive four CDs during the school year. Every iCD is packed full of actual Web sites organized by subject area including: science, mathematics, language arts, world cultures, and more! You'll get great multimedia Web sites appropriate for every subject area and every grade level!

You have total control!

When you use the Educator's Internet CD Club, you can feel confident that your students will always have access to the sites you've designated. You also don't have to worry about students accessing any "inappropriate material" — because there isn't any — just pure information developed for classroom use.

Here's what you'll get:

- Actual Internet Web Sites — Six to eight different subject areas chock full of the best Web sites edited and reformatted for classroom use.
- Lesson Plans — Each subject area contains ready-to-use lesson plans.
- Activity Sheets — Gradable activity sheets for each subject area make assessment easy.
- Teaching Tips — Dozens of ideas, "mini-lessons," and added resources to further help you integrate the Educator's Internet CD Club into your classroom.
- Educator's IdeaBank — Lesson plans for any curriculum, classroom software, project ideas and other "teacher-only" resources that will help you enhance all of your educational programs.

Here's how the iCD Club works:

When you join the Educator's Internet CD Club, you'll receive four CD-ROMs — one iCD will be sent to you every 7–8 weeks during the school year. As a Charter member of the iCD Club, you'll pay the special Charter Member rate of ONLY $129 for the year (a $40 savings off the regular rate).

SAVE $40

Special Charter Membership Offer Regularly **$169**

$129 Item No. CCD00
Annual Membership includes 4 CD-ROMs
Plus FREE Teachers Resource PowerPak CD

Plus, as an iCD member, you'll also be able to buy **subject-specific CDs** as they become available at the discount membership price of ONLY $19.95 — A 50% savings off the regular price of $39.95. Subjects include math, science, astronomy, social studies and more!

Netscape 2.0 included!

Each iCD PowerPak comes equipped with 2.0 *(for educational use only)*, the latest in Web browser technology. And we've included six multimedia player programs.

Special Bonus CD FREE, if you act now!

As a limited time offer, you'll receive absolutely FREE with your membership, the Teacher's Resource PowerPak CD — a $39.95 value! This CD is packed with "teacher only" resources and Internet teaching tips and techniques. Includes actual Internet Web sites for teachers and multimedia software. Includes 30 days FREE Internet access featuring Netscape Navigator™ software.

"This is a way to get more kids to use the Net and its wealth of information, even for those who only have one or NO phone lines! It makes the Web portable."

— Barb Falkenburg
Library/Media Specialist
Edgewood, MD

"You're going to love using iCD in the classroom — brilliant multimedia resources, lesson plans, and project ideas — all classroom-ready for your immediate use."

(800) 638-1639

24 hour Fax Line (717) 393-5752
URL: http://www.classroom.net

Child Safety on the Internet CD-ROM

Free software to get you up and running on the Internet right away

Here is your CD-ROM, jam-packed with free software to get you onto the Internet and using its resources in minutes! There are seven main items on the disc:

1. **Internet access software.** From EarthLink Network,® this includes EarthLink Network TotalAccess™ software with Netscape Navigator.™ The software entitles you to 10 days free, unlimited dial-in Internet access with no sign-up fee.

2. ***Child Safety on the Internet* HotPage.** Contains "live" Internet links to many of the best online sites listed throughout this book.

3. **HyperStudio™ multimedia software demo.** Enables you to use the multimedia files you find on the Internet to create colorful, interactive slide shows. This demo version also includes close to 200 MB of clip art, video clips, sounds, and other multimedia files.

4. **Monstrous Media Kit™ for Macintosh.** Multimedia authoring software that is perfect for students who are new to computers and want to create fun, informative interactive presentations with sounds and video.

5. **CyberPatrol™ Internet access filter software.** A highly flexible and effective means for blocking access to inappropriate online sites. The version on this CD-ROM is enabled for a full 30-day free trial.

   "TO SURF AND PROTECT"

6. **SurfWatch™ Internet access management utility.** Used by parents and teachers to control children's access to the Internet. When SurfWatch is installed on a computer, children have less chance of accidentally or deliberately being exposed to unwanted material.

7. **Electric Library™ software.** Provides an outstanding online research collection. The software on the CD-ROM is enabled for a full 30-day free trial—a whole month's access to a complete online research library.

LICENSE AGREEMENT AND LIMITED WARRANTY

READ THE FOLLOWING TERMS AND CONDITIONS CAREFULLY BEFORE OPENING THIS SOFTWARE MEDIA PACKAGE. THIS LEGAL DOCUMENT IS AN AGREEMENT BETWEEN YOU AND PRENTICE-HALL, INC. (THE "COMPANY"). BY OPENING THIS SEALED SOFTWARE MEDIA PACKAGE, YOU ARE AGREEING TO BE BOUND BY THESE TERMS AND CONDITIONS. IF YOU DO NOT AGREE WITH THESE TERMS AND CONDITIONS, DO NOT OPEN THE SOFTWARE MEDIA PACKAGE. PROMPTLY RETURN THE UNOPENED SOFTWARE MEDIA PACKAGE AND ALL ACCOMPANYING ITEMS TO THE PLACE YOU OBTAINED THEM FOR A FULL REFUND OF ANY SUMS YOU HAVE PAID.

1. **GRANT OF LICENSE:** In consideration of your payment of the license fee, which is part of the price you paid for this product, and your agreement to abide by the terms and conditions of this Agreement, the Company grants to you a nonexclusive right to use and display the copy of the enclosed software program (hereinafter the "SOFTWARE") on a single computer (i.e., with a single CPU) at a single location so long as you comply with the terms of this Agreement. The Company reserves all rights not expressly granted to you under this Agreement.

2. **OWNERSHIP OF SOFTWARE:** You own only the magnetic or physical media (the enclosed SOFTWARE) on which the SOFTWARE is recorded or fixed, but the Company retains all the rights, title, and ownership to the SOFTWARE recorded on the original SOFTWARE copy(ies) and all subsequent copies of the SOFTWARE, regardless of the form or media on which the original or other copies may exist. This license is not a sale of the original SOFTWARE or any copy to you.

3. **COPY RESTRICTIONS:** This SOFTWARE and the accompanying printed materials and user manual (the "Documentation") are the subject of copyright. You may not copy the Documentation or the SOFTWARE, except that you may make a single copy of the SOFTWARE for backup or archival purposes only. You may be held legally responsible for any copying or copyright infringement which is caused or encouraged by your failure to abide by the terms of this restriction.

4. **USE RESTRICTIONS:** You may not network the SOFTWARE or otherwise use it on more than one computer or computer terminal at the same time. You may physically transfer the SOFTWARE from one computer to another provided that the SOFTWARE is used on only one computer at a time. You may not distribute copies of the SOFTWARE or Documentation to others. You may not reverse engineer, disassemble, decompile, modify, adapt, translate, or create derivative works based on the SOFTWARE or the Documentation without the prior written consent of the Company.

5. **TRANSFER RESTRICTIONS:** The enclosed SOFTWARE is licensed only to you and may not be transferred to any one else without the prior written consent of the Company. Any unauthorized transfer of the SOFTWARE shall result in the immediate termination of this Agreement.

6. **TERMINATION:** This license is effective until terminated. This license will terminate automatically without notice from the Company and become null and void if you fail to comply with any provisions or limitations of this license. Upon termination, you shall destroy the Documentation and all copies of the SOFTWARE. All provisions of this Agreement as to warranties, limitation of liability, remedies or damages, and our ownership rights shall survive termination.

7. **MISCELLANEOUS:** This Agreement shall be construed in accordance with the laws of the United States of America and the State of New York and shall benefit the Company, its affiliates, and assignees.

8. **LIMITED WARRANTY AND DISCLAIMER OF WARRANTY:** The Company warrants that the SOFTWARE, when properly used in accordance with the Documentation, will operate in substantial conformity with the description of the SOFTWARE set forth in the Documentation. The Company does not warrant that the SOFTWARE will meet your requirements or that the operation of the SOFTWARE will be uninterrupted or error-free. The Company warrants that the

media on which the SOFTWARE is delivered shall be free from defects in materials and workmanship under normal use for a period of thirty (30) days from the date of your purchase. Your only remedy and the Company's only obligation under these limited warranties is, at the Company's option, return of the warranted item for a refund of any amounts paid by you or replacement of the item. Any replacement of SOFTWARE or media under the warranties shall not extend the original warranty period. The limited warranty set forth above shall not apply to any SOFTWARE which the Company determines in good faith has been subject to misuse, neglect, improper installation, repair, alteration, or damage by you. EXCEPT FOR THE EXPRESSED WARRANTIES SET FORTH ABOVE, THE COMPANY DISCLAIMS ALL WARRANTIES, EXPRESS OR IMPLIED, INCLUDING WITHOUT LIMITATION, THE IMPLIED WARRANTIES OF MERCHANTABILITY AND FITNESS FOR A PARTICULAR PURPOSE. EXCEPT FOR THE EXPRESS WARRANTY SET FORTH ABOVE, THE COMPANY DOES NOT WARRANT, GUARANTEE, OR MAKE ANY REPRESENTATION REGARDING THE USE OR THE RESULTS OF THE USE OF THE SOFTWARE IN TERMS OF ITS CORRECTNESS, ACCURACY, RELIABILITY, CURRENTNESS, OR OTHERWISE.

IN NO EVENT, SHALL THE COMPANY OR ITS EMPLOYEES, AGENTS, SUPPLIERS, OR CONTRACTORS BE LIABLE FOR ANY INCIDENTAL, INDIRECT, SPECIAL, OR CONSEQUENTIAL DAMAGES ARISING OUT OF OR IN CONNECTION WITH THE LICENSE GRANTED UNDER THIS AGREEMENT, OR FOR LOSS OF USE, LOSS OF DATA, LOSS OF INCOME OR PROFIT, OR OTHER LOSSES, SUSTAINED AS A RESULT OF INJURY TO ANY PERSON, OR LOSS OF OR DAMAGE TO PROPERTY, OR CLAIMS OF THIRD PARTIES, EVEN IF THE COMPANY OR AN AUTHORIZED REPRESENTATIVE OF THE COMPANY HAS BEEN ADVISED OF THE POSSIBILITY OF SUCH DAMAGES. IN NO EVENT SHALL LIABILITY OF THE COMPANY FOR DAMAGES WITH RESPECT TO THE SOFTWARE EXCEED THE AMOUNTS ACTUALLY PAID BY YOU, IF ANY, FOR THE SOFTWARE.

SOME JURISDICTIONS DO NOT ALLOW THE LIMITATION OF IMPLIED WARRANTIES OR LIABILITY FOR INCIDENTAL, INDIRECT, SPECIAL, OR CONSEQUENTIAL DAMAGES, SO THE ABOVE LIMITATIONS MAY NOT ALWAYS APPLY. THE WARRANTIES IN THIS AGREEMENT GIVE YOU SPECIFIC LEGAL RIGHTS AND YOU MAY ALSO HAVE OTHER RIGHTS WHICH VARY IN ACCORDANCE WITH LOCAL LAW.

ACKNOWLEDGMENT

YOU ACKNOWLEDGE THAT YOU HAVE READ THIS AGREEMENT, UNDERSTAND IT, AND AGREE TO BE BOUND BY ITS TERMS AND CONDITIONS. YOU ALSO AGREE THAT THIS AGREEMENT IS THE COMPLETE AND EXCLUSIVE STATEMENT OF THE AGREEMENT BETWEEN YOU AND THE COMPANY AND SUPERSEDES ALL PROPOSALS OR PRIOR AGREEMENTS, ORAL, OR WRITTEN, AND ANY OTHER COMMUNICATIONS BETWEEN YOU AND THE COMPANY OR ANY REPRESENTATIVE OF THE COMPANY RELATING TO THE SUBJECT MATTER OF THIS AGREEMENT.

Should you have any questions concerning this Agreement or if you wish to contact the Company for any reason, please contact in writing at the address below.

Robin Short
Prentice Hall PTR
One Lake Street
Upper Saddle River, New Jersey 07458